# THE ARTIST'S TORAH

Dear Jessica —
   I hope you'll find
some inspiration here!
All the best —

*[signature]*

# THE ARTIST'S TORAH

David Ebenbach

CASCADE *Books* · Eugene, Oregon

THE ARTIST'S TORAH

Cascade Books
An Imprint of Wipf and Stock Publishers
199 W. 8th Ave., Suite 3
Eugene, OR 97401

www.wipfandstock.com

ISBN 13: 978-1-62032-205-5

*Cataloguing-in-Publication data:*

Ebenbach, David.

The Artist's Torah / David Ebenbach.

xviii + 254 pp. ; 23 cm. Includes bibliographical references and index.

ISBN 13: 978-1-62032-205-5

1. Jewish art. 2. Judaism and art. 3. Bible. O.T. Pentateuch—Commentaries. I. Title.

N7415 .E2 2012

Manufactured in the U.S.A.

*For Rachel, my ner tamid;*
*and for Reuben, who asks the big questions*

# Contents

Contents

## Deuteronomy

# Foreword

## Rabbi Sandy Eisenberg Sasso

FROM THE EARLIEST VERSES in the book of Genesis we learn of the power of language to create, not just narrative or poetry, but a world. God speaks: *Let there be . . .* and there is. It takes naught but sparse language to bring into being not only light but earth and sky, plant and animal, man and woman.

It should come as no surprise then, that we find wisdom in the words of Scripture, not only about a sacred covenant, the fashioning of a people, its beliefs and values, but about the very art of creating itself.

And so we begin *in the beginning.* What appears as a simple phrase is not simple at all. The first word of Genesis in Hebrew, *b'reishit,* yields two different, even contradictory understandings. Does the text in Genesis 1:1 mean to say, "In the beginning, God created the heaven and the earth . . ." suggesting that before God's initial act, there was nothing? Or should we translate it as, "When God began to create heaven and earth, the earth being unformed and void . . . ," suggesting that the earth already existed but was unformed? In other words, is creation a crafting out of nothing or is it an ordering out of chaos?

What is the creative process that yields prose and poetry, dance, art, and music? Is it an act of breathing in what is—the chaotic swirl of feeling and thought, the jumble of smells and tastes, sounds and sights—and breathing out of form? Or is it a calling up from the emptiness, the void of nothingness, of absence, something new and altogether original? Might it be that the very first words of the Bible offer us the possibility that creation is both?

From the first words, we turn to the first story. What appears to be a simple account of the world's birthing is not simple at all. The author of the first chapter of Genesis seeks to capture the wonder of creation in majestic poetry. Yet no sooner than we have completed the poem, taken a breath of rest, then we begin again.

This time, in Genesis' second chapter, the world is formed anew in the rich mythic narrative of Eden, a Garden of Delights. It seems that no literary form can hold the grand process completely; each is a partial glimpse of the mystery of creation.

So it is that in the Bible everything begins as an art project. God is the Master Artist, potter and gardener, painter, and musician, creating with words and breath. We learn not only of God as Master Architect but of the human being created in the image of God. Might it be that the Bible wishes to teach us that our share in divinity is not merely as creatures formed by God, but as divine co-creators?

Through a unique understanding of Torah, matched with the wisdom of authors and musicians, dancers, painters, and sculptors, David Ebenbach offers stunning glimpses into the dynamics of the creative soul. As God celebrates creation and argues with it, builds and uproots, affirms and regrets, so *The Artist's Torah* illuminates our own joys and disappointments, struggles and triumphs. Ebenbach's insights cajole and comfort, challenge and demand. They are worthy of all who would dare to participate daily in the ongoing work of creation.

# Acknowledgments

GRATEFUL ACKNOWLEDGMENT IS MADE to the following journals in which two of these chapters (in modified forms) previously appeared: *Tiferet* ("*B'reishit*—The Roots of the Artist in the Tree of Knowledge"); *Whirlwind Review* ("*Sh'mot*—The Unknown").

This book would not exist without the incredible support of many people. Thanks to Sandy Eisenberg Sasso for her generous foreword, and to Christian Amondson and Rodney Clapp and everyone else at Cascade Books for all they've done to shepherd this book into print. Thanks to all the readers who encouraged me and this work when I was developing it aloud, in blogs, in bits and pieces. Finally, thanks to my family—to my parents, who raised me to be curious; to my sister, who has always been a model for me; to my wife, Rachel, my great love, whose support has been greater and more unflagging than anyone could expect or deserve; and to Reuben, my beautiful boy.

# Introduction

T HERE IS AN OLD story—two thousand years old, actually—in which a Gentile, perhaps a potential convert to Judaism, approached the pre-eminent rabbi Hillel and demanded he explain the contents of the Torah (the first five books of the Hebrew Bible) while standing on one foot—in other words, quickly. Famously, Rabbi Hillel found a way to summarize: "What is hateful unto you, don't do unto your neighbor. The rest is commentary."[1]

Of course, that commentary is pretty important; it's not as though everyone just stopped reading the Torah right then and there. In fact, Rabbi Hillel ended his famous response by saying, "Now go and study." It turns out that being kind to one another is much harder than it sounds—how else to explain so many of the problems in the world today? And so we study because we need to understand it more deeply than we can in the time that a person can stand on one foot.

As a creative writing teacher, I am sometimes put in a position not unlike a Rabbi Hillel when I am called upon to give eager students the secret to writing, and preferably in twenty words or fewer. When I'm thrust into this position I say, "There's only one secret to writing: Write. Go put words on paper." I could very easily add, "The rest is just commentary." And to that I could certainly add, "Now go and study." As it happens, sitting down to write—settling in to do any kind of art, in fact—is also much harder than it sounds. And so we need to understand it more deeply than we can in twenty words or fewer.

In fact, the artistic life raises big, challenging questions: What is creativity? Where does it come from? Who has it? What's the point of being creative? How does it work? How does the process vary from person to person? How does creativity get blocked and how can blocks be overcome? How should work be shared with others? What does it do in the world? Does the artist have any obligations to the world? And then, because I'm a

---

1. Telushkin, *Jewish Literacy*, 49.

Jewish writer, I have often found myself asking another question: What, if anything, does Judaism have to say about all this?

This may sound like a crazy question at first: why should Judaism, or any organized religion, have anything to say about the artist's life and work, especially when so many artists are disengaged from organized religion? Well, I think it's important to remember that Judaism emerged in an era when there was no word for "religion"—in other words, no idea of religion being separate from everything else in a person's life. It emerged in a time when every day, each action, all people were thought to be connected to the divine. In this understanding, anyone deeply engaged with the most powerful aspects of life—and that sounds like an artist to me—would be as mixed up with God as a priest would be, and could learn a lot from our tradition.

To do that learning, Jews have long turned first and foremost to the Torah. We have been called "People of the Book" because this text is at the center of our tradition and religious culture. The millennia-old text called *Pirkei Avot* (or, in English, "Sayings of our Fathers") advises us to "Turn it [the Torah] and turn it, for everything is in it." That's a bold statement—this document, written thousands of years ago, is supposed to have everything, *everything*, in it? Yes—that's what Judaism teaches. Indeed, our sages have even suggested that God read the Torah for instructions when creating the universe. So not only is it likely that artists can find themselves in there— we're part of everything, aren't we?—but if God is supposed to have used the Torah for help in creation, what better source of wisdom could we consult for help with questions on the creative process?

Of course, there are many views on the Torah, and while many people believe it to be the exact word of God (at least when it's in the original Hebrew), many other people think that the Hebrew Bible was written not by God but by people. For our purposes here, I'm not sure it makes all that much difference. Even if the words came from people, there's little doubt that these people were engaged with the weightiest possible practical, moral, and spiritual matters—with, however you define the term, the divine. There's also little doubt that the text, with its complicated relationships and ethical decisions and sibling rivalries and love and sex and violence and death, is still relevant to us today.

I'll admit, though, that, when I started writing this book, I managed to have my doubts all the same. Could I really find ideas and stories relevant to the artist's life all throughout the Torah? Not just in Genesis, that is, with its explicit interest in creation, but also in the wanderings of Exodus and Numbers, the focus on the Priesthood in Leviticus, the repetition in Deuteronomy? I wrote *The Artist's Torah* in part to delve into a sacred text for insights, and in part just to see if it could be done.

As it turned out, the problem wasn't going to be finding enough insight—my exploration unearthed views on the origin of creativity, the call to see creativity as a journey, the nature of sacrificing for one's art, the need for artists to engage with the senses and with emotion, the role of rules in a creative life, the ebb and flow of creativity, art and idolatry, the role of the artist in society, how to define and deal with success and failure, and much more. The problem was really going to be how to contain all the wisdom.

The Torah is a big, big book—not in the sense of word count, necessarily, but certainly in its scope and detail and complexity. When Hillel talked about "commentary," he was talking about a vast body of wisdom, both within the Torah and in response to it—wisdom that continues to grow and accumulate today. This is probably the main reason we read the text so slowly; each week Jews all over the world read one portion (or, in Hebrew, *parasha*) of the Torah, so that, by the end of the year, we've read the whole thing. Read it again, that is—each year at the holiday of Simchat Torah we return to the beginning and start over. It is a text so rich that one can read it for a lifetime and still find new insights.

This richness is the reason why I have broken the book down into so many chapters, each one representing one of the weekly Torah readings. As I discovered, each *parasha* has something distinct to tell us about creativity and the life that surrounds and supports creativity.

Of course, the Torah isn't the only good source of information in the world. In this book I've also gathered the wisdom of a broad array of Jewish artists, including quotes and ideas from painter Marc Chagall, sculptor Louise Nevelson, composer Arnold Schoenberg, songwriter Paul Simon, choreographers Anna Sokolow and Meredith Monk, filmmaker Woody Allen, poets Robert Pinsky and Muriel Rukeyser, and fiction writers Philip Roth and Allegra Goodman, in addition to a number of Jewish religious scholars. These artists and thinkers add a great deal to the conversation, perhaps in spite of—or more likely *because* of—the great diversity of their experiences and their attitudes. It's also striking how often their thoughts line up with what I'm finding in the lines of the Torah.

What I hope above all is that this book will be of use—of use to people who have lived as full-time artists for years and to those who are just beginning to explore their creativity; to people who consider themselves religious and to those who don't; to lovers of Torah and to those who view it with suspicion and mistrust and to those who've never encountered it before; to Jewish people and to everyone else as well.

To this end, I've concluded each chapter with questions. I use the line *In Your Mouth and In Your Heart* from Deuteronomy (30:14), a line that reminds us that Torah is not up in Heaven, too far away from us to be reached, but instead down here among us and in us. Whether we're talking about the creative spark or spiritual understanding, this book means to suggest that we contain these things already, and just need to see them more clearly. I end the chapters with questions so that you'll have the opportunity to look inward.

At that point, it's up to you. As I said, there's really only one secret to doing art: you have to do it. The rest *is* just commentary—but, as I've found in the journey of writing this book, it's powerful commentary indeed. And so I invite you to do what I did:

Go and study.

# Genesis

# B'reishit

## The Roots of the Artist in the Tree of Knowledge

Genesis 1:1—6:8

*Man has become like one of us, knowing good and bad . . .*

GENESIS 3:22

WHAT MAKES A PERSON an artist? What makes a person start painting, choreographing, composing, writing, or snapping photographs, as a way of expressing what is irresistibly compelling about the universe? What makes a person even *notice* that the universe's details are worth expressing in this way?

The reason these questions matter is because our answers can change our lives. If we believe that art requires madness or genius or an expensive education, we'll just decide that art is for other people. If we believe that art is something only children do, we'll grow out of it and leave it behind. But what if we were to believe that art is part of all of us, part of what makes us human?

Painter Marc Chagall once wrote, "Art seems to me to be above all a state of the soul."[1] In other words, art is not something outside us, to be acquired—it's something within us, to be discovered. And although success in an art form requires an artist to learn skills and traditions, the creative

---

1. Chagall, *My Life*, 115.

orientation itself is a natural state, not a learned one. When choreographer Anna Sokolow trained actors to dance, she observed that, while "it may seem to the actor that he is learning how to move and how to use his body . . . what he really learns is to be simple, honest and human."[2] Art is, in fact, our heritage as a species—a heritage that, in Jewish understanding, dates back to the very beginning of time.

The first *parasha* (portion) in our annual cycle of Torah readings returns us to the story of *Gan Eden*, the Garden of Eden—a story that has meant many things to many people. To some Christians, for example, it is the account of how, with a bite of fruit, people committed the Original Sin, the one that hangs on humankind to this day. There are also Jews who, while they might not put quite as much emphasis on the moment, regard it as our earliest spiritual failure. To others, it is an allegory describing how men and women have become mutually estranged and suspicious, or a prooftext for misogyny, or a sensational story of rebellion, or the place where snakes and apples (or was it a fig?) got a bad rap. In Jewish tradition, it is also seen as the time that started our calendars running.

That's right—as I write these words the universe around me, according to Jewish tradition, is 5,772 years old, and the sages derived that count by calculating backwards, from generation to generation, to the birth of *ha-adam*, the first human being, in the Garden. Now, let me say that I personally take this story as divine metaphor—a tale that, while not factual in a literal sense, nonetheless connects us to what is universal and Godly in the universe—and so I don't worry about squaring the exact year count with a Darwinian account of evolution. What I *do* think about is the enormous significance we place on the story of ha-Adam's emergence in *Gan Eden*—such significance that we locate the beginning of our calendars—of *time*—right then and there.

So what was it that, in this story, began with the emergence of *ha-adam*? Note that, by the time he made his first appearance, the Garden of Eden was already a lush and vibrant natural utopia, with all species of plants and animals having been in place from nearly the beginning. Thus, his arrival didn't mark the beginning of life. When *ha-adam* arrived, he was already surrounded by the fullness of creation.

So is it possible then that this moment, commemorated by the number on our calendars, doesn't mark the actual beginning of cosmic or geological

2. Warren, *Anna Sokolow*, 202.

or evolutionary time but of something different, yet equally profound? A rabbi once suggested to me that that number instead reminds us of a crucial turning point—not in the history of the Earth but rather in the maturation of the human species. Specifically, as we'll see, the Garden of Eden can be seen as the place where, more than anything, we as a species became *aware.* Aware, that is, of creation, of ourselves, of God—and this awareness is what fuels and defines the deepest human experience.

I approach this issue, above all, as an artist, a writer, a person for whom awareness is perhaps the overarching point of existence. We fulfill our highest potential not when we are wealthy, necessarily, or when we're physically strong, or even when we're happy, in my opinion—no, we fulfill ourselves when we are in deep connection with the universe around us. This is the one true summit in the writer's life, the artist's life, and, in fact, all human life. What this awareness actually *is*, we can explore through the central turning point in the story of the Garden of Eden.

According to the story, *ha-adam* was in a state of real innocence before partaking of the forbidden fruit, and so was the woman who would come to be called Eve. The thirteenth-century sage Ramban wrote that "man's original nature was such that he did whatever was proper for him to do naturally, just as the heavens and all their hosts do."[3] Indeed, before eating from the Tree of Knowledge of Good and Evil, there was no backtalk from these humans, and, like all the other animals around them, *The two of them were naked, the man and his wife, yet they felt no shame* (Gen 2:25).[4] The early parts of this story show us a man and a woman no different from the rest of creation—all-natural and perfectly content. Probably they were so content, in fact, that they never even stopped to reflect on the fact of their contentment.

The fruit changed all that. With one bite, these two brought down on themselves an all-time devastating curse from God. They had to say good-bye to their easy contentment, trading it in for something else entirely: *suffering.* Suffering throughout their lifetimes, and through all the generations of humankind.

But how did God plan to ensure that this misery would continue through the generations? Through constant efforts to put stumbling blocks

3. Ramban, *Commentary*, 72.

4. Unless otherwise noted, all quotes from the five books of the Torah are from the 2004 Etz Hayim translation from the Jewish Publication Society.

in our path? Through regular visitations of plagues? Through a physical battle to the finish between deity and mortals? No—tradition teaches that, in the moment of eating of the forbidden fruit, suffering became an unchanging part of human nature itself. It would never have to be renewed by God, because it had become part of the fabric of our very existence. Everything changed, *in us*, in that moment. As the *midrash* (Torah commentary) explains, when Adam *knew* after being ejected from *Gan Eden* (as in, *the man knew his wife Eve*, Gen 4:1), "He knew how he had been robbed of his tranquility" (*Bereshith Rabbah* 22:2).

So what exactly was it that changed about us, to guarantee all this suffering, when we ate the fruit from the tree of knowledge of good and evil? The answer is contained in the name of the tree itself. After the man and woman ate, the Torah tells us, *the eyes of both of them were opened* (Gen 3:7), and God later exclaimed, *man has become like one of us, knowing good and bad . . .* (Gen 3:22). This tree, then, lived up to its press—but the wisdom it delivered wasn't quite what Eve had been expecting when she reached for that tempting fruit.

The very first experiences of wisdom included an embarrassed awareness of their own nakedness, and great fear at hearing God approach. God, the One that had previously been to them a parent, a creator, a nurturer, now promised them that where before they had seen utopia, now they would see toil and thorns and thistles—and suffering. One *midrash* on these verses quotes this line from Ecclesiastes: *For as wisdom grows, vexation grows; To increase learning is to increase heartache* (1:18).[5] We became aware, and not just of the good in the world, but also of the evil.

Yet remember that each year at the holiday Simchat Torah, when we return in our Torah-reading to this part of our story, we don't mourn—we dance. Remember that this moment of eviction from paradise is not just a fall—it is also the beginning of the remarkable path of human history, as we understand it.

In *gan Eden* all had been perfect—there was no need for the humans to produce, to work, to improve the world, and so of course they did not do any of these things. In the difficult world outside the garden, however, there was a pressing need for the humans to better their world—and they began at their task right away. Immediately after the expulsion we learn that Adam and Eve will be having a child. Cain won't turn out to be the easiest child,

---

5. Unless otherwise noted, all quotes from the rest of the Hebrew Bible are from the 1985 translation from the Jewish Publication Society.

but nonetheless this is an awe-inspiring moment, because this is an act of creation by humans—the first ever. These two have now done something that up until this time has been solely God's domain. And here's the key: as we saw earlier, the word used to describe the first human conception is the verb "to know"—Adam and Eve are now in a position to truly "know" one another, precisely because of the wisdom that has guaranteed them so much suffering, and it is this knowledge that makes them creators, akin to the God that created them.

According to the great Torah scholar Rashi, when the snake tried to persuade Eve to eat of the forbidden fruit he said, "Every craftsman hates his fellow craftsmen. He [God] ate of the tree and created the world."[6] Ramban calls this slander on the snake's part—but the eating of the fruit has done exactly what the serpent claimed it would. It has turned human beings into crafters and creators, in the image of their God.

The loss of Eden was therefore not the end of human civilization, but in fact the beginning. In the perfection of the garden, there could be no Torah scrolls, no Judaism, no sculpture or music; Eden was already perfect, and needed none of these things. Only afterwards was there a need—and only afterwards were there human beings capable of participating in meeting those needs.

This, as the descendants of these first rebellious humans, is our legacy—a legacy of partnership with God in building and rebuilding the world.

This book is about embracing this creative opportunity. It is about taking our heritage seriously, about understanding the calling to art, with its aspect of curse and its aspect of blessing. On the one hand, artists see what is broken in relationships, in work lives, in political and social systems, and everywhere else in the universe around us. On the other hand, seeing these truths (along with the equally real truths of beauty and compassion and holiness) allows us to express them, so that others might know that they are not alone in their understanding of the world. This is the calling of the artist—and it *is* a calling, in every sense of the word. It means calling things what they are, and calling out the truth, loudly, across the empty spaces that separate us from one another, so that others might hear it. It is a calling that every one of us is able to hear, and to receive.

6. Chabad.org.

"To be a poet," Piercy says, "is to open your eyes to everything around you."[7] As poet Allen Afterman puts it—and he, like Piercy, could very easily be talking about any art form: "Poetry is the downward motion of enclothement, of capturing. Thus poetry is related to the concept in Torah of catching light, of catching arrows in midair; ultimately, of catching the expanding universe."[8] What we're talking about again is a kind of awareness, openness to the world around us.

Most artists who've been at their craft for a while know that, although this awareness is as natural a habit as breathing, it can take a lot more effort to acquire and maintain than breathing does. We have been raised to pay attention first and foremost to the practical details of life, from the basics of food and shelter to the more abstract realities of money and prestige, and so we have to cut against that, over and over, to pause to smell roses—or garbage. Often we'd rather not make a pause like that. Do we really want to see all the brokenness in the universe? "I think when I get blocked," says songwriter Paul Simon, "when I have writer's block . . . what it is is that you have something to say but you don't want to say it. So your mind says, 'I have nothing to say. I've just nothing more to say. I can't write anything. I have no thoughts.' Closer to the truth is that you have a thought that you really would prefer not to have."[9]

The first thing is to make the difficult commitment to the truth, even when the truth is uncomfortable in some way. "As a *lyricist*," Simon explains, "my job is to find out what it is that I'm thinking. Even if it's something that I don't want to be thinking."[10]

Consider what all this means. Consider that the past 5,772 years have been leading up to this moment. That you are a descendant of the first scientist, the first inventor, the first artist. And when you were born you carried into the world the deeply human ability to see the world clearly, to know it, and to call out your knowing.

7. Moyers, *Fooling with Words*, 184.
8. Afterman, *Kabbalah and Consciousness*, 75.
9. Zollo, *Song-Writers*, 98.
10. Ibid.

*In Your Mouth and In Your Heart:*

What beauty do you see in the world around you? What brokenness? Can you envision creating a piece of art that would honor and express both? Get started on it.

# Noach

## Two Pockets

### Genesis 6:9—11:32

RABBI BUNIM, A HASIDIC teacher of the late eighteenth and early nineteenth centuries, told his students that they should carry two scrolls with them, one in each pocket. One should read, "I am dust and ashes," and the other should read, "the world was created for me." For sure this challenged his students to adopt a balanced view of their own importance; more importantly, though, it also reminded them about an enduring tension in Judaism. Ours is the religion where joyous weddings culminate with the shattering of a glass to remind us of brokenness, and ours is the religion that asks us to respond to death and loss with the Mourner's Kaddish, a prayer consisting only of praise, with no mention of death at all. In the midst of creation we are consistently confronted with destruction and in the face of destruction we are reminded of creation.

Take *Parashat Noach* for example. This is the second portion in the Torah, right on the heels of *B'reishit*; we have barely finished hearing about seven days of creation, just gotten through generations and generations of begetting—and already we encounter a deeply frustrated God saying to Noah, *I have decided to put an end to all flesh . . . I am about to destroy them with the earth* (Gen 6:13). And so comes the flood—water from above, water from below, enough to cover the highest mountains by a sizable margin. The scope of the destruction defies imagination: *And all flesh that stirred on earth perished—birds, cattle, beasts, and all the things that swarmed upon the earth, and all mankind. All in whose nostrils was the merest breath of life, all that was on dry land, died. All existence on earth was blotted out.* (Gen 7:21–23)

However, the destruction *isn't* total; as the Torah says, *Noah was left, and those with him in the ark* (Gen 7:23), including his immediate family and many pairs of animals. God has been unable to fully follow through on the threatened *end to all flesh*, and it's a pretty big concession; because God allowed these few to survive, the world will soon be repopulated with all the same creatures that populated it before the flood. Even the most consistently vexing animals—humans—will be back in full throng.

Of course, they'll all be the descendants of Noah, a *righteous man . . . blameless in his age* (Gen 6:9), which perhaps gave God a good feeling about starting over with him. But even Noah's family contains the same tension between creation and destruction that we see throughout the Torah. He is the descendant of Seth, the son that Adam and Eve begat *in place of Abel* (Gen 4:25), a kind of stand-in for the favored son. At the same time, Noah's wife Naama is actually a descendant of the very Cain who killed Abel in the first place. That means that their sons, who will be the forebears of all the peoples of the earth, are a volatile mix of both lines.

According to the Jewish mystics known as the Kabbalists, volatility is built into the nature of the world. When God created the world, in this account, it was through a divine light that poured into the void. Vessels called *sefirot* were created to contain the light, but many were unable to hold it, and instead shattered. The shards, still coated with some of the divine light, fell to our world. Part of the Kabbalistic message, then, is that our world is a mix of these apparent opposites, too.

These thinkers, though, also ask us to rethink our understanding of destruction. The mystic Menahem Azaria of Fano offered an analogy in which the *sefirot*, described as "points of light," are compared to seeds: "And just as a seed cannot grow to perfection as long as it maintains its original form—growth coming only through decomposition—so these points could not become perfect configurations as long as they maintained their original form but only by shattering."[11]

Creation and destruction, we learn, are not antagonists but partners. God's light shatters and nurtures growth at the same time; Adam and Eve lose the Garden of Eden and gain the ability to reproduce; the flood wipes the face of the earth clean so it can be filled again. This double edging

11. Matt, *Essential Kabbalah*, 96.

continues throughout the Torah. Later in *Noach*, in fact, we see humanity coming together to build the tower of Babel, high enough to reach Heaven. This is a tremendous creative achievement, but sages also believed this was an attempt to wage war against God. Then God thwarts the attempt by scattering us across the earth and turning our one human language into many languages—an act that can be viewed either as leaving humanity in confusion or as unleashing our full potential for cultural richness and diversity.

Of course, every day we see the double edge in our own lives. Losing a job or ending a relationship means starting a new kind of life, sometimes with opportunities better than the original ones, but always new and different. Reconciliations among family members sometimes happen at a deathbed. Then, too, the great joys of life—marriage and parenthood, for example— ask us to let go of old identities and build new ones. As Judith Taylor puts it in her poem "Mood Sonnet #4," "To break out of a life you must have the humility to destroy it."[12]

Nowhere is this more vivid and constant than in the artist's life, where every day of work is a blend of destruction and creation. The creation part of things, of course, is the most obvious; art is often directly concerned with finding or making something new, or finding a new way to express things. When painter Marc Chagall said, "I want to see a new world,"[13] when Isaac Bashevis Singer said that "literature is capable of bringing new horizons and new perspectives,"[14] when choreographer Anna Sokolow set up the "fresh and new" as her goal,[15] they were all talking about the same thing.

This can be seen as a spiritual and religious goal as well. Think of Isaiah's words: *Sing to the Lord a new song* (42:10). But what does it mean to make something new?

Chagall revealed what he considered the goal of art, in saying that he wanted us "plunging into chaos . . . shattering . . . turning upside down the familiar ground under our feet."[16] And so art requires the same kind of shattering we encounter in the Kabbalistic story of the world's origins. Art is simultaneously creation and destruction. But what exactly is destroyed in the process?

12. Taylor, *Selected Dreams*, 15.
13. Chagall, *My Life*, 94.
14. Allen, *Nobel Lectures*, 163.
15. Sokolow, "I Hate Academies," 38.
16. Chagall, *My Life*, 101.

Making something new happen in an art in some sense means that we have to throw out our old understandings. I think of Arnold Schoenberg and his invention of the twelve-tone method of music composition. Before that, according to Leonard Bernstein, "Schoenberg was in a blind alley. He had stretched tonality to such a point of agony that he couldn't stretch any more without actually tearing it to pieces. So tear it he did, and destroyed it entirely. And out came atonal music."[17] This, of course, upended many composers' understandings of how music could work.

Every poem that changes our understanding of the line break, every sculpture that makes us rethink how form can take up space, every dance that gives a new vision of the possibilities and limits of movement—every really *creative* piece of art—in some ways destroys what art used to be.

The effects only spread from there, if an artist's work is effective. The "chaos" that Chagall talks about is meant to overturn the earth we walk on—and so often that is the effect of good art. When an artist sees a "new world," s/he often feels, as musician and contemporary composer John Zorn says, "compelled to tell the truth" about it[18]—and that means that everyone who encounters the art is confronted with that unexpected vision too. "What we're doing," Zorn says, "is we're creating something that is a little bit scary to most people. It challenges their view of the world." Maybe that means that the world itself ends up changed.

Certainly the artist ends up changed, if everything goes right. I'd take it further than Zorn: as artists we're doing something that is *very* scary, even to us. It challenges our view of ourselves. It asks us to respond to the truth we see, without and within. It asks us to be willing to grow—to destroy what we've been so that we can be something new. The writer Gertrude Stein advises, "A very important thing—and I know it because I have seen it kill so many writers—is not to make up your mind that you are any one thing."[19] And so we, too, can be turned upside down, or any which way— just like the ground under our feet.

I think this is one reason some people avoid the arts. It's easier, in fact, to make your mind up permanently about things, to embrace the known and keep the unknown at a distance. The person who wants to escape destruction—a synonym here for change, for letting go of the past—has to avoid creation as well. Neither one can go long without involving the other.

17. Bernstein, *Joy of Music*, 202.
18. Milkowski, "John Zorn."
19. Preston, "Conversation with Stein," 167.

Maybe this is also why so many artists claim they don't have a choice about what they do. The implication is that, if they had a choice, they'd do something else. But how many really mean it? Sure—a photographer, for example, who puts down the camera forever has a chance to forget just how ephemeral our powerful moments can be (how much like dust, that is), and how much a captured vision can shake the earth (which was created for me). That person can try to walk through life with pockets totally emptied. Yet the floods and towers of the Torah, the begettings and blottings out, all suggest that to do so is to give up something that is a deep part of what it means to be human. To be an artist is to set that option aside utterly. To be an artist is to get into the powerful work of creation, and to judge your success in part by whether or not your work opens the heavens and the fountains of the deep—by whether or not it invites the flood.

---

### In Your Mouth and In Your Heart:

What does your creative work do that hasn't been done before? What traditions would you most like to turn upside down in your work? Go ahead.

# Lekh L'kha

## The Stranger and the Journey

### Genesis 12:1—17:27

IT HAS BEEN OBSERVED by many creative writing teachers that there are only two stories in the world: on the one hand, you have Someone Goes on a Journey, a storyline found everywhere from *Gilgamesh* and *The Odyssey* to *Huckleberry Finn* and *Star Trek*; on the other, there's A Stranger Comes to Town, which you can see in, for starters, *Beowulf*, *Pride and Prejudice*, and *Beloved*, not to mention countless horror movies. Sometimes, as in the case of *Parashat Lekh L'kha*, we get both plots at once. In this Torah portion, God plays the role of the stranger, coming to town to tell Abram (who will become Abraham later in the *parasha*) to leave his home and head out into the world. In some ways, then, this is the ultimate story—visitation and journey all at once.

Interestingly, many commentators find themselves stuck just a few words into this tale. It begins: *The Lord said to Abram, lekh l'kha* (Gen 12:1). Those last two words, which make up the title of the *parasha*, are difficult to translate. The first word, *lekh*, is a clear command to "go," but the second word—which seems to literally mean "to you" or "for you"—is harder to understand, especially because the command would make perfect sense without it. In the story, God could just say *Go*, but doesn't.

This is going be a big journey for Abram. He's going to leave his father's dwelling place and travel to a land that God promises will belong to all his descendants, a people that will be uncountably numerous and great. That makes it a big journey for *all* people who consider themselves inheritors of Abraham in one way or another—and that's why it makes sense that so many Torah scholars have stopped to ask why God starts the journey off with that complicated command.

It would make sense for artists to ask this question, too. Artists often feel visited by a kind of compulsion—I *must* make music; I *must* dance, or "one is an artist by necessity," as composer Leonard Bernstein said[20]—and our path, too, is a journey, one that could just as easily begin with the imperative *lekh l'kha* as Abram's did.

Rashi, the great eleventh-century Torah scholar, looks at this command and sees God telling Abram, "Go forth *for yourself.*" In other words, Abram should go forth for his own good. God is definitely offering some incentives:

> *I will make of you a great nation;*
> *And I will bless you;*
> *I will make your name great,*
> *And you shall be a blessing.*
> *I will bless those who bless you,*
> *And curse him that curses you;*
> *And all the families of the earth*
> *Shall bless themselves by you.* (Gen 12:2–3)

Of course, many of these rewards—like the great nation, for example—will come after Abraham is dead. You can see a parallel in the artist's life: if an artist achieves greatness, the work will outlive her or him, and there's always the possibility of fame as well. Yet in both cases there's a more immediate reward as well, in the meaning of the journey itself.

One Kabbalistic interpretation of the command is "Go *to* yourself"; in other words, travel inward as you make your way through the world. Come to know yourself. As I mentioned earlier, in this *parasha* Abram becomes Abraham, the name by which we know him best, and which has been translated as "the father of many nations." In this change, he has become his truer self—has fulfilled the destiny that his inner nature demanded. So, too, do artists become their truer selves as they pursue their callings; Allen Shawn, the biographer of Arnold Schoenberg, says that we learn from Schoenberg—and we could learn this from many different practicing artists—to live "according to the law of life which compels us, if we would live and grow, to become ever more fully and nakedly what we essentially are."[21]

---

20. Bernstein, *Joy of Music*, 43.

21. Shawn, *Schoenberg's Journey*, 83.

Because of their inward nature, both of these journeys are in some sense solitary. In describing painter Amedeo Modigliani, for example, poet Anna Akhmatova said, "He seemed surrounded by a dense ring of solitude."[22] Sculptor Louise Nevelson said, "An artist by his very nature works alone. He spends most of this time by himself."[23]

This may be part of the reason that Rabbi Samson Raphael Hirsch translated the Torah's command as "Go *by* yourself." As it says in the Plaut commentary on the Torah, "One must become a stranger in the world to view it clearly."[24] Composer John Zorn sees that as the role of the artist as well. He says, "I think the outsiders, the individualists, the people who have a messianic belief in themselves and are able to stick with their vision despite all odds . . . they're the ones that are really going to make a difference in the world."[25]

Here we see again the importance of the journey. That may be one final reason for the strange construction of God's message. Maybe God, above all, wanted to make the command as urgent as possible. Consider the fact that *lekh* and *l'kha* have the exact same spelling in the Torah scroll, which is written without vowels. A Hebrew reader encountering these words for the first time, without vowels, might see them as saying "To you, to you," or, more plausibly, as "Go, go"—in either case a repetition that emphasizes the pressing nature of the order. Maybe God is saying, *Go—GO, already.*

This feels deeply Jewish; we are told by God much more often to *do* things than we are told to *feel* things or to *understand* them. As a result, we've been following these commandments since they were first uttered, while the emotion and comprehension have only developed over time, in the millennia of Jewish life and study that have followed the Torah's writing. And so, as with any *mitzvah* (commandment) we are asked to observe, it is even more important for Abram or for the artist to just get started than it is to immediately and deeply appreciate the journey on all the many levels contained in this rich command.

Of course, as artists, as independent spirits, we don't like being told what to do. We don't like hearing, *Because I said so.* The very urgency and individuality of our artistic drive makes us resistant to the idea of God or any other stranger coming to town from parts unknown to give us direction.

22. Meyers, *Modigliani*, 89.
23. Lisle, *Louise Nevelson*, 225.
24. Plaut, *The Torah*, 102.
25. Milkowski, "John Zorn."

But what if God was not some external taskmaster but some inner voice, something not in conflict with our innermost instincts but in partnership with them? After all, the translation of *go to yourself* suggests that it would be impossible to fulfill this *mitzvah* in a way that was inconsistent with one's core self. To deny one's nature in going forth is to not go forth at all.

If this is true, the rewards and the insights will start to become manifest once the journey is underway. Right now, though, the important thing is to get started.

---

### *In Your Mouth and In Your Heart:*

Imagine that the universe somehow told you to *lekh l'kha*—where would you and your creative work go? What paths would you take? And ask yourself: is it possible that the universe is already saying *lekh l'kha*? How will you start the journey?

---

# Va-yera

## The Sacrifice

### Genesis 18:1—22:24

*P*ARASHAT *VA-YERA* IS ONE of the busiest in the Torah; in it, Abraham gives us a lesson in hospitality and shows us how to argue with God, and then Sodom and Gomorrah are destroyed, Lot's wife is turned into a pillar of salt and Lot's daughters try to repopulate a world they think has been utterly destroyed; meanwhile, Sarah manages to get pregnant and birth Isaac at ninety years of age, and Abraham even takes time to argue with Abimelech about wells. As we return to this part of the text each year, there's a lot to draw our eyes. Yet one story seems to overshadow all the others. In Hebrew, this episode is called the *akedah*—the binding.

At the end of this *parasha*, the same Abraham who, just four Torah chapters earlier, haggled on and on with God about the fate of Sodom and Gomorrah, is now following divine orders without question—bringing his beloved son to Mount Moriah, intending to make Isaac a human sacrifice. The plain meaning of the text is that this biblical hero is willing to kill the child that is the future of his people, the son he waited for until he was a hundred years old, the child he loves so dearly. God stops the sacrifice just before it happens, of course—but that doesn't make it easy to shake this moment: a God making an impossible demand, and a father, following a voice or a vision, with a knife over his son's throat, absolutely ready to kill.

One temptation for contemporary Jews is to dismiss this story as evidence that the Torah is hopelessly dated—that it's a relic from a brutal period in human history, one that's (thankfully) long gone. After all, in this day and age, it's hard to imagine getting an order like this from a God like

Genesis

that—and harder still to imagine following it. With this view, a book that can contain a story like this one looks completely irrelevant to us. There's a reason, after all, why many Jews don't ever read the Torah anymore.

Of course, this is a constant tension even for the Jews who do still read it; should we be trying to connect to all the parts of the Torah, or just the ones that seem most relevant or tolerable? If we decide the latter, the *akedah* is likely one of the chunks we're going to want to skip. If we decide the former, though—and, as Rabbi Menahem Nahum of Chernobyl said in the eighteenth century, "Everything in the Torah must apply to each person and to every time"[26]—we're going to have to find a way to connect to the hard stuff.

But let's back up a second. Is it really so difficult for us to relate to this particular story?

Okay—it feels extreme. It makes us uncomfortable. Yet the truth is that, as artists, surely we know a little something about great sacrifice.

At the most basic level, the pursuit of art demands time, energy, and some space to work. It means diverting resources that could go to other endeavors—and often without much hope of substantial financial compensation in return. There are other compensations, of course—but what are we prepared to give up in order to get them?

This question becomes a lot more intense when one's creative side starts seeming more like a vocation than just an avocation—a calling rather than a hobby. As art moves to the center of a life, and as one's goals for it become bigger and more challenging, its demands can become increasingly loud and insatiable. We look around at our lives, lives that also juggle families, friends, jobs, leisure time. What are we prepared to sacrifice?

A few years back, I was fortunate enough to be able to be a stay-at-home writer for a while. Time was abundant; when I was at home, I could write and write and write. My freedom even meant that, when I wasn't writing, I could travel and read to audiences from my first book of short stories, which had just come out.

Then our son was born. Anybody who has had a child knows that becoming a parent transforms a life completely. In one sense, this meant that I went from being a stay-at-home writer to being a stay-at-home Dad who wrote on the side. This brought me joys I had never predicted—and it also meant that time (not to mention sleep) was suddenly precious and scarce.

26. Green, *Menahem Nahum*, 212.

Most pressing, it was suddenly uncertain that I could simultaneously do right by my son and do right by my art.

What are we prepared to sacrifice?

Writer Saul Bellow went through marriage after marriage—five of them—and divorce after divorce. Architect Louis Kahn moved back and forth fleetingly between three simultaneous families, none of which knew about any of the others. Sculptor Louise Nevelson found it impossible to both do art and maintain a stable family at all. This pain and disconnection around relationships, of course, leads us toward another image of artists, as those who are deeply, constitutionally unwell. Indeed, mental illnesses like depression and social anxiety hounded Nevelson as well as writers Isaac Bashevis Singer, Allen Ginsberg, and Franz Kafka. The life of painters Chaim Soutine and Jules Pascin ended in suicide.

Or take the case of painter Amedeo Modigliani. As a teenager, Modigliani ignored his schoolwork in order to do his art. Later, he sacrificed his well-being by living in poverty despite coming from a well-to-do family, refusing to find ways to earn money in case they might threaten his artistic integrity. He was a womanizer, a drug addict. He neglected his children, refused to seek treatment for the tuberculosis that plagued him all his life. "Beauty herself makes painful demands," he wrote, "but these nevertheless bring forth the most supreme efforts of the soul."[27] Amedeo Modigliani died at the age of thirty-five. Although his "supreme efforts" were eventually appreciated, it didn't happen in his short lifetime.

In the light of these examples, the *akedah* starts to sound a little more familiar—and a little scarier.

Of course, this is only if we stick to the surface reading of this Torah story: God tells Abraham to kill Isaac; Abraham gets ready to obey; God calls it off. On the surface, it's a story about a God who demands unthinking obedience to even the cruelest commands and about a person who follows orders—no matter how disturbing—without question. Rabbi Michael Lerner, however, has offered us a very different understanding of this story. "The greatness of Abraham is *not* that he takes his son to Mount Moriah . . . so that he can sacrifice his son. No. The greatness of Abraham is that he doesn't go through with it."[28] Lerner suggested that Abraham mishears the original command, which in the text comes from "*ha elohim*"—translatable

27. Meyers, *Modigliani*, 30.

28. Lerner, *Jewish Renewal*, 45.

as "the gods." This may refer to the cruel gods he knew as a child growing up among idol makers; with those early experiences he was expecting to be asked to do violence. When the second command comes for Abraham to let Isaac go and do him no harm, it comes from a single messenger of *yod-hey-vav-hey*—the name of Abraham's new God. This is a subtle-seeming but actually colossal shift. Abraham, in seeing his son on the altar, grows enough to hear a new divine voice and to take on a new religious path—one in which he is most definitely *not* called on to sacrifice his son.

It's easy to make this same mistake in an artistic life, to set out to sacrifice the wrong thing. As children we grow up among idol-makers, too, among people who tell only the most dramatic stories about artists—stories about alcoholism, drug abuse, mental illness, broken families, poverty, and suicide. We are asked to idolize these lives. Yet even Modigliani once said, "Your duty is never to waste yourself in sacrifice. Your *real* duty is to save your dream."[29] He may have ultimately failed at this duty himself, but he was never calling for us to follow his sad example.

Meanwhile, there are other models for an artistic life. Painter Marc Chagall's happy marriage to Bella, choreographer Anna Halprin's healthy and artistically productive response to her own diagnosis of cancer, and writer Chaim Potok's ability to hold down a real job—these don't make for juicy story-telling, and so we usually don't hear about them. Yet these artists exist, and they can be our models—not our idols, but our models.

Of course, even if we're not being asked to abandon our families or our well-being, that doesn't mean that art comes for free. Nothing important does, I suppose. Even in the story of the *akedah*, after Abraham unties his son they don't just climb down the mountain and head home; they still have a sacrifice to make. But now that Abraham is perceiving things clearly—behold!—he sees a ram caught in a thicket and offers that up to God in place of Isaac. Artists, too, have to have clear enough vision to find something to offer up in place of their own destruction.

When composer John Zorn says, "we make a lot of sacrifices to do what we do,"[30] he's talking about more than needing a little time and space to write music. It can be remarkably difficult, however, to know what else it might take. Composer Leonard Cohen says:

29. Meyers, *Modigliani*, 30.
30. Goldberg, "John Zorn."

> Well, things come so damn slow. Things come and they come and it's a tollgate, and they're particularly asking for something that you can't manage. They say, "We got the goods here. What do you got to pay?" Well, I've got my intelligence, I've got a mind. "No, we don't want that." I've got my whole training as a poet. "No, we don't want that." I've got some licks, I've got some skills with my fingers on the guitar. "No, we don't want that either." Well, I've got a broken heart. "No, we don't want that." I've got a pretty girlfriend. "No, we don't want that." I've got sexual desire. "No, we don't want that." I've got a whole lot of things and the tollgate keeper says, "That's not going to get it."[31]

At one time or another, this is how it feels to many of us earnestly engaged in the attempt to create; we search frenetically for the toll, offering up anything and everything we can think of, perhaps even emulating some of our most destructive idols in the process. Each time Cohen's tollgate keeper says *no*—but the keeper finally adds: "We want you in a condition that you are not accustomed to. And that you yourself cannot name. We want you in a condition of receptivity that you cannot produce by yourself."[32]

You can see how this connects to the *akedah*. Imagine Abraham saying, "I've got my son," and God, "No, we don't want that." What God wanted was for Abraham to be receptive, open—to let go of his past. When he manages that, all of a sudden the proper sacrifice is visible to him, there in the nearby bushes. He doesn't have to hunt for it—he just has to *see* it.

We've already talked about the kind of receptivity required for the artist's life. What's new here is the idea that we might not be able to attain it by ourselves, and that it might involve some sacrifice.

Left to his own devices, still listening to the voices of his past, Abraham might have killed his son. Left to our own devices, listening to melodramatic artistic legends, we might engage in behaviors destructive to ourselves or others. When we think we already *know* the way it prevents us from *seeing* the way. Creativity, after all, requires that something new happen—and nothing new can happen when we've already got everything figured out. And so, no—we can't produce this receptivity by ourselves. We above all can't produce it *through* our selves. We can only produce it by getting the ego out of the way of the openness that's asked of us—and therein lies the sacrifice, too. We sacrifice our certainty, our egos, our feeling that we know what to do before we start.

31. Zollo, *Song-Writers*, 335.
32. Ibid.

When my son Reuben was three months old, I wrote a poem—the first writing I'd done since his birth. Looking back, it's not surprising that the subject of the piece was the arrival of my son. At the time, though, I had no idea what to expect. Over the next two months, I wrote eight more poems, five of them about Reuben, and three of those in what I imagined would have been his voice if he could speak—one was entitled "The Newborn Explains His Unhelpful Sleep Patterns." It was still difficult to find the time to work, and the first year of my son's life was by no means my most prolific, but I did write. By the time he was six months old I was beginning a book-length fiction project—a project fueled by the experiences of parenthood.

To make that happen I didn't have to sacrifice my family, and I didn't have to sacrifice my well-being; I needed to be receptive to what was going on around me. I did that by letting go of the way I had forged before becoming a father, and finding a new one.

And—behold!—the gates opened.

---

### In Your Mouth and In Your Heart:

What things in your life seem to be in conflict with your need to create? What do you need to sacrifice in order to do your work—and what do you *not* need to sacrifice? If you need to make some changes, make some changes—the right ones.

---

# Hayyei Sarah

## Clothes for the Abstraction

### Genesis 23:1—25:18

JEWS HAVE OFTEN BEEN referred to as People of the Book, because of the central importance of the Torah in our religious and cultural lives. Yet the reverse is true, too—the Torah might best be called the Book of the People. These scrolls describe events that take place not in Heaven but on Earth, and the stories are generally the stories of human beings muddling their way through life. In fact, one of the most interesting things about these pages is the way God sometimes disappears from direct view, leaving the action to us, the divine visible only through our interactions and our relationships with one another.

In *parashat Hayyei Sarah*, for example, the implication is that God is involved with the events at hand, but not in a speaking or acting role. Instead, the human characters of the Torah are at the center of things—and their timeless humanity comes through at every turn.

Some of these stories involve loss. First, Sarah passes away, and Abraham returns from a journey *to mourn for Sarah and to bewail her* (Gen 23:2). At the end of the *parasha*, Abraham dies, and his sons Isaac and Ishmael come together to bury him. As is the Torah's habit, however, the interpersonal losses are often balanced by an emphasis on new or renewed relationships. Take Isaac and Ishmael, estranged brothers, who have found a way to come together for their father's funeral. Then, too, there's the lengthy story about Rebecca and Isaac coming together. In the middle of the *parasha*, before his death, Abraham sends his servant Eliezer to find a wife for Isaac, and Eliezer leaves town, finds Rebecca and brings her to meet Isaac. When they do meet, the word "love" is used for the first time in the Torah to describe the feelings in a marital relationship, and we hear that Isaac is consoled by this love, enough to begin to heal from the loss of his mother. All in all, these are our stories—the stories of our living, our dying, the actions we take through it all.

Yet these are also God's stories. Although not in the foreground here, a divine presence is still in the text fairly continuously. Above all, we see this in Eliezer's mission. Before sending him off, Abraham says, *[God] will send His angel before you* (Gen 24:7). We never see this angel, but its effects are soon felt. When Eliezer gets to a good spot, he prays for a sign. (This is the first prayer to be found in the Torah, and it's worth noting that it's a prayer intended to bring about a human relationship.) When Rebecca appears, Eliezer gets the sign he wanted, and doesn't take the form of some supernatural event—instead he knows he's found the right woman because she is so kind as to give him and all of his camels water. God is here in this *parasha*, but our awareness of God comes not as a result of awe-inspiring miracles and wonders, but from concrete, earthly things, such the decent and hospitable actions of human beings.

For contemporary readers, this kind of connection to God makes sense. We may *davven* (pray) or find inspiration in the Torah's pages, but we don't generally expect God to show up in a flash of lightning to boom out proclamations or direct our lives face to face. God has been described by modern thinkers as "The power that makes for salvation" (Rabbi Mordecai Kaplan),[33] the "eternal Thou" (Martin Buber)[34] or simply as a verb rather than a noun (Rabbi David Cooper)[35]—generally a God that can't be actually touched or seen or heard. In fact, the painter Mark Rothko observed that it's impossible to encounter God directly. He noted that it's that way with all abstractions: "Like the old ideal of God, the abstraction itself in its nakedness is never directly apprehensible to us. As in the case of God, we can know its manifestation only through works, which, while never completely revealing the total abstraction in the round, symbolize it by the manifestation of different faces of itself in works of art."[36]

As I mentioned above in discussing Rebecca's kindness, God can only be encountered if made concrete in some way in the world. Good human

33. Kaplan, "God as the Power," 72.

34. Buber, "I and Thou," 63.

35. Cooper, *God Is a Verb*.

36. Rothko, *Artist's Reality*, 64.

actions accomplish this—and, as Rothko tells us, so does art. Art is one of the methods at our disposal for making God present in a real way in the world. Or, as Rabbi Elizabeth Bolton puts it: "Our struggles with Judaism are about a search for meaning in life through a lived tradition, involving exploration at countless levels of learning, teaching, thinking, and experiencing. Art renders the search visible and tangible, communicating what is discovered through dancing, singing, drawing, creating, designing, building."[37]

How does art do this? According to Rothko, the artist "tries to give human beings direct contact with eternal verities through reduction of those verities to the realm of sensuality, which is the basic language for the human experience of all things."[38] By "the realm of sensuality," Rothko just meant the realm of our five senses. He added, "For sensuality is the one basic human quality necessary for the appreciation of all truth."[39] In other words, we *can't* appreciate God—or anything abstract—unless it becomes available to our senses.

Perhaps for this reason, the Torah doesn't just say something like *Rebecca was very nice* and expect us to believe it's true. Instead, we get to know her through concrete actions. When we read *Quickly emptying her jar into the trough, she ran back to the well to draw; and she drew for all [Eliezer's] camels* (Gen 24:20), we can picture her doing it, and in that tangible picture of earnestness we can really know her.

As Bolton suggests, the same kind of thing happens when we encounter art. For the most part, art is inescapably sensual; we hear music in our ears (or even feel it in our body if it's loud enough), take in the colors of paint or the contours of a sculpture or the leaps of a dancer through our eyes. Sound, color, shape, movement—the realm of the sensual. Written art (unless it's read aloud) is at the greatest disadvantage in this respect, as black marks on white paper don't offer much of a sensory experience by themselves. But even writers work to evoke the sensual, as the old adage "Show, don't tell" suggests. Again, the Torah doesn't just tell us that *Rebecca was nice*—it *shows* us her character. In this way, writers try to join their fellow artists in making the abstract concrete.

---

37. Bolton, "Toward a Jewish Theology," 19.

38. Rothko, *Artist's Reality*, 25.

39. Ibid., 27.

This is what completes poet Allen Afterman's description of poetry as "the downward motion of enclothement, of capturing."[40] The first step in doing this is the kind of awareness we talked about in response to *parashat B'reishit*. The second step is to take that awareness and make it concrete—to, in a paraphrase of Afterman, give it clothes. What could be more tangible than that? The notes on the guitar, charcoal lines, the developed photograph—these are all the clothes for the abstraction to wear, so that it can be encountered in the world.

There is no other way for the artist; we are bound simultaneously to abstract truths and to the earthbound limits and opportunities of the five senses. We work so that a higher reality can *feel* real to ourselves and others. If we approach the work with this understanding, our art can be the kind of sign that Eliezer prayed for—the concrete evidence that there's something in the universe worth our devoted attention.

---

### *In Your Mouth and In Your Heart:*

How can your creative work better reach the five senses? Where does it lose itself in abstraction, and where is it vividly concrete? Create something that really touches those senses.

---

40. Afterman, *Kabbalah and Consciousness*, 75.

# Tol'dot

## The Art of Imitation

### Genesis 25:19—28:9

A S I'VE NOTED BEFORE, artists often feel the need to throw out old conceptions, old methods, old approaches, and to replace them with something that hasn't been thought or used or tried before. Many of us seem to be fueled by the sentiment found in Isaiah: *Sing to the Lord a new song* (42:10). Of course, this raises a lot of questions for the artist, like: What does "new" really mean? Is it possible to create something completely new, something so original that it's a complete break from the old? And if that's the goal, to move away from the known and toward the unknown, is there anything to be learned from the artists who have come before us? Is there anything to be gained from modeling ourselves after others, from imitation?

The word "imitation" carries some negative associations—the word "cheap" goes with it easily. And even if you manage to make a "perfect like-ness" of something, that tends to impress people less than doing something truly innovative. Critics attack art they see as derivative, a boring recycling of old ideas.

Yet most artists, at least during some stage of their careers, actively try on the styles of others. First of all, it's unclear that an artist can ever really create something that's absolutely new. Critics see links between ev-ery revolutionary artistic movement—cubism, jazz, modern dance—and the work that's come before it. So even if "derivative" is meant to be an insult, it probably also describes every piece of art that's ever been created. Imitation is what happens when artists acknowledge that fact and make it happen on purpose. So what dangers do we flirt with in doing this—and what opportunities?

*Parashat Tol'dot* gives us a window onto this issue. Here, we meet Isaac and Rebecca's children—two boys named Jacob and Esau. They are twins, though not identical twins. In fact, the Torah goes out of its way to emphasize the differences between the boys. Even in the womb they fight with one another, and Esau emerges hairy and red, and Jacob (born second) is smooth and pale. Esau grows to become a hunter, while Jacob spends most of his time in his family's tents. Even the parents do their part to separate the boys; Isaac prefers Esau and Rebecca prefers Jacob. Turn after turn, the text distinguishes between the brothers, and later commentators get into the act, too, painting Esau as the height of wickedness and Jacob as a model of morality. Given this sharp contrast, it might surprise a first-time reader to see that the story of the *parasha* hinges on a case of mistaken identity between them.

The twenty-seventh chapter of Genesis opens by describing Isaac's later years: *Isaac was old, and his eyes were too dim to see* (27:1). He's worried that his death is around the corner, and so he wants to bless his first (and favored) son Esau before it's too late. He sends Esau out to hunt—Isaac loves to eat what the boy brings home—and promises to bless him when he gets back. Rebecca overhears, however, and wants *her* favored son, Jacob, to get that blessing. Her plan is for Jacob to impersonate Esau, bringing Isaac game and wearing his brother's clothes, as well as hairy goatskins on his arms and neck—and the plan works. After some initial ambivalence about a son that feels and smells like Esau but sounds like Jacob, Isaac goes ahead with his blessing:

> *May God give you*
> *Of the dew of heaven and the fat of the earth*
> *Abundance of new grain and wine.*
> *Let peoples serve you,*
> *And nations bow to you;*
> *Be master over your brothers,*
> *And let your mother's sons bow to you.*
> *Cursed be they who curse you,*
> *Blessed they who bless you.* (Gen 27:28–29)

This was the blessing intended for Esau, but Jacob is the one who ends up with it. This turn in the story is really provocative. For one thing, we can certainly question Jacob's morality here—Esau's distress when he gets home is vivid—and we also might feel that Jacob deserves what he gets when he's the victim of someone else's trickery in the next *parasha*. One point, though, is beyond debate: it's hard to argue that Rebecca's plan is a failure. Jacob, afraid of his brother, leaves home soon after, but he leaves with a very powerful blessing—much better than the one he would have gotten if he hadn't engaged in imitation.

Yet the Torah expresses some uneasiness with the concept of imitation. Jacob himself is worried that his father will see through the ruse and see him as a *m'taateia* (Gen 27:12)—a *trickster*, as translated by the Etz Hayim Torah,[41] or a *mocker*, as translated by the ArtScroll.[42] This is no small thing he's worried about. Rabbi Mordecai Gafni goes so far as to connect the word *m'taateia* to idolatry, which is, among all sins, the one denounced perhaps the most often and the most harshly by the Torah. Idolatry always involves a denial of God, and, in Gafni's view, imitation denies God because it means an at least temporary denial of the true self imparted by God.[43] It is therefore no trivial consequence, no spanking or time-out, that Jacob is worried about when he resists Rebecca's plan at first.

So why does he go through with it? Well, there are probably a few different reasons. First of all, Esau's blessing is going to be good, and Jacob might just want it, even if it means pretending to be someone he's not. But he also does it at the urging of his mother, and she has reasons of her own. For one thing, she got a prophecy from God at the beginning of the *parasha* that told her that the younger brother would be the one to rule over the older one. And so, seen that way, she's trying to help Jacob become the person he was always meant to be. And so there's the paradox: for Jacob to fulfill his own personal destiny, he has to pretend to be someone else first.

Part of the reason he's successful is that he is, in fact, only pretending. It's not as though he actually thinks he's Esau—he knows the whole time that it's a disguise. Even when he protests, he doesn't say "I don't want to be a trickster"; he says, *I shall appear to him as a trickster* (Gen 27:12). In other words, he's not worried that he's an idolater. He's only worried that he'll be seen that way.

The way that Jacob avoids idolatry is by never losing track of who he is. When he brings the food to his father, he says *Anochi Esav b'chorecha* (Gen 27:19), and although the Etz Hayim Torah translates this as *I am*

41. Lieber, *Etz Hayim*, 155.
42. Scherman, *The Chumash*, 137.
43. Fogelman, "Toldos (Generations)."

*Esau, your firstborn*, the ArtScroll also notes Rashi's point, which is that this line can be reasonably translated as *It is I* (who brings this to you); *Esau is your firstborn*.[44] In many cases like this, the commentary points out, Jacob uses ambiguous language that could be interpreted multiple ways, one of which is the truth. Again, we could debate the morality of this, but either way Jacob never loses track of who he is, and so never denies the true self he was given by God.

There is, however, another way in which imitation can go wrong. If one danger is self-denial, the companion danger is denial of the humanity of the other. After all, the person we're imitating also has a self created by God, and it can be easy to forget that in the act of impersonation. In the Torah portion, Jacob does a good job of hanging on to his own selfhood while standing in Esau's clothes, but his attention to his brother's soul is considerably less intent. Jacob steals his brother's blessing in full knowledge that Isaac has only one first-son blessing to give. The one Esau gets as a consolation prize is nowhere near as wonderful:

> *See, your abode shall enjoy the fat of the earth*
> *And the dew of heaven above.*
> *Yet by your sword you shall live*
> *And you shall serve your brother.* (Gen 27:39–40)

Thus Jacob has helped himself at the direct expense of his brother—and the Torah seems to be a little uncomfortable about it. In the next *parasha*, Jacob finds himself in the camp of his uncle Laban, who turns out to be the master trickster. For starters, Laban offers his nephew his daughter Rachel in marriage in exchange for seven years of work, but then substitutes a disguised Leah instead and makes him work seven more years for Rachel. The trickery goes on from there.

The Torah offers many clues that these later events have been brought on by Jacob's earlier actions. Some of them are linguistic. First of all, the word *serve*, the key word used in both brothers' blessings to establish their pecking order, is used to describe *Jacob's* status seven times in his negotiations and relationship with Laban. Also, when Jacob discovers that he's married Leah instead of Rachel, he asks Laban, *Why did you deceive me?* (Gen 29:25). The Hebrew word used for *deceive me—rimitani—*shares its roots with the word *b'mirmah*, or *in guile*, used to describe Jacob's stealing

---

44. Lieber, *Etz Hayim*, 137.

of Esau's blessing (Gen 27:35). Then, too, there is the matter of Leah being disguised so as to appear to be Rachel—a parallel with the brothers' story. This is clarified when Laban defends his swap by saying that the older daughter needs to get married before the younger—an emphasis on birth order that Jacob has recently upended.

All in all, this looks like an instance of poetic justice, of Jacob reaping what he has sown, all because he stole Esau's identity. In fact, the sowing goes on for quite a while. In a later *parasha* Jacob suffers because of the actions of his sons, including Joseph, who, in another important story, hides his identity to toy with his family a bit. This seems a further turnabout of Jacob's early behavior. Rebecca may have said that the consequences of their scheme would be on her, but they've fallen on Jacob instead.

So: how, in the act of imitation, do you hang on to the integrity of not just yourself but also the self of the other?

The distinction between failing and succeeding at this is probably the distinction between taking and learning. In putting on Esau's clothing, Jacob set out not to learn from Esau but to take from him—to *be* him long enough to get something that was intended for Esau. This is not what we usually mean when we talk about walking in someone else's shoes. What if Jacob had used the opportunity to really *understand* Esau? Certainly there were things Jacob could have learned. Esau is noted for his devotion to Isaac, for one thing, and his physical prowess and confidence both make him a force to be reckoned with, unlike Jacob, who responds to physical confrontation with trickery and fear most of his life. Both brothers have skills and weaknesses, and both have plenty to learn from the other.

What does this have to do with the artist? Everything. Whenever an artist engages in the act of imitation, s/he faces the same dangers Jacob faced. First of all, abandoning your own artistic instincts and style in order to take on someone else's can be an act of violence toward the self. Philip Roth describes his undergraduate literary efforts in this way: "I managed to extract from Salinger a very cloying come-on and from the young Capote his gossamer vulnerability, and to imitate badly my titan, Thomas Wolfe, at the extremes of self-pitying self-importance."[45] Interestingly, "there were no Jews in the stories, no Newark, and not a sign of comedy"[46]—several of the

45. Roth, *The Facts*, 60.
46. Ibid.

elements that would eventually come to define the writing of Philip Roth. He managed to get past this stage, of course, but what if he hadn't? We of course don't know the names of any of the writers who never stopped copying others—we're too busy reading the people they copy.

Sometimes this self-denial comes from real pain. Choreographer David Gordon describes what happened to him after some of his work was received extremely harshly by an audience, with people walking up to him to boo him more directly than they could from their seats. He stopped dancing altogether for a while, and when he finally did join a troupe again, an improvisational group run by Yvonne Rainer, he refused to actually improvise, to draw on his own material. Instead, "everything I did in that first Grand Union year was Yvonne Rainer material. Everybody else was inventing stuff, but not me. I just did her *Trio A* faster, slower, in a corner, in a box, upside down, and backward. I did not want to be responsible for making new material. I was responsible for my performance of Yvonne's material and that was it."[47] And why? He says, "The others already thought of themselves as downtown artists; I thought of myself only as a fellow who was smart and had some kind of talent."[48]

The other danger is that taking on someone else's style to gain favor rather than to learn can amount to a kind of plagiarism or theft. The literary community is occasionally shaken when an author is discovered to have lifted or lightly paraphrased passages from someone else, and the ones who get away with it have done the same wrong. Ironically, this tends to circle back on the artist; in using someone else's style to succeed, you can become dependent on it and end up abandoning your own. Thus, just as Jacob becomes a victim of impersonations throughout his later life, the thieving artist does, too.

Yet there are also blessings to be had through some kind of engagement with imitation—and you don't have to be untrue to yourself, or even steal anyone else's good fortune, to get them. When you need to grow, you try things on, but not because you're mixed up about who you are or because you want to take someone else's place. When artist Amedeo Modigliani's work started to show the influence of his friendship with sculptor Constantin Brancusi, it wasn't because of self-denial or self-loathing, and Modigliani didn't think he secretly *was* Brancusi. He took on this influence to try it on, to see what would happen, what he would gain, by doing so. He

47. Morgenroth, *Speaking of Dance*, 45.
48. Ibid.

was adding to his artistic self, not abandoning it. Neither was he trying to obliterate Brancusi in the process.

The goal, in the ideal case, is learning—learning from another's style in order to develop one's own. Composer Arnold Schoenberg "believed that in order to develop the instincts one needs to write in a new style, one has first to become fluent in a known idiom where the elements and their uses can be more rationally discussed and evaluated." Therefore he "never spoke about modern music to any student who could not, let's say, write a string quartet in Brahms's style well."[49]

And so there's a right way to do imitation, and there's also a wrong way. The nice thing is that, unlike Jacob, we don't have to get it right from the very beginning. His early mistakes haunted him for the rest of his life, but we may be living in more forgiving times. Philip Roth's derivative early efforts didn't lead to a lifetime of derivative work; they were instead the first steps toward something he could claim as his own. When David Gordon was refusing to explore his own material, he was still growing. While toying with Rainer's material in different ways, he also found himself going to Broadway musicals to see how different actors played the same roles. "I wanted to understand what interpretation meant,"[50] he says. As it turns out, that kind of thing is very important to a choreographer, who needs to understand that one choreographer's vision will look different when performed by different people. When he finally got back to his own material, Gordon knew things that he hadn't known before.

So it often is with artists. We try things on sloppily, sometimes from a desire to learn but other times from a desire to leave some part of us behind or from an envy that makes us want what our heroes have. The key to making it through these times is an awareness, somewhere in us, of the integrity of our own souls and the souls of those we want to emulate. In that awareness, our imitation becomes a point of meeting, a place where two people with the same passions and the same goals can sit down for a while to talk, not like lord and servant, not like thief and victim, but like brothers.

49. Shawn, *Schoenberg's Journey*, 183.
50. Morgenroth, *Speaking of Dance*, 45.

*In Your Mouth and In Your Heart:*

Which artists do you admire the most? How can you learn from those artists without losing your own unique stamp?

# Va-yetzei

## What's in a Name

### Genesis 28:10—32:3

I F YOU WANT TO know what the Torah thinks about the point of creation, you don't have to look much further than the many stories where a child is born. In those moments, we get a window on the *why* of creativity. What does it mean to these mothers and fathers to have brought newness to their lives and to the world?

In *Parashat Va-yetzei* we see childbearing like we've never seen it before. Jacob's two wives and their two handmaids bring forth a total of eleven sons and a daughter, with only Benjamin yet to come in a later chapter. These births are full of drama, because motherhood is such a powerful experience and also because these women are in (pro)creative competition with one another. Each time, we learn something about how the mother feels about the experience. The main clue in each case is the child's name.

If the Torah is an accurate lens onto the traditions of the time, it was apparently the custom for parents to name their babies shortly after birth. These children weren't named in honor of dead relatives; they were instead branded with whatever feelings marked the parents' experience of meeting their child for the first time. Through those feelings, you learn a lot about what creation means to the parent.

Take Leah for example. She's married to Jacob, but only because of her father Laban's trickery. She sees her children largely as a way to get Jacob to love her the way that he loves her sister Rachel. The name Simeon contains some of the Hebrew letters in the word for "hear," and seems, for Leah, to represent God having heard her plight. The name of her son Judah shares roots with words for praise and thankfulness; Leah is grateful to God for giving her a chance to be loved. Levi's name has unclear origins, but his birth causes her to say, *"This time my husband will become to attached me"* (Gen 29:34) and the text indicates that his name is connected to that sentiment. Her first son, whose name Reuben means simply "See—a son," at first expressing a pure kind of joy about a child, leads her to say, *"The Lord has seen my affliction . . . now my husband will love me"* (Gen 29:32). This is a persistent motivation for Leah; even by the time she bears a sixth son, she names him Zebulun, which in the Ugaritic language means "to raise up." *"This time my husband will exalt me"* (Gen 30:20), she says. Sadly, the Torah never suggests that Jacob eventually comes to love her.

Clearly being an unloved wife is awful for Leah, and the joy of creation is distorted as a result. There are signs, though, that she's capable of forgetting about her troubles to focus on her kids. As I said, the name Reuben implies at least a moment of straightforward delight. Then, two of her later sons, Gad and Asher (born by her handmaid Zilpah, and technically considered Leah's children), are given names that spring from words for "luck." Neither time does she refer to being unloved, or seeing her children as a vehicle to love—only to good fortune. When Leah subsequently bears another child of her own—son Issachar—his name suggests "reward," which makes the fact of his existence a prize unto itself, rather than a means to an end. Perhaps most movingly, her final child is a daughter she calls "Dinah," which calls up echoes of the word for "judgment"; the great Torah commentator Rashi says that Leah knows that Jacob is destined to have twelve sons, and so prays during her final pregnancy that she will have a girl so that more of the sons could come from Rachel. If this is true, she has—remarkably—passed up an opportunity to squeeze some affection out of her husband.

For her part, Rachel is well-loved by Jacob from the beginning, but struggles with fertility. She begs her husband to impregnate her, but he reminds her angrily that such things are in God's hands. She then gives him her handmaid Bilhah, who has a son that Rachel calls Dan, also close to the word "judgment"; she sees Dan as evidence that she has been judged worthy of children. The next son, Naphtali, seems to be named to evoke a successful scheme or competition. Rachel herself eventually has a son of her own, and she calls him Joseph, which in Hebrew hints at things being taken away and things being added, and so she says *"God has taken away my disgrace"* (Gen 30:23) and *"May the Lord add another son for me"* (Gen

30:24). She sees these births as crucial for vindication, for status relative to her sister and in the eyes of God and the community. Of course, in an era when women were judged primarily by their success in bearing male children, we can hardly blame her for her attitude—but this does unfortunately make her kids means to an end rather than an end unto themselves. When she eventually faces death in childbirth, her bitterness peaks, and she names her last child Ben Oni, which means "son of my mourning." Jacob renames him the less grim Benjamin (which either means "son of the south" or "son of my old age") but the Torah has already recorded the mother's first impulse.

One take-home message is that there is enormous pressure on these two women, and the effects of that pressure are easy to see, and generally tragic. And so Rachel spends her married life trying to create so that she might be judged favorably, and she dies bitterly in the attempt. Leah, on the other hand, creates in an apparently futile quest for love. There are, though, moments when the births seem surrounded with a purer joy, especially for Leah. All in all, these two women showcase a range of motivations that in some ways characterize all creative experiences.

Just about everybody wants acceptance and recognition, and most artists are no exception. That's the bind, of course; we choose a path that means pushing boundaries, doing things that aren't done, and seeing things in a new way, yet we don't necessarily mean to cut ourselves off from others. As composer John Zorn says, "It's hard to stay on the outside wanting to be on the inside, climbing up the cliff, just hanging on by your fingernails."[51] At the very least, most of us want some kind of recognition from our peers in the art world, and that desire can come to dominate all our other motivations for doing the work. Writer Natalie Goldberg says, "Often we use writing as a way to receive notice, attention, love."[52]

On the other end of the spectrum is the kind of motivation that has nothing to do with gaining approval. Instead there's a desire to create for creation's sake. This is how Woody Allen lives his life as a film-maker: "All I do is work, and my philosophy has always been that if I just keep working, just focus on my work, everything else will fall into place. It's irrelevant whether I make a lot of money or don't, or whether the films are successful or not."[53] Choreographer and composer Meredith Monk says, "I think

51. Milkowski, "John Zorn."
52. Goldberg, *Writing Down*, 57.
53. Allen and Bjorkman, *Woody Allen*, 192.

discovering is the only thing that keeps me going. You feel like you're part of something much bigger than yourself."[54] Painter Marc Chagall says, "There's only one thing that guides my hand, and that's the urge to paint."[55] These folks are like Leah when she first sees her first son, when her initial excitement is about the baby himself rather than what he can do for her. We generally set these motivations up as being more noble or healthy than the art-for-love alternative.

And what about the artists who do their work specifically to help others? There are the dances of Anna Halprin that have no audiences, aimed at transforming the dancers—often people with no dance background—themselves. There's Hannah Senesh, who says, "Perhaps, through writing, I will be able to contribute something towards human happiness."[56] Is *this* the best reason to create?

It's probably not an either/or situation. Undoubtedly we each have many different reasons for doing what we do. As Goldberg observes, "'Why do I write?' It's a good question. . . . [and] over time you will find that you have given every response."[57] There are the moments when we're desperate for attention, and the moments when we're caught up entirely in the joy and intensity of the work itself. There are moments when we create out of boredom, out of suffering, other moments when we do it because we think we have something valuable to contribute.

It may not matter very much. Look at the children of Leah, Rachel, Bilhah and Zilpah. They had their problems, sure, but they also grew up to do some fairly impressive things. They may have been partially means to an end for their desperate mothers, but they became ends in themselves.

So it is with art. The choreographer David Gordon first started with dance because he wanted to attract the attention of a dancer he thought was cute—and he stayed in it because of Valda, another woman, one that eventually became his wife.[58] Once he was hooked, though, it became an enduring passion for him, something driven from within.

Halprin has always had many reasons fueling her choreography. Speaking of her participatory non-audience pieces, she says, "I used to be discouraged that people in the dance world would just slough this work off

54. Morgenroth, *Speaking of Dance*, 98.

55. Coleman, *Creativity and Spirituality*, 97.

56. Senesh, *Life and Diary*, 19.

57. Goldberg, *Writing Down*, 113.

58. Morgenroth, *Speaking of Dance*, 44.

as therapy and say that I wasn't doing art. But I could see how important this work was and how limiting it is to say that there's only one way to dance."[59] "Why limit yourself?" she notes elsewhere. "Why not be able to use art for various purposes?"[60]

Goldberg suggests that it can be a useful exercise to consider why we do what we do, especially because there's often an inner voice that keeps demanding to know. "Why are you wasting your time?" it asks.[61] Every once in a while, it might be worth it to toss out a few answers, just to quiet the doubts. But that's all you're doing—quieting your doubts. In the end, Goldberg tells us, the motivations don't matter as much as the work. "Leave the why for psychologists," she says. "It's enough to know you want to write. Write."[62]

Or, in the words of songwriter Bob Dylan, "It doesn't really matter where a song comes from. It just matters where it takes you."[63] Born of revenge, of competition, of ambition, of love, of compassion, of hope—in a world that has so much to gain from art, the most important thing is that new work is born at all.

---

### In Your Mouth and In Your Heart:

Why do you create? Does it matter?

---

59. Ibid., 39.
60. Ibid., 31.
61. Goldberg, *Writing Down*, 116.
62. Ibid., 113.
63. Cott, *Bob Dylan*, 436.

# Va-yishlah

## The Struggle

### Genesis 32:4—36:43

*P*ARASHAT *VA-YISHLAH* CONTAINS ONE of the most remarkable and mysterious episodes in the Torah. Jacob and his family are traveling, father-in-law Laban and his deceptions behind them, brother Esau and his anger ahead of them, and they reach a river. Jacob sends all the people and possessions across the river and spends the night by himself on the near bank, and then we read: *Jacob was left alone. And a man wrestled with him until the break of dawn* (Gen 32:25). Later lines make it clear that this "man" is actually an angel. Despite his antagonist's divine origins, however, Jacob holds his own. Eventually, dawn comes and the angel begs to be let go, and Jacob refuses, saying, *I will not let you go unless you bless me* (Gen 32:27). (Jacob is, as always, the master of extracting blessings from the unwilling.) The blessing this time is that his name will be changed to *Israel*, rooted in the words *yisrah* (to strive) and *el* (God), because he has *striven with beings divine and human and* [has] *prevailed* (Gen 32:29). Arthur Waskow has translated this name as "God-wrestler."[64] Ultimately, this will refer not only to him, but also to the whole nation of people who are his descendants. And so this is who we are as people of Israel: those who wrestle with the divine and emerge blessed.

We should pause to think of the implications of a name like this. After all, we could have been called "God-lovers," "God-followers," or even "God-avoiders," or any of a number of other things—and indeed our relationship to the divine takes many forms in our lives—but our primary relationship

64. Waskow, *Godwrestling*.

42

has a very particular character. To be "Israel" means to become an active force in the realm of the sacred, to become people who struggle instead of accepting passively or turning away in fear or disgust—and whose struggles make us equal to the holy forces we're engaging.

This is the way that writer Saul Bellow talks about the search for meaning: "Out of the struggle at the center has come an immense, painful longing for a broader, more flexible, fuller, more coherent, more comprehensive account of what we human beings are, who we are, and what this life is for. At the center humankind struggles with collective powers for its freedom, the individual struggles with dehumanization for the possession of his soul."[65] This is not a description of submission or docility. According to Bellow, this active hunger for truth is one reason why some people turn to artists for help; in his eyes the world is waiting for the kind of hard-won wisdom that comes from full, vigorous, personal engagement with the universe—the kind that comes from art.

Indeed, writer Natalie Goldberg makes art sound like a contact sport: "What people don't realize is that writing is physical. . . . You are physically engaged with the pen, and your hand, connected to your arm, is pouring out the record of your senses. . . . My writing hand could knock out Muhammad Ali."[66] Or witness sculptor Louise Nevelson at work, in the words of Alan Gussow, one of her fellow art school students: "My God, what energy! She reveled in the inks and papers. She threw down textures of fabrics, worked with enormous physicality, literally throwing herself into the work. The most lasting impression was that she got dirty. I mean very dirty. It was as if she enjoyed wallowing in the blackness."[67] This is a description of a particular artist, but in some ways it feels like the prototypical description of artists generally—we're used to thinking of the creative process as involving this kind of passionate, even bodily engagement. Visual artist Judy Chicago, for example, has frequently used the word "struggle" to describe her relationship to her art, and she's not alone. It's so engrained into our understanding of how creativity works that art historian Jeffrey Meyers calls it the "conventional pattern of art pupils: study, revolt, struggle, success."[68]

The real question is *why*. Why is this a good way to get at the truth?

65. Allen, *Nobel Lectures*, 138.
66. Goldberg, *Writing Down*, 50.
67. Lisle, *Louise Nevelson*, 172.
68. Meyers, *Modigliani*, 24.

A strong possibility is that the artist really has no choice about it. To my mind, one of the most important things about this story is the exact phrasing (in English and in Hebrew) of the line *a man wrestled with him until the break of dawn* (Gen 32:25). It doesn't say *Jacob wrestled with a man*; it says the reverse, and in so doing it makes the point that this *man*, this angel, is the one initiating this struggle. Jacob, in other words, doesn't go looking for trouble; trouble finds him.

In the upcoming commentary on *Parashat Mi-ketz*, we'll see artists describe their frequent experience of being overtaken by inspiration, having it come at them unexpectedly and unstoppably. I've already talked about the need to get to a state of receptivity so that those creative bursts can happen to us. And so Jacob's experience does feel typical—he's left alone, and truth strikes. This doesn't happen every day—not even to Jacob—but it can happen sometimes, if the person is receptive.

What really stands to Jacob's credit, though, is how he responds. In the past, when he has encountered difficulty, he has usually tried to get around it somehow rather than confront it directly. He got his father's blessing through trickery and ran from his brother before Esau could exact revenge. More recently he ran from his nemesis Laban. This time, though, he holds his ground. The particular truth he faces, in the form of this angel, is powerful, powerful stuff—probably even quite dangerous. (Remember that the angel is supposed to be an instrument of God, and by this point we've been told that God is the one who flooded the earth, shattered the tower of Babel, incinerated Sodom and Gomorrah, and so on.) In some ways truth always has this threatening quality. Yet he does not run from it, and does not let it overwhelm and destroy him. Instead, he engages with this angel, and not only avoids being overpowered but even manages to get a (literal) grip on it so that he can extract his blessing, his meaning, from the encounter.

This is how we all must work. We must not only be open to whatever comes—we must also be prepared to grapple with it. What this means is that we can't turn away or deny the truth of what we see in the world, and can't allow it to run us over or destroy us. We must hold our ground and engage with the truth of our experience, try to get it down on canvas, in movement, in music, on paper. Sometimes, in doing so, we face things about ourselves or the world that are disturbing or frightening, and there's some chance that we'll be wounded by the encounter, as Jacob was—but the main lesson of his experience is that one emerges from this kind of engagement wiser, stronger, and more fulfilled overall. Shortly after this encounter, Jacob will finally face Esau—successfully. (Of course, then Jacob will run away again, but nobody ever claimed that wisdom was easy to hold on to.)

One more thing, though—the encounter ends with a demonstration of some limits. After Jacob has gotten his blessing, he asks the angel's name, and the reader might expect that this adversary, now defeated, would have to do whatever Jacob asks—but the angel refuses to give a name. In fact, the response is *"You must not ask my name!"* (Gen 32:30). There are some things, in other words, that Jacob can't know, even after such courageous and determined struggle. Artists understand this well; even after a great triumph, one where an artist has worked incredibly hard and extracted some invaluable truth, there is plenty more that's still not known. That's as it should be. The truth is a wonderful thing—but what Jacob tells us is that the blessing isn't to be found there. The blessing comes from the struggle itself.

---

*In Your Mouth and In Your Heart:*

What truths about the universe do you struggle with the most? How can that struggle appear in your creative work?

---

# Va-yeishev

## Prophecy

### Genesis 37:1—40:23

ONE OF THE THEMES of the Hebrew Bible—the collection of texts that includes the Torah, the accounts of various prophets, and other writings—is that people aren't all that happy about having the truth thrown in their faces. Whether it's Elijah and his stark predictions getting on King Ahab's nerves, Moses endeavoring to teach the stiff-necked Israelites in his care, or Jeremiah haranguing the people to put their trust in the divine, we see that people resist when they're asked to face reality.

We get our first taste of that theme in *parashat Va-yeishev*, the Torah portion where Joseph comes into his own. Things start with him bringing *bad reports* about his brothers to his father Jacob (Gen 37:2), and then we hear about two of Joseph's dreams—one in which his brothers' sheaves of grain bow down to his sheaf and another in which *the sun, the moon, and eleven stars* bow down to him (Gen 37:9). Being a teenager with questionable judgment, he promptly describes these dreams to the people in his family, and they bristle. Jacob says, incredulous, *"Are we to come, I and your mother and your brothers, and bow low to you to the ground?"* So his brothers were wrought up at him, and his father kept the matter in mind* (Gen 37:10–11).

This jealousy boils over one day when the brothers see Joseph approaching them in the field. *"Here comes that dreamer!"* they say (Gen 37:19). They plan to kill him, and although eldest brother Reuben talks them out of that plan, the other brothers still get serious revenge, stripping Joseph of his special tunic (a gift from Jacob), tossing him into a pit, and

46

finally selling him into slavery with some passing traders. The ironic thing is that all of Joseph's predictions will ultimately come true, and the brothers will find themselves full of guilt and regret. In the meantime, though, they're just happy to be rid of their family prophet.

In these pages, I talk again and again about our relationship with the truth—our obligation to the truth. We have to be willing to see the world as it is, in all its complexity, and make sacrifices to do so. We have seen how much that demands of a person, how challenging it can be to stay in earnest pursuit of truth. As we've observed, this can be a solitary journey, a journey so focused on being one's most honest self that it sets one apart from others.

Yet art is not *ultimately* solitary, because there's also the need to share our vision with others. In the words of poet Stanley Kunitz, "In my interpretation, the poem is on its way in search of people. For its complete fulfillment it has to find an audience, it has to be invited into some other person's mind and heart."[69] Or, as poet Allen Aftermath puts it, "The Jewish way is to know the world, to deny nothing . . . and sing."[70]

There are obviously a whole host of challenges when the artist, at the end of a private quest, turns back to others and gives voice to her or his discoveries. In 2002 the National Endowment for the Arts surveyed more than seventeen thousand Americans to see what interest they had expressed in the arts over the previous year. The results were not encouraging. Only 27 percent of respondents had been to an art museum that year. Forty-five percent of the respondents had read at least one novel or short story, but only 12 percent had read a poem—about the same percent of people who had been to a non-musical stage play, a performance of classical music, or a jazz performance. Four percent of people had seen ballet, 6 percent had seen another kind of dance, and 3 percent had been to the opera. Meanwhile, about half the respondents watched an average of three or more hours of television a day, and 95 percent watched at least an hour a day.[71] To put those numbers in some perspective, seven times as many people found time for a thousand hours of television that year than for just one performance of modern dance. Artists have something of broad value to share, but they're having trouble finding a mass audience. Why?

69. Moyers, *Fooling with Words*, 12.

70. Afterman, *Kabbalah and Consciousness*, 212.

71. NEA, *Reading at Risk*, 4–5.

There are probably a lot of reasons, ranging from issues with education in the United States and a lack of general cultural emphasis on the arts to ways in which artists themselves fail to reach out to people—but we also have to consider the nature of art itself. Painter Mark Rothko makes a distinction between art and decoration: "The function of art is to express and to move. The function of decoration is to embellish. . . . We should of course expect a road sign to be pleasant rather than ugly. Yet the pleasantness is greatest when it merely performs its function without destroying its surroundings. Therefore decoration is the expression of good taste. A picture can be the direct castigation of good taste."[72] In other words, art is not just window dressing, not just entertainment, not just a pleasant experience. Its goal is to reach people, to affect them—and, at the core, art has an inherently unsettling, prophetic nature. As writer Isaac Bashevis Singer said in his Nobel Prize speech, "I am not ashamed to admit that I belong to those who fantasize that literature is capable of bringing new horizons and new perspectives—philosophical, religious, aesthetical and even social. In the history of old Jewish literature there was never any basic difference between the poet and the prophet."[73]

It can be an intense experience encountering prophecy. Poet Allen Ginsberg, described as a "prophet" and a "visionary" by fellow poet Anne Waldman, liked "setting fire to people's imaginations that he met along the way. . . . you saw the world differently after you spent some time with him," according to popular songwriter Bono.[74] Painter Augustus John described the experience of encountering Amedeo Modigliani's sculpture in a related way: "The stone heads affected me strangely. For some days afterwards I found myself under the hallucination of meeting people in the street who might have posed for them. . . . Can 'Modi' have discovered a new and secret aspect of 'reality'?"[75] This is hardly the same experience as turning on the television to watch a goofball sit-com where problems are raised and then reassuringly resolved in the space of a half-hour. According to visual artist Judy Chicago, "If ideas make people comfortable, they say, 'That's nice.' If ideas have any power," on the other hand, "they're going to make people uncomfortable because they're going to cause you to think about things you haven't thought about."[76] And so maybe people tune out because

72. Rothko, *The Artist's Reality*, 129.

73. Allen, *Nobel Lectures*, 163–64.

74. Ginsberg, *Life and Times*.

75. Meyers, *Modigliani*, 78.

76. Levin, *Becoming Judy*, 384.

they'd rather be settled than unsettled, and maybe the artist plays the role of the crazy-seeming street-corner preacher, shouting until hoarse while people cross the street to avoid hearing.

King Ahab did everything in his power to silence Elijah; the Israelites ignored and challenged Moses at every turn. The prophet is inherently a revolutionary, fighting for a vision of life that isn't in place—and art, which fights for truth in a world full of reassuring illusions, is revolutionary, too. We must expect a little resistance. That doesn't mean, however, that our "new horizons and new perspectives" have no worth to the world. In the words of writer Saul Bellow, "Perhaps humankind cannot bear too much reality, but neither can it bear too much unreality, too much abuse of the truth."[77] If he's right, the artist fills a basic human need to stay in contact with the truth, at least some of the time.

One open question, though, is whether there's a right way and a wrong way to spread prophecy. Joseph obviously creates enemies when he recounts his dreams freely as a young man, and the experience of his brothers' retribution does seem to change him; never again do we see a scene of him relating one of his own dreams to others. Instead, for the rest of his recounted life in the Torah, he sticks to interpreting the dreams of others. From this we might learn that prophecy is not just about telling our own truth but also speaking to the truth of others.

Yet we should not see this as a call to see only the good in others, to talk only about what's immediately uplifting. Certainly we should not see this as a call to be reassuring. When Joseph is asked to interpret the dreams of two of Pharaoh's fallen chamberlains, he predicts a return to grace for the cupbearer but an execution for the baker—and he tells them their futures, right to their faces. The Torah does not report the Chamberlain of the Bakers' reaction, but we can bet that he had been hoping to hear something more cheerful. Yet the man was destined for the gallows, and Joseph's responsibility to the truth made him say so. As artists we have much the same responsibility. To repeat poet Allen Afterman's words, "The Jewish way is to know the world, to deny nothing . . . and sing."[78] We broaden our song beyond ourselves to make sure it addresses others, but we do not edit it so that it lies. We sing whatever the song requires. And just as the words of Isaiah, Jeremiah, and Elijah have stayed with us through the centuries, we hope that our own song lives on, penetrates now or in the future whatever deafness fills the world's ears.

77. Bellow, Nobel Lecture.

78. Afterman, *Kabbalah and Consciousness*, 212.

*In Your Mouth and In Your Heart:*

What unique truth do you have to share with the world? What particular vision do you have that nobody else quite has? How can that vision be made tangible to others in your next work of art?

# Mi-ketz

## Feast and Famine

### Genesis 41:1—44:17

Pᴀʀᴀsʜᴀᴛ Mɪ-ᴋᴇᴛᴢ ɢɪᴠᴇs ᴜs a vision of Egypt at two very different times. We start with seven years of tremendous agricultural abundance, with more than enough food for all the people of Egypt, and then we move into seven years of severe shortage. Joseph, based on Pharaoh's dream, predicts these two periods in advance, and ends up being the country's steward during both, gathering the extra during the abundance and distributing it during the famine. His contributions are crucial—but while his wisdom gets them through the difficult stretch, it doesn't prevent it from happening in the first place. That's the lesson: plenty and scarcity are simply parts of the cycle of existence, and cannot be dodged.

Similarly, for most artists, there are times when inspiration and work come easily—almost too easily to even keep up with it—and there are times when everything seems to stop. These feel very much like opposites, but the extremes have things in common. Above all, there's the feeling that the process is essentially out of our control—just as even Joseph's advance knowledge of God's plan couldn't stop it from unfolding.

Consider the abundant periods, the stretches of time when inspiration seems bottomless. Sculptor Louise Nevelson described a period of incredible productivity this way: "At that time, if I'd had a city block, it wouldn't have been enough, because I had this energy that was flowing like an ocean into creativity."[79] This is an abundance that is bigger than the artist, one that works through her but is not subject to her dictates. As composer

---

79. Lisle, *Louise Nevelson*, 210.

John Zorn said, "When I'm writing, sometimes it gets to that place where I feel like the piece is writing itself and I'm trying not to get in the way."[80] Sometimes it can feel as if the work is itself doing the controlling. "A poem usually begins with an image or an idea that starts to resonate, to become compulsive," said poet Allen Afterman. Eventually, "it more or less forces itself out."[81] Or, in the words of writer Elie Wiesel: "Writers write because they cannot allow the characters that inhabit them to suffocate them. These characters want to get out, to breathe fresh air and partake of the wine of friendship; were they to remain locked in, they would forcibly break down the walls. It is they who force the writer to tell their stories."[82]

Of course, this is a happy kind of "force"; what creator really minds being in the service of her or his work? The real problem is what happens when the feeling of plenty starts to die down, as it eventually must. Here's how choreographer and composer Meredith Monk described the experience: "The time between finishing a piece and starting the next one is always hard. It's a time of emptiness."[83]

What are you supposed to do to address that emptiness, if so much of the process is out of your control? Composer Leonard Cohen offers a fairly scary account of what's required: "Nothing works. Nothing works. After a while, if you stick with a song long enough it will yield. But long enough is way beyond any reasonable estimation of what you think long enough may be. In fact, long enough is way beyond. It's *abandoning*, it's abandoning that idea of what you think long enough may be. Because if you think it's a week, that's not long enough. If you think it's a month, it's not long enough. If you think it's a *year*, it's not long enough. If you think it's a decade, it's not long enough."[84]

But before we let this take us deep into despair, note one of the most important parts of this quote: "if you stick with a song long enough it will yield." This is where we see that there is some part of this process of inspiration that *is* in our hands. Specifically, there's the matter of showing up at the easel, the desk, the piano, the studio, day after day, in the fat times and in the lean. Cohen says that creative work—songwriting in his case—is "something you do every day and you can't get too far from it, otherwise

80. Goldberg, "John Zorn."
81. Afterman, *Kabbalah and Consciousness*, 211.
82. Wiesel, "Sacred Magic," 262.
83. Morgenroth, *Speaking of Dance*, 96.
84. Zollo, *Song-Writers*, 334.

you *forget what it's about.*"[85] Or, in the words of writer Gertrude Stein, "The way to resume is to resume."[86]

The point is not that we can really *force* something to happen; the point is that we need to be there at work when inspiration does finally strike, and that it's more likely to do so, in fact, if we're there. Poet Marcia Falk observed, "The poem's moment cannot be summoned, but it can be readied for."[87] The discipline of showing up day after day is part of the process of becoming ready. Think of Joseph, unable to overturn God's will but working hard to get people through the difficult times. There are things we can do.

More surprisingly, the actual creative scarcity itself can be part of that process as well. Consider the Torah's understanding of the famine in Egypt. In the story, the famine strikes at a time when Joseph is separated and estranged from a family that has no idea what's happened to him. His father, for one, believes him to be dead. One result of this agricultural disaster (which is not terribly destructive, thanks to Joseph's wisdom) is that it brings people from all over the world to the land that Joseph has been overseeing, because he's made sure that there are large stores of food left over from the abundant years. This brings about a family reunion—and that family reunion leads to the Israelites settling in Egypt, which leads to the Exodus story, which leads to revelation, the moment when God gives the Torah to the people at Mount Sinai. Seen this way, the famine is the event that's *required* in order to ultimately bring about the covenant between God and the Jewish people.

In the artist's life, the dry period is often an essential part of the cycle of creativity. After a time of inspiration, having given ourselves fully to the work, we return to the world somewhat dazed. We may have lost the sense of discipline that we didn't need when things came so easily. Caught up in the moment, we were unable to think ahead or to take a big-picture look at all the work we'd been doing, unable to plan our next moves, to be thoughtful about an overall direction for the work. Work that comes during the fat times can be exciting but ungoverned and sloppy. The lean times, on the other hand, can be a time to get grounded again, to do some planning, to revise and rework, to get back into the habit of showing up no matter what, to get perspective and to turn back from the work to the world, which is the

85. Ibid., 338.

86. Preston, "Conversation with Stein," 160.

87. Falk, "Response," 83.

source of the work in the first place. According to her biographer, Louise Nevelson "eventually realized that blackness and brightness inevitably gave way to each other,"[88] and "she attributed the eventual depth of feeling in her work to what she called her 'sharp exhaustions,' before her recuperative powers began working once again."[89]

Above all, the famine gives us the opportunity to feel gratitude for the feast, to recognize that abundance is a connection to something larger than ourselves. And of course reverence is the main part of what makes us open to further inspiration. In other words, to mature artistically you have to get beyond the view that cherishes plenty and curses scarcity; both are part of the same process, and to lose one probably means losing the other.

Of course, as we said at the beginning, the process is largely out of our control anyway. There will be times when the work pours through us like a miracle, and there will be times when things don't happen, no matter what we do. The job of the artist is to be like Joseph, the person who sees both parts of the cycle coming, and who, in both times, shows up to work day after day—the person who finds a way no matter what the universe hands down.

---

*In Your Mouth and In Your Heart:*

Do you feel creatively abundant right now, or tapped out? What purpose is this particular time serving in your creative life?

---

88. Lisle, *Louise Nevelson*, 136.

89. Ibid., 140.

# *Va-yiggash*

## The Bones

### Genesis 44:18—47:27

Ancient Egypt has a powerful place in Jewish communal memory. *Mitzrayim*, the name of the nation in Hebrew, can be translated as "the narrow place"—a place of constriction. Indeed, this is the place we associate with oppression, abject servitude, despair; the place where Israelites were slaves for hundreds of years; the place we are happy to leave behind each year in our Torah readings from the Book of Exodus and at our Passover seders. Our understanding of liberation and freedom and moral responsibility root in our intense biblical stories of trials in Egypt.

For these reasons, we read *parashat Va-yiggash* with a certain discomfort; in these pages, Jacob and his family are all summoned to Egypt by Joseph, and the mood is high—Jacob is reunited with all his children, and they're given the choice Egyptian land of Goshen to pasture their flocks, a promising spot to ride out the final stretch of the famine that's covered the earth. All in all, it seems like a whole pile of good news—but those of us who've read ahead know that things are going to get bad soon enough, and we are not surprised when God talks to Jacob and twice refers to the journey as going "down" to Egypt. "Down" is the word typically used in the Bible when our ancestors made this particular trek, and clearly that word means more than "South."

Still, along with our discomfort is our knowledge that this downward journey is part of the path that leads us to the sweet freedom and to the heights of Mount Sinai. When God speaks to Jacob on the road, God says *Fear not* and promises that this is part of the plan to make of the Israelites a *great nation* (Gen 46:3).

Of course, those of us rooting for the Israelites tend to wonder at this point why they have to endure so much before becoming that *great nation* that we've been hearing about for so long. If God, after all, is capable of absolutely anything, couldn't we just skip all the oppression and get right to the happy part? Because that doesn't happen, we have to suspect that there's something meaningful about that experience down in Egypt, something we actually *need* in order to fully embrace the good things yet to come.

Naturally, I see this as an opportunity to read the Torah as metaphor. Who among us *hasn't* occasionally been to some narrow place in our lives? The question is what we get out of the experience.

Our guide ought again to be Joseph, the person who knows the most about this journey. Of all our ancestors, he tastes slavery first, being sold into servitude in Egypt by his brothers—and he's the first to rise out of the condition as well, eventually becoming Pharaoh's most trusted and empowered advisor. But these heights—wealthy, respected, powerful—do not mark the end of his experience of *Mitzrayim*. Joseph dies in Egypt, and *A new king arose over Egypt who did not know Joseph* (Exod 1:8). Reduced to near-anonymity, his bones are nonetheless carried out of the land by Moses, eventually to be buried in the promised land in the book of Joshua. That's the point—Joseph leaves not as the Pharaoh's vizier but as bones—and so his story shows us that great glory may not be the sign that we are done with *Mitzrayim*; in fact, we may not be done until we are stripped clean.

How similar this sounds to the experience of choreographer and composer Meredith Monk: "I feel that in some ways now my work is getting more transparent and things are actually falling away rather than getting bigger and bigger. Everything is getting more down to the bone and more pared away. Not smaller and smaller, but more essentialized."[90] For her, this is a positive, even crucial development. In this process, she learns "what the piece really needs and what you can throw away."[91] In discussing her work on her first memoir, visual artist Judy Chicago described the art of writing in the same way: "I rewrote the book eight times, and each time I peeled away more. I had first hidden behind a lot of rhetoric."[92] Poet Allen Afterman had a similar process: "The poem has to be stripped away, until

90. Morgenroth, *Speaking of Dance*, 92.

91. Ibid.

92. Levin, *Becoming Judy*, 269.

I discover its essence."[93] He writes draft after draft, cutting out the "blood, ego, cliché."

In the view of these artists, paring down to bones is not ultimately loss; it may be a temporary loss of temporary things like a habitual dance move or a favorite image, but ultimately it is a reduction of oneself and one's work to their essences, and from that comes the best art, the art that is most directly and simply in contact with the "eternal truths . . . the essence of being" that writer Isaac Bashevis Singer once talked about.[94] Sculptor Louise Nevelson, in her signature shorthand, wrote: "Today in Modern Art we have freed ourselves totally & completely from t representational, from t literal and dug right down deep into t core, right down to t place where creation is unadulterated, where we have cleaned & scrubbed it to its primordial place. For me this is t place of t beginning-ness. The place of pureness, t first place, t one-ness & there you are. It is t place you [tap] life itself."[95]

But it is not only about boiling down. This process also gives you a new starting place, somewhere simpler from which to spread out again. Monk said: "You always know when your work is coming from your center, your core source, and you always know when it has come through you. That's when it feels like the grounding is right and then you can build off that."[96] "Build" is a key word there; Monk works *from* her essence toward fresh possibilities. Similarly, composer Gustav Mahler—not known for simplistic music—started often from "a story in its simplest and most essential form (a fairy tale, a ballad, a popular strophic song) and uses it as a departure point for a musical journey. . . . His invention flourishes precisely in the void created by this process."[97]

And so the bare bones are often the armature for the next sculpture we mold. We get rid of the "blood, ego, cliché" not to vanish but in order to create something more true.

This is all about being true to oneself. Here's Chicago on her memoir again: "I would get feedback from my friends that the best parts—" in other words, the places where she was down to essentials—"were when I was being exactly myself."[98] Or, in the words of writer Paul Rosenfeld on

93. Afterman, *Kabbalah and Consciousness*, 211.

94. Singer, Nobel Lecture.

95. Lisle, *Louise Nevelson*, 182.

96. Morgenroth, *Speaking of Dance*, 92.

97. Berio, "Mahler's Parable," 103.

98. Levin, *Becoming Judy*, 269.

iconoclastic composer Arnold Schoenberg: "If we ourselves see anything in Schoenberg's career, it is nothing if not the development of a man according to the law of life which compels us, if we would live and grow, to become ever more fully and nakedly what we essentially are."[99] This is probably true of most artists—certainly of all great artists.

It's also true of our ancestor Joseph. When his bones are buried in Shechem, in the promised land, it is not an afterthought to a once-important life; it is the ultimate fulfillment of his life's purpose. He is the person through whom God works to bring Israel down to Egypt so that it can become an enslaved nation, so that it can become a great nation; once that's been achieved, he can take his rightful place in the soil of the nation's promised land. He becomes part of its fertility, in ways that would never have been possible if he hadn't been brought up out of that narrow place—or, more importantly, if he had never gone down there in the first place.

---

*In Your Mouth and In Your Heart:*

What is the essence of your creative work? At its most basic level, what's it really about? Can you envision creating a piece of art that would capture that essence directly and simply? Get started on it.

---

99. Shawn, *Schoenberg's Journey*, 83.

# *Va-y'hi*

## What Will Call to You

### Genesis 47:28—50:26

REACHING THE END OF the book of Genesis means reaching a major
turning point. In *parashat Va-y'hi*, the book's final *parasha*, we see a
small group of Israelites—a single extended family of seventy—settling into
a life in the land of Egypt. They are few enough that we know something
of their individual histories and personalities. When we cross the bridge
to Exodus, however, we will find that our ancestors have in the interim
multiplied and become a massive people, a people that is said to number
600,000 when they finally leave Egypt again. It's a shift between, among
other things, the person and the community.

As if to emphasize that we're on the verge of leaving the close-up view,
*parashat Va-y'hi* goes out of its way to particularize Jacob's twelve sons; towards the end Jacob offers deathbed messages for each of them, and spends
time characterizing them one by one. There's *unstable* Reuben (Gen 49:4)
and *wild* Joseph (Gen 49:22), and Judah is compared to a lion cub (Gen
49:9), Issachar to a donkey (Gen 49:14), and Dan to a snake (Gen 49:17).
Only Simeon and Levi are lumped together as *a pair*, bound together by
*wrath* (Gen 49:5,7); the rest of the brothers get unique descriptions and
each is told a different fortune.

It's important to notice a couple of things. First of all, these messages
are not blessings. When Jacob summons his sons, he says *come together
that I may tell you what is to befall you in days to come* (Gen 49:1). In other
words, he is not trying to shape the future so much as to forecast it. His
predictions range from seeing Zebulun living along the sea and Asher

producing tasty food to expecting Dan to become an avenger and Issachar a *toiling serf* (Gen 49:15). Now, according to the ArtScroll, the more literal translation of Genesis 49:1 would be *I will tell you what will call to you.* We know, of course, that what calls out to us says a lot about who we each are. Thus it's no surprise that the range of predictions is very wide for this very varied collection of sons.

The other important thing is that he has all his sons around him as he addresses each one. The experience of any given son is not only of hearing a description of himself but also of hearing how his brothers are described. There's got to be a feeling like *Ah—so this is what's in store for me, and that is what's not in store for me.* I am like this, not like that. For any given son, the other brothers represent lives and destinies that don't belong to him.

And so, just before we turn our attention to the massive people Israel of the book of Exodus, we are reminded what it means to be an individual: to have unique strengths, unique weaknesses; above all, to have a particular past and a particular future.

Imagine if you were summoned to Jacob's bedside to hear his account of you, his predictions for you. How would you be described? What forecast would you hear? What would you be told about the character of what you would go on to produce?

The experience of this *parasha* suggests that you would walk away from that encounter with a sense of your particular strengths and weaknesses and how those characteristics were going shape a very individual future. You would also know that certain things would *not* be destined. You would see a life with a great deal of promise and some very important limitations. You would know that you are who you are.

There can be a sense of inescapability here. In another scene, Jacob blesses Joseph's sons Ephraim and Manasseh, and he crosses his arms to lay his right hand on Ephraim, the younger boy, and his left hand on Manasseh, the older, getting ready to give the better blessing to the secondborn. This isn't the way it's supposed to go (and Jacob ought to know this), and Joseph tries to correct Jacob, but Jacob insists on doing it this way, giving the strong impression that he's reversing the order because it describes their futures more accurately. Ephraim, in other words, gets the better fortune because that outlines the future that he's destined for, and there's no getting out of it. Jacob once upended this system, but he's apparently the only one who gets to do it. The rest of us are, in some sense, stuck with who we are.

This message can feel uncomfortable. After all, aren't we capable of change? I think many of us would agree that we are. But that's not really the question. The question is whether we're capable of *infinite* change, whether we're capable of being absolutely anyone, whether we can leave ourselves entirely behind and take up whole new lives that are in no way shaped by our respective pasts and our long-held personality traits. The answer is probably *not*—and, seen in that light, it begins to make more sense, this idea of each of us having a unique blessing, a unique destiny.

We could still imagine artists struggling with this idea, however. After all, doesn't creativity itself imply a kind of limitless possibility, of being able to do anything or perhaps even *be* anything? As it happens, most artists in practice see that this is not so.

Composer Arnold Schoenberg wrote, "Everything I have written has a certain inner likeness to myself."[100] Artists are inescapably unique, and the work they produce is inescapably unique. New York Times writer John Canaday once wrote of sculptor Louise Nevelson: "If [Nevelson] had to be placed in a standard textbook classification, you couldn't do it. . . . You would have to saw her in two and file one half under 'Mystic-romantic' and the other under 'Rational-classical' but all you would prove is that she is in a class by herself."[101]

The difficult thing about this idea is that it comes with limits. Nevelson describes her embrace of visual arts (as opposed to acting or dance, other fields in which she dabbled) as being "pushed into it because the other things didn't add up. There was nothing else to do."[102] It can be hard to think that you're in a particular art form because the other ones just didn't work out, and yet that's sometimes what happens.

It can be even harder, though, to confront the limitations you have in your chosen art form. Choreographer David Gordon said, "I wish I were a little more sophisticated."[103] Meredith Monk, a choreographer and composer, said, "I have a very idiosyncratic body" and "I was not terribly agile as a child and had trouble with simple coordinations like skipping and jumping, perhaps due to my inability to fuse two visual images together."[104]

---

100. Shawn, *Schoenberg's Journey*, 232.

101. Lisle, *Louise Nevelson*, 198.

102. Ibid., 69.

103. Morgenroth, *Speaking of Dance*, 53.

104. Ibid., 88.

Of course, this is partly a matter of what you choose to see in yourself. Your uniqueness comes with limits, sure—but it also comes with blessings. Monk said, "I was always able to sense somatic rhythms"[105]—something a lot of other people could never claim. Choreographer Anna Halprin believed that "if people have a personal reason in their life to dance, it's going to have a heart, a meaning that is so profound that, even just witnessing it, you feel it too,"[106] and this personal stamp would not be available if everybody was exactly the same. When you shift your focus so that you see the benefits of your individuality, good things start to happen. In Nevelson's words: "When I let my inner vision guide my hands, there are no errors"[107]

Even the limitations themselves can be productive for an artist. To return to Meredith Monk: "Necessity is the mother of invention, so in a way my limitations became a kind of strength. I had to find my own style, my own way of thinking about movement, my own way of structuring in space."[108] Creative people, faced with a constraint, find a way to work—a way that expresses their distinct understanding and approach to the world. Composer Allen Shawn wrote, "Artists find their voice at the point at which what they cannot do, or don't do, ceases to matter."[109] In that triumph, the world gains a perspective it never had before, and not just in the art but in how it represents a particular way to *be* in the world.

And so we stand with resolve at Jacob's bedside, determined in our progress toward self-understanding—and, through that lens, our progress toward understanding (each in our own way) so very much more.

---

*In Your Mouth and In Your Heart:*

What are your creative strengths and weaknesses? How do they show themselves in your creative work? What kind of work would you produce if you lived with your weaknesses and played to your strengths?

---

105. Ibid.
106. Ibid., 30.
107. Lisle, *Louise Nevelson*, 196.
108. Morgenroth, *Speaking of Dance*, 88.
109. Shawn, *Schoenberg's Journey*, 299.

# Exodus

# *Sh'mot*

## The Unknown

### Exodus 1:1—6:1

I HAVE SUGGESTED MANY times already that being an artist is to be engaged with some larger-than-ourselves something that we might call "God"—that to be an artist is to be like God, to become closer to God, to be led forward by God. Yet I have sometimes avoided the word "God," replacing it with something like "the divine" or "what is meaningful," because I know how many distracting assumptions and associations people have (including me) when they encounter the word. It's high time we look at it directly.

In the first *parasha* of Exodus, Moses has an encounter with God, one in which he's asked to lead his people out of Egypt. Moses offers up many protestations and excuses to try to get out of the job—he's not a good speaker, nobody's going to believe him—but his most interesting response comes in chapter 3, line 13: *"When I come to the Israelites and say to them, 'The God of your fathers has sent me to you,' and they ask me, 'What is His name?' what shall I say to them?"* Moses wants to know who this God *is*, if he's going to follow the divine charge, if he's going to head back to Egypt for the fight of his life.

The answer is more interesting still. God says, *Ehyeh-Asher-Ehyeh*—a name that is difficult to translate, but which could mean "I Am Who I Am," "I Will Be Who I Will Be," and "I Am That I Am,"[1] not one of which is really a solid answer. In that way it resembles the name of God we see used most often: יהוה. This is a name with no vowels, something like YHVH

1. Lieber, *Etz Hayim*, 330.

in English, virtually untranslatable. Thus it is no surprise that God in this *parasha* refuses to become concrete for Moses—the prophet's first (though not last) lesson in the unfathomable nature of the divine.

Composer Allen Shawn wrote: "At the core of Judaism is the idea of the oneness of God and of the unknowability and unrepresentability of that oneness. It seems to me that a part of the meaning of Judaism is this abstraction, this deep sense that we do not know. The not knowing is itself sacred."[2]

And so if I continually claim that art is an engagement with the divine, we may have a problem: how can we engage with something unknowable?

The truth is that most artists, religious or not, would tell you that art is very often a fumble in the dark. Painters Adolph Gottlieb and Mark Rothko, in a letter to the *New York Times,* wrote, "To us art is an adventure into an unknown world."[3] According to choreographer Meredith Monk, "Part of the process is hanging out in the unknown."[4] This very often means that artists don't even know how they do what they do. Sculptor Louise Nevelson "had great difficulty talking articulately about art because her approach was essentially intuitive."[5] Marc Chagall, a painter who knew himself well enough to write his own autobiography, nonetheless admitted that his own drive to paint is a bit mysterious, saying that it was "something I was born with and don't really understand myself."[6]

Notice that these artists don't really *mind* the mystery. Choreographer Meredith Monk again: "With each form that I make, particularly the interdisciplinary forms, I'm excited that I don't know what the form is going to be when I start. . . . I think discovering is the only thing that keeps me going. You feel like you're part of something much bigger than yourself."[7]

But there's more at issue here than unknowability. More importantly: if artists are people who try to, in Rothko's words, "give human beings direct contact with eternal verities through reduction of those verities to the realm of sensuality"[8]—in other words, if we are the people who try to *represent* those truths here on earth—what do we do with the fact that

2. Shawn, *Schoenberg's Journey*, 233–34.

3. Gottlieb and Rothko, Letter.

4. Morgenroth, *Speaking of Dance*, 91.

5. Lisle, *Louise Nevelson*, 118.

6. Coleman, *Creativity and Spirituality*, 97.

7. Morgenroth, *Speaking of Dance*, 91, 98.

8. Rothko, *Artist's Reality*, 25.

the divine, the underlying meaning of the universe, is, as Shawn tells us, *unrepresentable*?

Shawn himself has an answer for this: "Paradoxically, another aspect of the practice of Judaism is a very real dialogue with this abstraction, the addressing of God in a very personal way."[9] Moses, after all, is in dialogue with God throughout this *parasha*, both before he asks for a definition of the divine and afterward, when Moses is still without a clear definition to hold on to. He will learn from God what he's supposed to do with his life and what meaning can be found in that kind of life, but he will never have a God that is as concrete as a golden statue of a calf.

Neither will we artists ever have a universe that makes itself so thoroughly known as to be exhausted of all enigma. And thank God for that—what then would we paint or write or sing about?

Our role is not to solve "God." Our role is to hang out in that unknown, to be in dialogue with the divine mystery—and to view our art as reports on the conversation.

---

*In Your Mouth and In Your Heart:*

Do you find your own creative process to be mysterious? Does it focus on mystery at all? What's the role of mystery in your work?

---

9. Shawn, *Schoenberg's Journey*, 234.

# *Va-era*

## The Soft Heart

### Exodus 6:2—9:35

THE LIFE OF THE artist seems to demand toughness. On the one hand, there are the necessary set-backs and challenges in the work itself, and on the other hand there are the many rejections and difficulties in attempting to get one's work accepted in the world. A fragile ego might not survive these trials.

The difficulty, however, is that toughness can be a problem of its own.

In *Parashat Va-era*, Moses confronts the Pharaoh of Egypt and demands that the Israelites be released. Pharaoh, of course, refuses, and his stubbornness becomes one of the driving forces in this story; every time it seems that he's about to become reasonable, we hear that he has *va-yechezak lev*—translated generally as having stiffened or hardened his heart—and will not let the people go. And the plagues begin to rain down on him.

For our purposes, it's important to note that *va-yechezak lev* means more exactly something like "strengthened the heart," because of the presence of *chazak* (strength) in the first word. And so it's the *strong* heart that's given to stubbornness, and to all the curses that follow. Would Pharaoh have gotten a better ending to his biblical story if he had instead been soft?

This is one of the paradoxes of the artist's life—one needs a tough heart to protect oneself, and yet one desperately needs to live life in an unprotected way, too. Composer and choreographer Meredith Monk says: "There are examples of artists who have armored themselves. They can end up becoming caricatures of themselves. That's one choice, to continue the fixation, the armoring, to maintain that defensive stance. I think the other side of it is to allow yourself to become soft and vulnerable. You have to pick yourself up all the time, but that becomes something that you can share with other people. Then I think the work has a lot more to say and its power is enduring."[10] Songwriter Paul Simon offers a similar warning when he talks about the "protected" mind, the one that won't allow you to engage with the thoughts that are nagging at you—a mindset that leads to writer's block.[11]

In the words of songwriter Bob Dylan, "You must be vulnerable to be sensitive to reality."[12] That sensitivity is crucial to creativity; as poet Yehuda Amichai tells us, we have to "live openly, not to shrink from fear from anything."[13] Composer John Zorn says "You've got to remain flexible."[14] If the artist's calling includes a calling to be open—and we've seen this over and over again—how can a person with a hard heart really be an artist?

Another thing we learn in this part of the Torah is just how a heart turns hard. In this *parasha* Moses confronts Pharaoh a number of times, and each time Pharaoh's heart stiffens, frequently because Egypt's magicians are able to reproduce the wonders that Moses presents as signs of God's power. They can turn staves into snakes, can make water run red, can fill the land with frogs. And so Pharaoh feels contented with his own powers (his sorcerers are just an extension of his own might)—and he thereby closes himself off to the possibility of experiencing wonder at something greater than himself.

The habit of toughness carries a great deal of momentum. Even when the magicians fail to reproduce the plague of lice, Pharaoh shores up his resolve and refuses to let the people go. And soon enough the momentum gets out of Pharaoh's control altogether. In the wake of each of the first five plagues, he hardens his own heart, but when the sixth plague ends, the text reads *the Lord stiffened the heart of Pharaoh* (Exod 9:12). Then the man gets one more shot to soften up, after the seventh plague, but of his own free will he makes the same choice to be stubborn, and from then on the hardening is always attributed to God. In other words, a habit like this can get so ingrained that the person loses control of his or her own fate.

As we know, Pharaoh is ultimately destroyed—and most understandings of this story have it that he has largely destroyed himself. The

10. Morgenroth, *Speaking of Dance*, 98.
11. Zollo, *Song-Writers*, 98.
12. Cott, *Bob Dylan*, 180.
13. Cohen, *Voices of Israel*, 34.
14. Goldberg, "John Zorn."

implication is that a person cannot survive a hard heart. But can a person—can an artist—survive a soft one? I began this commentary talking about the many challenges that confront the artist day after day. Beginning writers regularly tell me they don't have the ego strength to send their work out to publishers—not long ago I heard it from someone new, in fact. But I think about Pharaoh and I wonder if ego strength is really what's called for. I think about Monk's words and wonder if the pain of the struggle is what an artist *needs* to experience, what an artist needs to be able to share. Strength, after all, didn't do Pharaoh much good. But still—how does a person survive the pain?

Of course, not everyone does. Artist's biographies are full of tales of drug and alcohol abuse, depression and anxiety, violence and suicide. It's clear that destruction can lie in the direction of the soft heart, too.

But not everyone succumbs—and probably the way to survive as an unarmored person is to take such pleasure and excitement and growth from the work itself that the challenges and wounds are manageable—worth it, really. Zorn says, "I'm not striving for happiness, I'm trying to get some work done."[15] This is probably what Piercy means when she says she believes in "receptivity and work."[16] The receptivity is what makes the work possible, and the work is what makes life possible.

This is a scary idea, I'll admit, the idea that vulnerability is necessary. What *Parashat Va-era* teaches us is that there is no real alternative. Vulnerability is a risk—but hard-heartedness is a guarantee: with every stiffening of that muscle, the universe shrinks a little around you, until you stand in the midst of a wondrous world—like Pharaoh in the split Red Sea—only to find it crashing down on you, all around.

---

*In Your Mouth and In Your Heart:*

Envision creating a piece of art that would leave you vulnerable—what would it look like? What will creating it open up for you? Give it a shot.

---

15. Ibid.

16. Moyers, *Fooling with Words*, 180.

# *Bo*

## Leaving a Sign

### Exodus 10:1—13:16

*P*ARASHAT *BO* FINDS GOD at war with Pharaoh, a war that Pharaoh is destined to lose. In fact, the imbalance of power is so dramatic that a reader might wonder why God doesn't just lift all the Israelites out of Egypt in a flash, skipping all the negotiations with Pharaoh, all the plagues. We get our answer starting in Exodus 10:1–2: *Then the Lord said to Moses, "Go to Pharaoh. For I have hardened his heart and the hearts of his courtiers, in order that I might display these My signs among them, and that you may recount in the hearing of your sons and your sons' sons how I made a mockery of the Egyptians and how I displayed My signs among them—in order that you may know that I am the Lord."* In other words, according to this story, God *has* to go through all of this because it's not just the result—free Israelites—that counts. It's also God's legacy.

One of the things I like very much about the Torah is that the God of the Torah is (if you'll pardon me for saying it) imperfect. We see impulsiveness, vindictiveness, pettiness, vanity, and all sort of other things that we can easily relate to. And why not? Genesis told us that we were made in God's image—and human beings are anything but perfect, right? Why shouldn't God be complex in the same way that people are?

Certainly we human beings wrestle with the desire to leave a legacy behind. We are, after all, impermanent—a thought that can be terrifying. And so we naturally wonder: can we mark the world in some way so that we'll live on in the minds of others?

Artists may feel this especially keenly. On the one hand, artists do what they do because the work itself is so fulfilling; on the other hand, there's something seductive about the idea that one's work will affect others and will continue to have an impact long after we are gone. Poet Hannah Senesh wrote, "Perhaps, through writing, I will be able to contribute something towards human happiness."[17] Composer John Zorn talks about making "a difference in the world."[18] Fellow composer Allen Shawn wrote that artists try to "make things that can survive without them."[19]

That said, some argue that this is a deep misunderstanding of the point of creative work. Filmmaker Woody Allen says, "Some artists think that art will save them, that they will be immortalized through their art, they will live on through their art. But the truth of the matter is, art doesn't save you. . . . I mean, it doesn't profit Shakespeare one iota that his plays have lived on after him. He would have been better off if he was alive and his plays were forgotten."[20] This is what leads Allen to emphasize the importance of the work rather than how the end results are received by others, rather than any tangible external rewards that come as a result.

Indeed, in considering one's legacy there is a real danger that the artist will lose sight of the work itself, that a focus on the future will destroy the moment in which creation can take place. Zorn warns us against getting "distracted by the normal human need for . . . understanding and appreciation. Those are distractions from doing the work."[21] The irony is that one can become so focused on creating something that will leave a mark—a focus on outcome rather than process—that one has trouble actually making the art in the first place. *Wanting* to produce a legacy is hardly a legacy in itself.

But what if it *doesn't* get in the way of doing the work? What if an artist finds the idea of lasting impact motivating? Visual artist Judy Chicago once wrote this about the drive for recognition: "One doesn't get up at 5 AM & push past one's limits & really put oneself on the line without wanting some reward."[22] As I suggested in the commentary on *Parashat Va-yetzei*, it may not matter why you create as long as you actually create.

17. Senesh, *Her Life*, 19.

18. Milkowski, "John Zorn."

19. Shawn, *Schoenberg's Journey*, 194.

20. Allen and Bjorkman, *Woody Allen*, 103.

21. Goldberg, "John Zorn."

22. Levin, *Becoming Judy*, 187.

It certainly worked out for God—we *do* talk to our children about the Exodus story at Passover every year, just as God said we would. What's more, we're happy that Hannah Senesh produced poems like "Eli, Eli," pieces that became songs that do contribute to the well-being of people, generation after generation. The same goes for lasting works of all artists. And take Amedeo Modigliani, who only painted in his head, rather on canvas, when he was especially depressed about the likelihood of selling his work.[23] Think of all the work we lost! We're better off because of people who tried to leave a mark, and worse off when the mark was never left at all.

I can't help but wonder, though. Isn't the work affected, shaped, by the motivations that fuel the doing of it? A strong focus on a certain outcome—becoming famous, say, or even helping others—necessarily takes a little focus off the process. And it can be a kind of trap. Turning back to the Torah and jumping ahead a few *parashiyot*, we see God ready to obliterate the Israelites after they create a golden calf, and Moses stops it from happening by confronting God about how it would look to others: *"Let not the Egyptians say, 'It was with evil intent that He delivered them, only to . . . annihilate them from the face of the earth'"* (Exod 32:12). The argument isn't that it would be wrong, but that it would leave the wrong kind of sign behind. Now, I'm not suggesting that the Israelites should have been wiped out, naturally—but I'm saying that God is backed into a strange corner; by placing importance on legacy in *Parashat Bo*, God sets up a dynamic where this ostensibly omnipotent being is later prevented from taking action by the thought that it might impair that legacy. What if an established artist similarly avoids taking a creative risk, for fear of damaging her or his legacy?

It always comes back to the work. Only you can be sure when thoughts of the future are helping the present, and when they're getting in the way. Just know that having a well-reviewed show isn't the same as actually painting, and winning the Pulitzer isn't the same as writing.

As I've already said, there's only one real secret to being an artist: make art. The rest might be a distraction or maybe an extra motivation—but it's never the point.

23. Meyers, *Modigliani*, 46.

*In Your Mouth and In Your Heart:*

Do you want to leave a legacy behind? Does that motivate your creative work? What if you knew that nobody would ever know about your creative work—ever? Would you still continue to create?

# B'shallah

## Fear

### Exodus 13:17—17:16

WHEN I TEACH CREATIVE writing classes, I start by telling my creative writing students what I hope will happen for them during the semester. This includes all sorts of things: I want them to grow as writers, come together as a writing community, try things they haven't tried before—and, above all, at some point I want them to write something that scares them. Courage, I want them to know, is essential in life, and especially in an artistic life—and that includes the courage to take on their fears directly. Many of my students struggle with this—but the ones who succeed produce some of the most exciting work they'll write all semester long.

*Parashat B'shallah* offers us a vivid analogy to this process. In it, the Israelites flee Egypt but quickly find themselves boxed in, the Sea of Reeds in front of them and the Egyptian army galloping at them from behind. They are, according to the text, terrified (Exod 14:10), and Moses cries out to God, who tells him that the people simply have to go forward—forward into the sea. Then God settles in between the Israelites and the Egyptians, separating the two overnight (Exod 14:20), and gives them plenty of time to dwell in their fear.

In the text itself, Moses finally raises up his arm and God splits the sea so that the Israelites can pass through, but a fairly well-known midrash tells the story differently. According to this account, the waters did not split until one Israelite—Nachshon, son of Amminadab—waded in. Some say that he was in the water up to his nose before the sea was parted. It's hard to imagine what happened to him on that long night of fear, but some way or another he came to an understanding by the morning: miracles only happen when we are willing to go forward into what scares us.

Many artists share this view. As I've noted before, painter Marc Chagall expressed his dissatisfaction with the world of art that surrounded him in this way: "I felt we were still playing around on the surface, that we are afraid of plunging into chaos."[24] His choice of metaphor could remind us of the Israelites faced with the Sea of Reeds.

There are always artists who share Chagall's desire to plunge in. Choreographer David Gordon tells this story of his childhood: "When I was a kid, living the Lower East Side tenement life, my mother would say, 'Go for a walk with your brother. Take your brother for a walk. Hold his hand.' I would take him out and work hard to get lost so that he would get scared and so would I. I'm still trying to get lost. In making a new work, I attempt to start someplace that I haven't started before. . . . I do what it takes to upset the balance of knowing."[25] Here you have an artist who goes beyond accepting that his work might be difficult or frightening and actually *invites* the things that scare him into his creative process. He continues: "I picked the sections of the music that were the hardest for me to understand how to deal with and began working on those sections first. . . . I needed to be the most frightened to start with."[26]

Fear is often part of the process. Choreographer and composer Meredith Monk said, "In making a new piece, the first feeling is fear. It's terrifying to hang out in the unknown. But you go ahead anyway on blind faith. There's usually some point in the process where my interest and curiosity take over."[27] She sounds like Nachshon here, wading in, hoping for the best, and finding that her blind faith indeed leads to something good.

I've had this experience myself. When I write fiction, I often write about the things that people experience but are uncomfortable talking about—loneliness, lust, desperation. I find that *I* am uncomfortable writing about some of the things I write about—but it's an exhilarating kind of tension. Dwelling in frightening places gives me a charged, intense kind of energy to write.

Consider that in our Torah stories fear often comes before our greatest moments of triumph. Jacob quakes as he thinks about confronting Esau and

24. Chagall, *My Life*, 101.

25. Morgenroth, *Speaking of Dance*, 48–49.

26. Ibid., 52.

27. Ibid., 96.

his army; Mount Sinai, the site where God gives the Torah to the people, is surrounded by thunder and lightning before revelation begins; the people balk at entering the promised land. In all these cases people succeed by allowing themselves to enter the fear, to pass through it or to live with it. As artists, we have to open ourselves up to this experience.

What frightens you? What do you desperately *not* want to deal with in your work? What wall of water stands in your way?

Nachshon, entering the Sea of Reeds, didn't first put on scuba gear, a snorkel, an inner tube, something to reassure him that everything would be okay. He just stepped, vulnerable, into the water. Neither can we just try to solve the problem so that the fear goes away. That wouldn't do anything for us; the miracle happens when we go forward into fear. So:

What are you afraid of?

---

*In Your Mouth and In Your Heart:*

Envision creating a piece of art that would take you right into the heart of something that frightens you very much. Get started on it.

---

# Yitro

## The Individual and Communal Natures
## of Revelation

### Exodus 18:1—20:23

THE TORAH TELLS US that all Jews were present for the revelation, the giving of the Torah, at Mount Sinai—not just the Israelites who had wandered there from Egypt but all subsequent generations, too, including the present (Deut 29:13–14). All of us stood at the foot of the mountain with the thunder and lightning and the rolling clouds all around; all of us heard the sound of the shofar and of that resonating voice. All of us still tremble there today.

This is therefore in part a communal experience; all Jews are there, together. And the words that came down to us weren't meant for just one person but for every one of us. Yet there is something individual about the experience, too. When God begins speaking the *Aseret ha-D'varim*, what in English we usually call the Ten Commandments, God starts with "*I the Lord am your God*" (Exod 20:2), and, in Hebrew, the *your* is singular. This is how revelation begins—personally.

And so although we all have an experience of Sinai, no two of us have the same one. What we each do with that experience, how we act in its wake, varies, too; it makes sense that that experience would play out in different ways in different lives. It also makes sense that artists, who bring out and renew revelation in every age, would produce such a dizzying range of work. The choreographer Anna Sokolow displayed an intuitive understanding of that in the way she worked with dancers: "She trains dancers to give full physical form to their personal pain and anger as well as to more positive emotions. Precisely because she employs no systematic techniques or exercises to achieve these goals, the dancers must find their own way in. She does not teach them how to plumb their own depths, she simply demands that they do. It becomes *their* search, *their* quest for performance integrity, and when they find it, the results are long-lasting."[28]

There's something beautiful about this, about the idea that each one of us has a unique and personal grasp on the wisdom of the universe. Our tradition tells us that this grasp is an instinctive one; the Hasidic teacher Menachem Mendel of Rymanov taught that God didn't tell the people the entire list of the *aseret ha-d'varim*, but only spoke the first letter, a single *aleph*, and the people intuited everything else.[29] The wisdom here is that, when a person is in close relationship with the divine, the wisdom of the divine comes to that person naturally, readily, speedily, without the need for detailed explanations.

You can see this happening in the frenetic productivity of sculptors like Louise Nevelson or composers like Arnold Schoenberg, both of whom tended to produce work in intense and continuous bursts. For one, "Schoenberg wrote much of his music at a feverish pace. He usually could not successfully complete a work once he had abandoned it."[30] Meanwhile, Nevelson's "approach to art remained essentially instinctive, impulsive, and deeply subjective; she favored instant aesthetic judgments, which underscored intuition and downplayed theory, and process rather than a perfectionist goal."[31] She valued "speed, spontaneity, and prolific output," and said, "It would offend me to think I would have to measure something, because I *feel* it."[32] This is revelation, instinct—not measured, rational planning. This is subjective and individual.

One of the interesting things about this process of creating art (and discovering wisdom) is that it can be hard to talk about. Composer John Zorn has said that he typically avoids interviews, partially because he's not sure what to say about what he's working on. "I do music," he says. "And a lot of times I don't really understand fully what it is that I'm doing at the moment. I understand 10 years later what it was. I gotta go on intuition a lot of the time."[33] It's hard to talk about revelation, especially because it's so extremely individual.

28. Warren, *Anna Sokolow*, 176.
29. Lieber, *Etz Hayim*, 441.
30. Shawn, *Schoenberg's Journey*, 95.
31. Lisle, *Louise Nevelson*, 128.
32. Ibid., 73.
33. Milkowski, "John Zorn."

Of course, this experience of being an individual can be a threatening one, as we've explored before. Composer Arnold Schoenberg puts it this way: "The young artist . . . believes that his work is at no point distinguishable from what is generally found to be good in art; and all of a sudden he is violently awakened from his dream, when the harsh reality of criticism makes him aware that somehow he is not so normal after all, as a true artist should never be normal; he lacks perfect agreement with those average people who were educable, who could submit wholly to the 'Kultur.' "[34] But this doesn't have to mean isolation. When painters Adolph Gottlieb and Mark Rothko wrote "It is our function as artists to make the spectator see the world our way—not his way"[35] they were suggesting that, even if the process of revelation can't be shared, the actual wisdom gleaned from the process might be able to be conveyed. Rabbi Reena Spicehandler puts it this way: "By sharing a highly personal version of an encounter with God, the poet helps readers expand their own spiritual potential. . . . Both the poet and reader are revealed as ordinary people who yet have the capacity to experience the transformative moment of prayer."[36] And so there's a bridge there, a little bit of community, when we as individuals offer one another the fruits of our individual moments of revelation.

There's also just the fact of being in this process, individually, together. The person next to me at the foot of Mount Sinai is having a different experience of the divine than I am, sure—but we are both having an experience of the divine. In his characteristically dense prose, painter Mark Rothko puts it like this when he discusses the similarities between the poet, the philosopher and the visual artist: "The preoccupation with these eternal problems creates a common ground which transcends the disparity in the means used to achieve them."[37] We are, each one of us, engaged in the same process. It plays itself out differently in each one of us, just as everything else does. But the result is the same—in every soul, a part or a version of the wisdom from atop the mountain. In the case of the artist, or anyone else who finds a way to share the revelation, that individual wisdom comes back to the community, whether on canvas or a sprung dance floor or in words or notes, a bond *with those who are standing here with us this day before the Lord our God and with those who are not with us here this day* (Deut 29:13)—a bond with the artist's generation and all those yet to come.

34. Shawn, *Schoenberg's Journey*, 130.

35. Gottlieb and Rothko, Letter.

36. Spicehandler, "The Poetry of Liturgy."

37. Rothko, *Artist's Reality*, 21.

*In Your Mouth and In Your Heart:*

How does your creative work reflect your uniqueness? How does it communicate that uniqueness to others?

# Mishpatim

## The Rules

### Exodus 21:1—24:18

To its critics (from without and within), Judaism is sometimes characterized as a religion of rules and regulations—to the exclusion, we are asked to believe, of real spirituality. It's certainly easy to get that feeling as you read *Parashat Mishpatim*; the Hebrew word *mishpatim* means rules, and this Torah portion catalogues commandment after commandment about matters as diverse as how to deal with a habitually violent ox to how to treat a sorceress and what happens to a person who insults his or her parents, along with more basic things like murder, theft, and sexual behavior. If the scholar Maimonides was right that the Torah contains 613 commandments, this one *parasha* can feel like it contains half of them all by itself.

People struggle with a *parasha* like this for a variety of reasons. For one thing, it doesn't tell any stories, and so it's a different kind of read than something like the sections we see in Genesis—the flood, say, or the binding of Isaac. But there's a deeper discomfort around even the idea of rules; a lot of us—especially, perhaps, artists—like to believe that there are no such thing as rules, or that they only exist in order to be broken.

Think of choreographer Anna Sokolow, who said, "I don't like imposing rules, because the person, the artist, must do what he feels is right, what he—as an individual—feels he must do."[38] In this, she certainly sounds like a few students I've taught, people who resist any notion that there are certain things that they *need* to do. Stories don't *need* plot, they tell me; poetry doesn't *need* imagery—the writer can do whatever s/he wants.

38. Sokolow, "I Hate Academies," 38.

It's hard to argue with that; after all, a poet *could* write a poem consisting only of the letter Y repeated over and over again. (Probably someone has already done exactly that.) It would be ridiculous for me to tell them that they're just not allowed to do certain things, because I said so, whether they like it or not. That would be tyranny, and tyranny doesn't lead to art. (Note Sokolow's word choice—she was concerned about "imposing" rules.) But of course that's not what many rules are actually about. In many cases, it's not that you're not *allowed* to do something—it's that you can only achieve the result you want, and avoid the results you don't want, by doing things in a certain way.

Take the example of a *mishpat* offered in Exodus 22:30: "*You shall be holy people to Me; you must not eat flesh torn by beasts in the field.*" The idea is not "*Don't eat torn flesh because I said so*"—the idea is that eating carrion—biblical roadkill, really—in some way automatically and naturally turns us from the holiness of our nature. And doesn't that make sense? Unless we find ourselves in a desperate situation, isn't there something less than sacred about chowing on a half-eaten and decaying animal left in pieces out in a field? Disobeying this particular rule is risky not because it'll lead to some arbitrary punishment from God but because it'll quite naturally lead to an outcome that the rule-breaker doesn't actually want. Complaining about it might be like stepping out of an open window and then griping that the law of gravity isn't fair.

Rules in art often address things nearly as basic and primal as gravity. I remember being in an art class as a schoolkid and being told not to use black to make shadows on a person's face, that brown made the shadows look more natural, more real. Now, if I had been *trying* to create an ashen pallor, or to disrupt our normal expectations of realistic color, the rule might not have applied to me—but I was trying to paint a believable portrait, and the role of the rule was just to tell me that I had to do things a certain way in order to achieve the particular effect I was after—not because the teacher said so, but because of the impact of color choices on the typical person viewing a painting. My desire to do things my own way wouldn't have made black a more *effective* choice, just as it wouldn't make the paint dry any faster or change the flexibility of my brush bristles.

The same goes for all the arts. Tonal music affects a listener differently from atonal music. Marble reacts in a certain way to the chisel. The dancer is always in relationship to the limitations of the body, the audience's associations with particular postures, and—yes—gravity. The desire to be rebellious doesn't change any of these basic facts. Even writers, who are working with something as socially constructed as language, are faced with thousands of years of history that have shaped the human relationship to their material. A writer can write a story without plot, a poem without imagery, but a writer can't force a reader to react the same way to these pieces as to a story *with* plot or a poem *with* imagery. We can control what we do, in other words, but we can't change the established relationship between the choices we make and the impact they have on an audience.

Knowing this, many artists base their art on responding to and working with the laws they encounter—and even some that they create. According to Glenn Gould, "the sources of [composer Arnold Schoenberg's] inspiration flowed most freely when stemmed and checked by legislation of the most stifling kind."[39] My students often discover that it's easier to write when the writing prompt I gave them is full of restrictions (e.g., a poem with ten lines, using six specified words, in dactylic hexameter) than if I just throw the assignment wide open and tell them, say, to write a poem on whatever they want.

Doing good work on a particular piece is sometimes inseparable from engaging with the rules at hand. Composer and choreographer Meredith Monk says: "Each of my pieces creates a kind of world and part of my job is to let that world come into being without my getting in the way. Another part of my job is to ask what the laws of this particular world are. And the piece answers it."[40] Part of creation is an openness to the fact that you don't know everything. Part of creation is an understanding that you will not necessarily be able to make all the rules yourself but that you will more likely have to deal with the pre-existing natural laws of the particular material and art at hand.

But what about all those artists who seem to break the rules? What about Sokolow, for example, and her resistance to being told what to do? Well, it's worth reading the rest of her quote, which ends with, "An art should be constantly changing; it cannot have fixed rules."[41] *Fixed* rules. An art should not have *fixed* rules. This makes perfect sense. If art is, among other things, the continuous effort to discover the natural principles of the world, then artists will continue to discover new truths about the laws that underlie art. Cubists discovered something new about how we see the

39. Shawn, *Schoenberg's Journey*, 203.
40. Morgenroth, *Speaking of Dance*, 92.
41. Sokolow, "I Hate Academies," 38.

world; modernist writers discovered something new about how we under-stand narrative—and then *post*-modernists took things further. I think of their efforts less as attempts to change the rules than to develop a broader, deeper, more complex and accurate sense of how the world might work. Composer Arnold Schoenberg, who wrote a great deal of atonal music in an effort to find other ways to hold music together, was on a "quest for a new musical law"[42]—not *no* law, but a new one.

Judaism's interest in rules is primarily about connecting to God and one another in the most ethical, the most appropriate, the most effective ways possible. When we follow the *mitzvot*, the commandments, and the *mishpatim*, the rules, we liberate the holy sparks in all the humble reality around us—not because God said so but because living in this way natu-rally makes the world holier and more meaningful. Even when we evolve as a religion, leave behind old ways for new ones, it's because we have uncov-ered still better ways to interact with the divine.

In our creative lives, we develop not by ignoring the natural laws of our work, but by wrestling with them, and, along the way, discovering new ones—which is just what we're supposed to do.

---

*In Your Mouth and In Your Heart:*

What rules in your particular medium of art strike you as the most important and undeniable? Which ones do you wrestle with the most? Which ones can you break effectively, and what new ones do you discover in their place?

---

42. Berio, "Mahler's Parable," 93.

# T'rumah

## Working Without a Blueprint

### Exodus 25:1—27:19

$P$ARASHAT T'RUMAH IS, TO my mind, one of the toughest reading experiences in all of the Torah. In it, we are presented with extremely detailed instructions for the building of the *mishkan*, the portable sanctuary that the Israelites would carry through the desert so that God might dwell there among them wherever they stopped. There are the four gold rings to be attached to the gold-overlaid table inside the sanctuary, the three cups on each of the branches of the menorah to be put on the table, each branch with calyx and petals, the fifty loops on each cloth hung to cover the *mishkan*, and then the coverings over the coverings, planks and many sockets, and then more rings and more cloths and more sockets. Line after line after line of something approximately as absorbing as the assembly instructions that come with your new do-it-yourself set of bookshelves.

In fact, my knee-jerk reaction is something like, *Hey—I'm not planning to actually build my own mishkan. I think we can skip some of the detail.* But of course, as usual, my first reaction to a piece of Torah misses the point, and only on deeper readings do I manage to notice that, as exhaustive as the instructions *seem* to be, they turn out to be missing a great deal. In fact, if the goal *was* to use this *parasha* as a blueprint for building the *mishkan*, the reader would quickly become frustrated.

We don't know the dimensions of the menorah we're told to build, for example, and we don't know the dimensions of the inner curtain or the uppermost coverings for the *mishkan*, either—and though we're told that these latter cloths should be made of *t'chashim* (Exod 26:14), we don't know for sure what *t'chashim*—often translated as "dolphin skins"—means. We don't know how many of the ritual utensils to make or what the text means by *corners* (Exod 26:23), or how to arrange the bars of the *mishkan's* wooden structure. The measurements are all inexact (at least to a contemporary reader), too—at one point we're told to make a molding that's a *hand's breath* in size (Exod 25:25), and the word *cubit*, a measurement of length that appears here many times, is "about 18 inches," according to the *Etz Hayim* Torah.[43] This all really threw me when I finally saw it. I mean, here we have instructions for the most important piece of architecture the Israelites will know—it even becomes the basis for the Temple in Jerusalem—and the text leaves out crucial details. So what can we learn from this?

I think what I learn is that there is no blueprint—not for the *mishkan* and not for other kinds of creative work, either. If there is no exact and exhaustive set of directions for this crucial piece of architecture, this highest product of the community, how much less so for the idiosyncratic creative conceptions of individual artists? Just as the Torah talks at length about the *mishkan* to give the reader a strong sense of how it should look and function but gives up at the level of final details, this book offers general principles for the creative life—but can't offer step-by-step instructions as to how to produce an accomplished painting or dance piece. There is no such thing as art-by-numbers.

This is partly due to the fact that, as we've explored before, each artist has a unique set of strengths and weaknesses, a unique set of inclinations and interests. Some writers outline and others just plunge in; some choreographers make extensive use of music or video from the early stages of putting a dance together and others leave additional media out of the dance altogether; some painters work and rework a painting to the level of perfectionism and others produce a painting in a continuous burst of energy and then leave the work behind after the final vigorous stroke.

For many artists, though, it goes deeper than just allowing for different methods for different people; many are suspicious of the idea of method itself. Even composer Arnold Schoenberg, who was known in large part for his fairly strict system for producing music, suggested that method alone is not enough: "It is said of many an author that he may have technique, but no invention. That is wrong: he has no technique either, or he has invention

43. Lieber, *Etz Hayim*, 42.

too. You don't have technique when you can neatly imitate something: technique has you."[44]

Others claim to dispense with method altogether, and instead operate from impulse. Filmmaker Woody Allen said, "The morning when I show up on the set, I have no idea of what I'm going to be filming, in what way I'm going to be filming. I like it to be spontaneous at that time."[45] Taken further, this approach can become an inarticulate and ungoverned frenzy of creation. Sculptor Louise Nevelson wrote about it this way: "every stroke creates a marriage between t[he] work and t[he] creator, all done in feverish heights. . . . When things like this are taking place, there is no inclination to think about technique."[46] This process is not ordered, not rational. Choreographer Anna Sokolow was known for saying, "Motion comes from emotion. . . . The technique will be there when you need it."[47]

The emotion, for many, is a kind of rapture that feels closest to love. For Nevelson, art "adds up to Structure, Technique, Material but & above & beyond all it is a Universal love affair for me and I'm in love with Art."[48] In response to criticism of his working methods, painter Marc Chagall said, "But these paintings are beyond technique: what counts is the love in the painting. . . . I've always done without theory or method."[49] There is, of course, no blueprint for love.

This is one reason why people wonder if art can be taught at all. Technique can be taught, certainly, but what about the rest? Well, while some artists resist the word "teach" around the practice of art, most seem to be very comfortable with the word "learn." Mostly this is a do-it-yourself kind of learning, one where you allow yourself to be shaped by your own personal experience. Poet Marge Piercy, who says "imagery can't really be taught," also says, "You have to stay open and curious and keep learning as you go."[50] The process of working can itself teach you something, as Sokolow suggests: "To learn to choreograph, you just have to mess through it

44. Shawn, *Schoenberg's Journey*, 182–83.

45. Allen and Bjorkman, *Woody Allen*, 65.

46. Lisle, *Louise Nevelson*, 104–5.

47. Warren, *Anna Sokolow*, 176.

48. Lisle, *Louise Nevelson*, 182.

49. Coleman, *Creativity and Spirituality*, 177.

50. Moyers, *Fooling with Words*, 179–80.

for a while."[51] And so you learn the part of art that is beyond technique by throwing yourself into it.

Certainly there is still room for method in all of this. The Torah gives us enough instruction to get us most of the way to building the *mishkan* but leaves some of it up to our imagination. So, too, does technique offer the artist useful tools. But tools can't do the work—they can only help the artist to do it. In the end, the artist works with no blueprint, no fixed plans, no certainties at all except the fact of creation happening and happening in whatever uncharted way it manages to happen.

---

*In Your Mouth and In Your Heart:*

Wake up early tomorrow and just start creating with no plan—start moving randomly around your room, throw paint any which way at the canvas, write whatever comes into your head. Does a purpose for the work start to emerge?

---

51. Sokolow, "I Hate Academies," 38.

# T'tzavveh

## The Worker and the Work

### Exodus 27:20—30:10

PEOPLE OFTEN CALL THE Torah the Five Books of Moses, and for good reason. First of all, the traditional understanding is that Moses is the one who received the words of the Torah from God. In addition, his name also seems to go with these books because he plays such a central role in them; although he doesn't appear until the book of Exodus, from that point onward he is, by far, the human who gets the spotlight the most. The Torah, which we think of as being the textual foundation of Judaism, is also largely the story of Moses's life.

This is why it's so interesting to encounter *Parashat T'tzavveh*, a *parasha* in which Moses does not say anything or do anything, one in which his name does not even appear once. There is no other *parasha* outside the Book of Genesis where Moses is this absent. It stands out.

Yet, despite Moses's absence, life goes on for the Israelites. Here we see God explaining how the priests should be dressed, how they should be anointed, how sacrifices should be made, how the incense altar should be set up. We receive these laws, laws that, like the other ones we receive, will apply to the people not only during Moses's lifetime but also after he is gone. The fact that he's gone during these pages allows the idea to sink in: Judaism will go on without Moses. Put another way, Judaism was, and is, bigger than Moses; it's not, after all, called Mosesism.

More importantly for our purposes, this *parasha* also shows us that a sharp line can be drawn between a person and his or her work. The work, if it is good, stands up on its own, whether or not you're there to explain or defend or promote it—and it lives on beyond and after you, too.

This is a simple enough idea—we continue to be affected by many inventions, innovations, political movements, works of art and so on, whose originators are long gone—yet it's easy to forget about the separability of creator and creation. People encountering a piece of writing, for example, tend to assume on some level that the speaker of a piece and the person who wrote it are one and the same. Writer Natalie Goldberg has written this on the subject: "Sometimes when I read poems at a reading to strangers, I realize they think those poems are me. They are not me, even if I speak in the 'I' person. They were my thoughts and my hand and the space and the emotions at that time of writing."[52] And so it's not even autobiography, in this view, if the piece was written about the writer, because that was just the writer (or some aspect or fantasy of her or him) at that time—and that poetic persona may bear no resemblance to the writer seen on some later night by an audience. The creation and the creator are not the same thing.

Some would argue that it's not just mistaken, this mixing up of the work and the person who made it, but also that it altogether misses the point of encountering the work. Painter Chaim Soutine "claimed that any reference to an artist's biography is motivated by an unhealthy curiosity about that artist's private affairs," according to art historian Avigdor Poseq, who adds, "One cannot quarrel with that—after all, what interests us is Soutine's work, rather than Soutine himself."[53] Songwriter Bob Dylan once said, "My background's not all that important though. . . . It's what I'm doing now that counts."[54] What he's doing now, of course, is the work.

The person encountering the art isn't necessarily the only one who has trouble making this distinction; sometimes the artist has the same problem. One thing you sometimes see in a writing workshop (a place where people give one another feedback on their stories and poems), for example, is the writer complaining, "But it really happened!" when a fellow workshop member questions the plausibility of a certain plot turn. Here the facilitator has to remind everyone that it doesn't matter what the writer *says* about the work—it only matters what the work does on its own. In fact, in my workshops I follow the common practice of asking the writer to remain silent during the discussion. I do this, among other reasons, so that we can be sure that we're discussing the piece at hand and not the author (or the author's "helpful" explanations). In the words of composer Arnold

52. Goldberg, *Writing Down*, 32.
53. Poseq, "Soutine's Fantasy," 111.
54. Cott, *Bob Dylan*, 20.

Schoenberg, "We want to see what the work of art has to give and not its external stimulus."[55] In the workshop, then, writers begin to appreciate that their work is separate from them. Goldberg offered this advice: "Don't identify too strongly with your work. Stay fluid behind those black-and-white words. They are not you. They were a great moment going through you."[56] Once it goes through you, it's out of your hands.

Imagine how Moses would feel looking at the Judaism of today—a Judaism which does not much resemble his religious experience. There is a dramatic loss of control when you let go of your work, leave it for others. This does not, how ever it sounds, have to be a bad thing. In fact, it's hard to see how this could be anything but a good thing. If we were to stay glued to a piece of work, trying to control what it does in the world, first of all we'd rob it of much of its greatness. Writer Norman Mailer said that art becomes manipulation rather than art when we can predict accurately how people will react to it.[57] Then, too, there's the problem of what clinging does to the artist: it prevents us from growing. Just as releasing the work allows it to become more than you envisioned, so too this allows us to grow beyond the work. As Goldberg said, "Instead of freezing us, it frees us."[58]

In these pages, while Moses isn't mentioned, I imagine him watching the Israelites from a little distance, just as he will at the end of the Torah look at the promised land from a distance, knowing he will not enter. There must be a feeling of loss, but I imagine there is also a feeling of awe, knowing what his work will go on to produce without him. May we all be so willing to let go, and may we all feel such awe in repayment.

---

*In Your Mouth and In Your Heart:*

Is there a piece you've made that you can't seem to release into the world? One whose impact or message you feel desperate to control? Consider sending it out there anyway—reading it in front of an audience, staging it, hanging it on a public wall—and then just backing away to watch it do its own work.

---

55. Shawn, *Schoenberg's Journey*, 79.

56. Goldberg, *Writing Down*, 33.

57. Mailer, *Spooky Art*, 162.

58. Goldberg, *Writing Down*, 32.

# Ki Tissa

## The Artist and the Golden Calf

### Exodus 30:11—34:35

THE IDEA OF ORIGINAL sin is basically alien to Judaism; there was no moment when we suddenly "fell" and remained forever fallen, and certainly Adam and Eve's mistake doesn't hang over us the way it hangs over the Christian imagination. Yet there is one episode in our ancient stories that does weigh on us a great deal. We find it in *Parashat Ki Tissa*: Moses has been up Mount Sinai talking with God so long that the Israelites are starting to think they'll never see either of them ever again, and they go to Aaron in a panic. They ask him to make them a God, a tangible, concrete one, for them to follow. Aaron complies, melting all their jewelry down to make a golden calf, and the people immediately begin worshiping it, even crediting this inanimate statue, freshly made, with having been the god that took them out of Egypt.

Predictably, the consequences are dramatic. Moses talks God out of mass violence against the people, but can't restrain his own anger completely—he starts by smashing the tablets of God's laws and then unleashes armed Levites on the rest of the Israelites, and the carnage is considerable. Much of the *parasha* after that is concerned with Moses's efforts to repair the relationship between God and the people. It's no easy task. God is in a state of righteous fury, astounded at the disloyalty of the people.

We who read this story retain some of that astonishment ourselves, to this day; God has, according to the tale, very recently demonstrated enormous power, and devotion to the people, in rescuing them from Egypt, and just warned them against sculptured images and worshiping other gods a few chapters earlier in the ten commandments. Not only that, but according to art critic Harold Rosenberg, "Jews were literally crushed by art while they were in Egypt, and the notion of sculpture must have induced tribal nightmares."[59] So how have the people slipped so far, so fast?

One of the things that this *parasha* demonstrates is how difficult it is to buy into monotheism, into a God that is in everything but that is no one particular thing. Even after being rescued from slavery by God, even after an awe-inspiring scene of revelation at Mount Sinai, the people still want something concrete to worship—something they can see and touch.

This is, in some ways, our central difficulty as Jews—and always has been. In the words of musicologist Talia Pecker Berio: "The entire Hebrew Bible can be seen as the story of a tormented struggle to overcome the temptations of idolatry and to reconcile the abstract nature of the Jewish deity with the human need for concrete rituals and earthly *space* for religious worship."[60] We can add "art" to this list of human needs; despite our ongoing desire to connect to the oneness of the universe, we are still moved by beauty and meaning in the particular—in a painting, say—and this is what puts art at the center of the tension around idolatry. Artists attempt to channel some of their awe into one particular manifestation of the divine, one work of art—and that's what makes many Jews nervous, what makes some forbid not only the worshiping of sculptured images but also the creation of them in the first place.

Isn't the artist, by definition, in flagrant violation of this most central of Jewish prohibitions?

Chaim Potok took this issue on directly in his two novels *My Name is Asher Lev* and *The Gift of Asher Lev*, both of which center around a painter born into a Hasidic community, torn between his creative urges and his people. In the first novel, the artist ultimately makes a choice that takes him out of community, and in the second he makes a great sacrifice for his people but still finds himself on the outside. In these books, there is no easy reconciliation between the drive toward art and the drive toward God. They are in serious conflict.

Photographer Frederic Brenner has faced this exact quandary: "As traditional Jew [*sic*], Brenner is caught in a fundamental dilemma: How to create not only pictures of Jews—an enterprise that is inherently suspect from a Jewish point of view—but a Jewish photography—that is to say, a

59. Lisle, *Louise Nevelson*, 39.
60. Berio, "Mahler's Parable," 95.

photography that does not idolize, that does not turn its subject into an object."[61]

Not everybody, however, sees this dilemma as unresolvable. Art historian Margaret Olin has noted that "the commandment against graven images does not straightforwardly aim at any and all image making. The injunctions that precede and follow it reveal its true target to be idolatry."[62] When we are warned against sculptured images, therefore, it might not be a call to stop all art; it might be a warning that, as we pursue art, we must be careful about how we relate to it.

One way of thinking about this is that we must not make the mistake of seeing a given object (perhaps a beautiful and inspiring art object) as being God itself. As writer Rodger Kamenetz put it, "'Idolizing' means mistaking the part for the whole—in Hebrew the word idol, *'pessel,'* means a fragment or broken piece. . . . The devotion that ought to go only to the One is given instead to the fragment."[63] This would have been a hard thing for the Israelites, who were fresh from Egypt and its many tangible gods portrayed in paint and stone on all sides of them.

It's tough for us, too—how much easier to just feel wonder at the moon or trees or stars, for example, than to take it further and feel a greater awe at the source and processes that lie behind it all.

Yet a mindful artist can still honor this ancient commitment to revering the oneness of the universe. Berio once said, "Judaism sublimates remembering through *evocation*."[64] One way to do this is to disrupt or avoid images that are literal, images that are intended to *capture* the world in fragments, and instead create images that *call up* something within us. Visual artist David Aronson has often done this; religion scholar Asjer Biemann "describes Aronson's fracturing of the figure—what he terms the imperfections of the artist's three-dimensional work—as 'an antidote to idolatry. . . . a shattered idol is no longer an idol of power. It is, in fact, more powerless than no idol at all. . . . The fracture negates idolatry.'"[65] Returning to Brenner, and his efforts to devise a Jewish photography: "He accomplishes this seemingly impossible task by placing his subjects into settings or poses, and at times both settings and poses, which clearly signal to both the subject and

61. Mayer, "Representing Acculturation," 87.

62. Olin, "Graven Images," 36.

63. Afterman, *Kabbalah and Consciousness*, xii.

64. Berio, "Mahler's Parable," 95.

65. Baskind, "David Aronson," in *Encyclopedia of Jewish Artists*, 25.

the viewer that beneath or alongside the fixed, black-and-white image on paper there is a process that very nearly contradicts what is actually visible to the eye."[66] This approach to art—shattering it, messing with it—keeps us awake, never lets us forget that we are looking at art, not God.

We get this model for art from the Torah itself, which, as it happens, is full of imagery and descriptions of art. According to art historian Laurie Lisle, "that art consisted of imaginative, surrealistic images—Joseph's coat, the burning bush, Balaam's ass, Aaron's rod. Other observers believe that it was no coincidence that Jewish artists emerged as the authority of the image was broken and non-representational art took hold in the twentieth century. In fact, the more avant-garde the art, the more respectful it would be of ancient Jewish law."[67] In other words, Jewish artists can avoid idolatry when imagery leaves behind the literal and embraces the abstract—anything that refuses to produce a concrete object for the viewer to worship.

But is there no way in for the artist who wants to produce realistic images? There is another Jewish teaching, one whose source I no longer remember, that is relevant here. To understand it, you have to know that traditional Jews wear a fringed ritual shawl while praying—a *tallis*—and that at one time the fringes, the *tzitzit*, were dyed blue. The teaching suggests that the sky—the whole vast expanse—can be seen as one blue *tzitzit* on God's *tallis*. This wisdom splits me open. What it means to me is that one can look at the sky with awe in such a way that it isn't the end of the feeling but a window onto even greater awe. The sky is beautiful, and it is a small part of the grand beauty of the universe as a whole.

In this way of thinking, even a literal image can avoid idolatry if it helps us see past its power to the power of everything behind it. Painter Mark Rothko, known best for his abstract paintings, said, "To feel beauty is to participate in the abstraction through a particular agency. In a sense, this is a reflection of the infiniteness of reality. For should we know the appearance of the abstraction itself, we would constantly reproduce only its image. As it is, we have the exhibition of the infinite variety of its inexhaustible facets, for which we should be thankful."[68] God is not any one particular thing, and, as Rothko suggests, if God *were* any one particular thing, we would just make copies of that thing over and over and worship it. In his view, art is actually the antithesis of idolatry because in an artist's varied

66. Mayer, "Representing Acculturation," 87.

67. Lisle, *Louise Nevelson*, 39.

68. Rothko, *Artist's Reality*, 64–65.

work we see evidence of the "inexhaustible facets" of the abstraction, the divine, that underlies them.

The problem, though, is that we all find it very hard to keep focusing on the intangible and inexhaustible and easy to lean for all our support on the facet in front of us. We need constant jolts to avoid the problem of idolatry. This is one reason that video artist Pier Marton interprets "the graven image interdiction as the forbidding of any image that would, through its formulaic cliché, lead to the grave," and therefore warns us against "kitsch" and "dead images."[69] Formulaic art lulls us, reassures us, allows us to get into an easy attitude that has no space for genuine awe. We have to keep making it new. Non-representational modern art was only a temporary solution; artists have had to keep pushing the edge in order to keep us awake, to keep us in contact with the possibility for awe. In Olin's words, "It would seem that the Second Commandment proscribes only tedious academic art. By following its precepts, Jews end up in the forefront of every avant-garde movement."[70]

And so is the second commandment *good* news for artists? Does it keep us from being lazy, keep us aware of our higher goals? Does it give us a license, in fact, to practice art, as one way among many to open doors to awe? Art historian Elisheva Revel-Neher says *yes*: "The question is not why, when, and how the Jews began to stand against the injunctions of the Second Commandment, but how and when they began to use precisely that Second Commandment to express in their art, consciously or in the dim background of their awareness, their faith in the transcendence of the One God and therefore their identity."[71]

We may not be fallen, but as we learn in this *parasha*, we have deep hungers that can take us away from a powerful relationship with the divine. It seems that, if we approach it with wisdom, art offers us a powerful answer to those hungers. We can create our art in an awareness that we are aiming for, in the words of Rabbi Elizabeth Bolton, "rather than perfection, connection."[72] We are not trying to reproduce God, but to connect to the divine, to connect to wonder, to awe, and to leave some tangible trace of our struggle and our experience—not so that others can worship it but so that they can join us in the attempt.

69. Olin, "Graven Images," 46.
70. Ibid., 45.
71. Revel-Neher, "Wisdom and Knowledge," 12.
72. Bolton, "Toward a Jewish Theology," 18.

*In Your Mouth and In Your Heart:*

Envision creating a piece of art that would be like God's blue *tzitzit*—
a window onto a greater awe and appreciation for things generally.
What would it look like? How can you avoid making it an object of
worship in itself? Try it.

# Va-yakhel

## The Wise Heart

### Exodus 35:1—38:20

$P$ARASHA VA-YAKHEL CONTINUES THE Torah's account of the building of the *mishkan*, the sanctuary, this time not with a set of instructions but instead a description of the work being carried out. This is a great opportunity for us—one of the rare places in the Torah where we see people in the act of creation.

It starts with Moses calling everyone who is "skilled" (Exod 35:10) to come make the various pieces that will become part of the *mishkan*— and one of the important things here is the way that "skill" is expressed in Hebrew. The Hebrew used in the Torah is *chakham lev*, which literally means "wise-hearted," from the root word *chokhmah*, or "wisdom." And so it's not just about having good hands, say—it's about something more profound than that. It is said that when God created the earth, God did so with *chokhmah*. It is no small thing, therefore, to demand that the people making the elements of the *mishkan* be *chakham lev*.

In Jewish mystical understanding, *chokhmah* is associated with insight, deep and intuitive—the quality that allows one to suddenly "get" something in a flash. Artists, too, are expected to be skilled in this way—not just competent, but wise in their hearts, filled with insight and driven by intuitive flashes. We saw in the commentary on *Parashat Yitro* how common this is for people who work in the arts.

So where does wisdom come from?

The Bible is clear that it comes either directly from God—*The Lord grants Wisdom* (Prov 2:6)—or through a certain kind of relationship with

God—*The beginning of wisdom is fear of the Lord* (Ps 111:10 and Prov 9:10). It is no accident, then, that Bezalel, the person designated as chief architect of the *mishkan*, has a name that means "in the shadow of God." He can be trusted with this appointment, despite being only thirteen years old (according to the *midrash*), because he is infused with the kind of wisdom that comes from being in good relationship with God.

This is where the important thing happens. Note that God doesn't build the *mishkan* directly. Note that God doesn't move Bezalel's hands for him. Instead, God infuses Bezalel with wisdom and lets him take over from there. An elaborate set of instructions have been given, but, as we've seen, those instructions are somewhat incomplete, and the rest is in the artist's hands. Indeed, as we go forward in hearing about the construction of the *mishkan*, we get a strong sense of the builder's independence. In the next *parasha*, *P'kudei*, where there are many builders, we frequently encounter the refrain *as the Lord had commanded Moses*, emphasizing that they did everything just as they were told—but in this *parasha*, where the builder singled out is Bezalel, we never read a line anything like that.

There are two possible implications of this. Maybe Bezalel didn't do just what he was told, but elaborated on the instructions and applied his own creativity. On the other hand, maybe he so instinctively did what God wanted that it didn't even need to be said.

I'm not so sure that these are different things. All the workers have some wisdom in their hearts, sure, but Bezalel, he who lives in shade provided by the divine, is the master of this kind of wisdom. For him, creativity is inherently about connectedness to the divine. What *makes* him wise is that he is in relationship with something larger than himself, and this wisdom allows him to exercise his own creative will in a way that really works. This is why God has singled him out by name for this task, even at the age of thirteen. And we shouldn't be surprised at his age, really—think of Marc Chagall as a child, already painting in a powerful fever;[73] a young Louise Nevelson collecting the castoff trash she would later use in her sculptures;[74] Meredith Monk in her earliest years using music to help her understand movement;[75] Judy Chicago's prodigy-level painting at a very young age.[76] Youth is not perfect protection against great wisdom.

73. Chagall, *My Life.*
74. Lisle, *Louise Nevelson.*
75. Morgenroth, *Speaking of Dance*, 88.
76. Levin, *Becoming Judy.*

In this understanding, *chokhmah* means knowing what it is you must do. Does this compulsion come from within the artist, or does it come from without, from the divine? Both. *Chokhmah* is the moment when those two things align, when your certainty about your next move is so exactly right that it can only come from honoring your own inner understanding and from honoring the wisdom of the universe that urges and shapes that understanding. They come together in the wise heart, and art—both new and old, individual and communal—is its flower.

---

*In Your Mouth and In Your Heart:*

What *chokhmah*—insight—do you have to offer the world? How does it show itself in your creative work?

---

# P'kudei

## A Place, or Places, for the Sacred

### Exodus 38:21—40:38

B Y THE END OF the Book of Exodus, we've spent quite a few Torah verses on the design and construction of the *mishkan*. As it happens, we'll be reading even more about it in later *parashiyot* as well. It's no accident that this portable sanctuary gets so much attention—as I mentioned earlier, this is the place where God is supposed to dwell, where the Israelite community will encounter the presence of God. Indeed, in *Parashat P'kudei*, after Moses has finished constructing the *mishkan*, we read the lines *The cloud covered the Tent of Meeting, and the Presence of the Lord filled the Tabernacle* (Exod 40:34).

Now, this Presence is, in the Torah, somewhat movable—whenever the cloud lifts up, the Israelites break camp, put the *mishkan* on their backs, and travel a bit, and then the cloud settles back down in their new camp. Yet, wherever they are in the wilderness, God always settles in the relocated *mishkan* again. So even though it's a temporary, portable structure, the Israelites always have to go to that same structure to interact with the divine. And this mobility is only temporary; when the Israelites enter the promised land, they will build a Temple in Jerusalem modeled after their makeshift wilderness sanctuary, and the Presence of the Lord will locate itself there immovably.

At least, that is, for a while. Looking back, we can see how impermanent this all was. The First Jerusalem Temple was destroyed by the Babylonians in 587 BCE, and though it was rebuilt, the Second Temple was destroyed by the Romans in year 70 of the Common Era, and that one hasn't ever been rebuilt.

Most scholars see the loss of a central Temple as one of the most important turning points in Jewish history; up to this point, we had worshiped our God through animal sacrifices, and by always coming to the same place. Our ancient festivals required pilgrimages; for Sukkot, Shavuot, and Passover we were asked to travel from anywhere and everywhere in Israel to the Temple in Jerusalem, in order to make our offerings. Religion was a highly centralized affair.

With the destruction of the Temple, this centralization was also destroyed. As we know, though, this wasn't the end of Judaism. Instead, we developed a new kind of Judaism, one that had festivals in our scattered communities instead of pilgrimages to far-off places; Torah study and prayer instead of animal sacrifice; rabbis instead of priests; and, instead of a single Temple, we pursued the sacred in our many synagogues, houses of learning, and our own homes. Amazingly, when we lost our cherished dwelling-place for God, we started to find God everywhere.

It's also worth noting that this change to Rabbinic Judaism was in some ways a return to the past. Before the *mishkan*, there was no single place where one was expected to have a holy experience; it could happen anywhere. In *Parashat Lekh L'kha*, God pops out of nowhere to tell Abram to leave his home, and then follows Abram and his wife on their travels. In *Parashat Va-Yetzei*, Jacob is shocked to discover God in an otherwise ordinary-seeming place where he spends the night. In *Parashat Sh'mot*, God appears to Moses in a burning bush. Before and after the *mishkan*, God can be anywhere.

So here we are shown two models of how to best encounter the divine. In one model, we can find it in any kind of place, and it often appears unexpectedly. In the other, there is one place to go to engage with the divine, and so that's where we go. Which model works best?

These days, we have to think of this more broadly than just in terms of religious experience; because we are in this post-Temple Judaism, we are inclined to recognize that holiness resides not just in rabbis and in prayer, but in a variety of other powerful things. One example, of course, is art. And so I come to this *parasha* wondering about the best way to encounter art—should art be centralized, or should it be everywhere?

Bob Dylan once offered an opinion on this subject so strong and so passionate that I think it warrants quoting at length:

Great paintings shouldn't be in museums. Have you ever been in a museum? Museums are cemeteries. Paintings should be on the walls of restaurants, in dime stores, in gas stations, in men's rooms. Great paintings should be where people hang out. The only thing where it's happening is on radio and records, that's where people hang out. You can't see great paintings. You pay half a million and hang one in your house and one guest sees it. That's not art. That's a shame, a crime. Music is the only thing that's in tune with what's happening. It's not in book form, it's not on the stage. All this art they've been talking about is non-existent. It just remains on the shelf. It doesn't make anyone happier. Just think how many people would really feel great if they could see a Picasso in their daily diner. It's not the bomb that has to go, man, it's the museums.[77]

Dylan is clearly a post-Temple kind of Jew—and he's not alone. Visual artist Judy Chicago once said, "Only by moving art out of the studio into the factory and ultimately into all suitable public places can the artist hope to affect society"[78]—and affecting society was, to her, the artist's duty.

Yet she didn't necessarily blame the museums. To Chicago, the nature of the art of our time is largely at fault: "Now art is made for a very small portion of society—and even if you were to take most art out of the context of museums, it has so little to do with anybody's life that nobody would look at it. So it might as well be in museums. The nature of art would have to change in order to have relevance to people's lives."[79] For this reason, Chicago called passionately on young artists for "expressive, accessible art."[80]

So it seems that there's a significant tide of sentiment in favor of the decentralized model, in favor of spreading the divine throughout space—an appropriate tide for Rabbinic times. This attitude has led to many, many wonderful phenomena—public murals, theater in the park, and street and subway musicians, for starters. I once took great pleasure myself in hiding hundreds of printed-out poems throughout the city of Philadelphia, and another time in mailing poems to random New Jerseyites in their homes, and more recently asking my students to do similar projects in Indiana. It feels good, and probably *is* good, to free art from its habitual dwelling places.

77. Cott, *Bob Dylan*, 54.
78. Levin, *Becoming Judy*, 128.
79. Ibid., 285.
80. Ibid., 300.

But the Torah presents both models because both are valuable—and there's plenty of reason to feel good about the art sanctuaries we do have. Nothing else can offer the concentrated experience of music like you get in a concert hall, and nothing else can offer the intensity of visual aesthetic stimulation you find in a museum. The outside world is a mish-mosh of many things—the beautiful, the functional, the commercial, and more—but a sanctuary like an artsy moviehouse or a gallery is a place where you can immerse yourself fully in the sacred. It's for this reason that I feel weepy in libraries. It's for this reason that writer Chaim Potok, in his novel *My Name is Asher Lev*, shows us a main character so entranced, so irresistibly compelled, by his visits to the Metropolitan Museum of Art. It's why Chicago herself sounds so manic after a visit to the museums of Europe: "Seeing all this work makes me realize that I haven't *begun* to assert my ego. Artists like Matisse, Léger, Picasso, Miró, Braque, Chagall, etc., moved into sculpture, pottery, mosaic, stained glass—all sorts of enormous projects, which demanded fantastic ego projection. I am learning so much here about the limits of my personality, my confidence, my ability to do what I want & the world be damned."[81]

We should do more to make these sanctuaries more available, accessible and inviting to a wider range of people—but that doesn't mean that they should be destroyed. We have on our hands two great ideas. From our reading—and our own experience—we can see the value of having a place where we can reliably encounter the divine, and we can also see the value of running into the divine in myriad unexpected places in our everyday lives. There seems little reason to choose between the models. If it were up to me, I'd say let's have more of both.

---

## In Your Mouth and In Your Heart:

What are your experiences with art sanctuaries like museums and galleries? What are your experiences with public art? What would it mean to you to have your own art displayed in one setting or the other?

---

81. Ibid., 216–17.

# Leviticus

# *Va-yikra*

## Form and Content

### Leviticus 1:1—5:26

THE DESCRIPTIONS OF ANIMAL sacrifices in the Torah are pretty bloody—
so bloody, in fact, that one often feels inclined to breeze past them as
quickly as possible (especially if one is, like me, a vegetarian). The Book
of Leviticus, which runs through the whole complicated system in some
detail, makes it hard to do so. There's just so much—and it *is* complicated.
There's one kind of sacrifice for one type of person, another for a different
type of person; one kind for this situation, and another for that situation. In
*Parashat Va-yikra* we encounter a dizzying variety of sacrifices, and refusing to wade through them would mean skipping the *parasha* altogether.

As it turns out, there's a basic but deep piece of wisdom that's demonstrated by all the detail. First of all, we learn something just by considering
the use of animals in sacrifices in the first place. The thirteenth-century
sage Ramban argued that sins happen when we give in to our "animal
nature"[1]—and so (if you view "animal nature" as problematic, which they
did) indeed it makes a certain kind of symbolic sense that our sacrifice
for doing something very wrong involves the complete burning—eradica-
tion—of an actual animal. Then, too, a sacrifice like this means that the person who's done something wrong, the person offering it, loses something
of value—his or her livestock—and gets nothing concrete back for it. That
makes sense, too—not from the animal's point of view, of course, but from
an Israelite's point of view.

---

1. Sprecher, "Mystical Message."

In that light, it also seems appropriate that an offering brought to celebrate *good* fortune does *not* involve a complete burning of the sacrifice. Instead, only the parts that the Israelites are forbidden to eat—the fatty parts—are burned, and the rest is shared with the priests in a celebratory meal. We also learn in this *parasha* that offenses against other people, rather than against God, are expiated not through sacrifices but through righting the wrong directly with the wronged person; a person guilty of fraud, for example, has to repay the defrauded individual, plus some extra. Finally, we are told in these chapters that people bringing animal sacrifices should choose the animal based on what they can afford—anything from cattle or sheep to birds or even grain. In all these cases, the form of our sacrifice varies according to who we are and what we're going through.

The take-home message from all this is that, if we are wise, we choose the form of our expression based on the content of our situation or feeling. So, too, in the world of art, where we often say that the form of our art ought to be tied to the content of what the art is about.

What does this mean in practice?

Mark Rothko said that the "chief preoccupation" of the artist "is the expression in concrete form of their notions of reality."[2] Yet this statement can only be the beginning of the process, because the artist then has to choose *what* concrete form the notions will have to take. Something big? Small? Bright? Dark? Slow? Fast? Artists often make these decisions on a creative-piece-by-piece basis, because different ideas have to take on different concrete shapes. For example, filmmaker Woody Allen was presumably thinking in this way when he chose slow, long shots for his somber film *September* and when he chose the disrupted, quick takes for his more anxious and jagged film *Husbands and Wives*. It's for that reason that Israeli writer Amos Oz says, "I hope never to become a servant to a specific form."[3]

Each artistic discipline offers up a range of choices in terms of form. In dance, classical ballet, with its leaps and its dancers on toe-tips, can suggest that we are closer to angels than animals, while dances low to the ground can convey a sense of difficulty or gravity (in every sense); poems with predictable rhyme and meter can offer a sense of order whereas poems with unexpected and frequent line breaks can suggest a disjointed or fragmented mood; harmonious music can make us see the world as harmonious while

2. Rothko, *Artist's Reality*, 21.
3. Cohen, *Voices of Israel*, 186.

dissonant music can create doubt in the possibility of harmony not just in sound but also in life itself.

This decision about form, as I'm implying, is about more than taste—it's about succeeding in conveying your notion. "Content dictates form," says Allen. "Because I am a writer, the only important thing for me is to tell the story effectively."[4] Effectiveness depends on choosing the most appropriate vehicle for your artistic impulse.

Rothko, who believed "that the subject is crucial and only that subject-matter is valid which is tragic and timeless," said, "We are for the large shape because it has impact of the unequivocal. . . . We are for flat forms because they destroy illusion and reveal truth."[5] He chose his *medium* of expression, in other words, because he felt that it reinforced what he was trying to express.

Composer Meredith Monk suggests something similar in explaining why she likes to combine vocal art with dance. "My personal impulse to tie together several artistic disciplines," she says, "was an affirmation of the richness of the human organism: a microcosm of a much more universal awareness."[6] That human richness she's talking about is conveyed in part by choosing a rich artistic form; if people are multifaceted, why not present art about them that has different artistic facets, from the auditory to the visual?

As Allen Shawn explains in his analysis of fellow composer Arnold Schoenberg's unfinished opera *Moses und Aron*, even leaving an opera unfinished can be a way of reinforcing content with form: "In order to communicate the sacred [which Shawn elsewhere calls 'unknowable'], Schoenberg's challenge was to find a concrete form of expressing not the inexpressible but 'inexpressibility' itself. Not to be able to fully form an opera on this very theme is to make the opera itself an expression of the powerlessness of man in the face of ultimate truths."[7]

Of course, there can be times when form and content clash—but still this ought to be on purpose. If you write a play set at a formal dinner party and everyone unrealistically shouts their otherwise polite and reasonable dialogue, you're saying something, probably about the tensions underlying the conversation. If you paint a canvas baby blue and then entitle it *Violence*, you're intending to say something with that contrast. Even in these

4. Allen and Bjorkman, *Woody Allen*, 326.

5. Gottlieb and Rothko, Letter.

6. Morgenroth, *Speaking of Dance*, 90.

7. Shawn, *Schoenberg's Journey*, 234.

cases, there's a strong relationship between the focus of your art and the way you present that focus.

So, choosing form is a big deal. How do you do it wisely?

To some extent it's a matter of instinct, and writer Gertrude Stein suggested that it's a matter of following one's emotions. "The great thing is not ever to think about form but let it come," she said.[8] And this makes sense, too; if the idea is to find a form that reinforces the joyous nature, say, of what interests you, you will be guided well by listening to your own joy. What container seems to hold it best, most clearly?

It takes time to get the right answer, but then the decision brings momentum. Allen again: "You know, when you write a short story or a novel, the very first sentence takes a long time to get. But then, from that first sentence, everything spins out. The second sentence reflects the first sentence, in rhythm and in other ways. And it's the same thing in a film. . . . And if later on you do something wrong, you immediately know you're wrong, because it's just not consistent with the way you've gone."[9]

As Stein said, it's probably best not to overthink this process. Yet it's crucial to develop instincts. Piece after piece, using trial and error to determine which forms are the best vehicles for your various content, you begin to know when you've got a fit and when you don't.

As that sense develops, the power of the work grows along with it.

---

### In Your Mouth and In Your Heart:

Plan a piece of art that roots in a personal experience full of strong emotion. Choose a form—loud, maybe, or vibrant, or physically overwhelming—that will make that emotion come through clearly.

---

8. Preston, "Conversation with Stein," 168.

9. Allen and Bjorkman, *Woody Allen*, 179.

# *Tzav*

## The Artist as *Kohen*

### Leviticus 6:1—8:36

**D**OES AN ARTIST HAVE any obligations toward other people?
Most artists do their work in solitude, and so an exploration of
the creative process usually focuses on creative people as individuals—but
at some point, most artists bring their work out into the world. The question
then is whether they have any obligations toward the people who live
in that world.

The question comes up now because *Parashat Tzav* focuses on the
group of people in the Torah most concerned with the life of the soul: the
*kohanim*—the temple priests. They are undoubtedly responsible for the Israelite people. At one point, the text tells us that these *kohanim* should be
anointed on their right ear, right thumb, and right big toe (Lev 8:23), and
the midrash suggests that this is a message to the *kohen*. The message is that
the *kohen* must use these body parts on behalf of the people—listening to
them, doing things for them, walking among them.

Can the *kohen* be a model for artists?

Certainly many artists believe that they exist in a relationship with
other people. For songwriter Leonard Cohen (no pun intended), people's
lives actually justify his work as he does it: "There's always someone affirming the significance of a song by taking a woman into his arms or by getting
through the night. That's what dignifies the song. Songs don't dignify human activity. Human activity dignifies the song"[10] Clearly Cohen has been
among the people, listening to the people around him. Many artists, in fact,

10. Zollo, *Song-Writers*, 331.

do walk among other people, do listen and *receive* from the world outside their studios. But what do they give back? Do they do anything for *others*, like the *kohanim* did?

Visual artist Judy Chicago argues that art can be of real value to people, can give them a voice they wouldn't otherwise have: "Maybe artists have to be like congress people—representatives of the needs, feelings, & aspirations of a group of people. At least that's what I want to be—to speak of the longings & yearnings & aspirations of women."[11] Poet Marge Piercy agrees: "To find ourselves spoken for in art gives dignity to our pain, our anger, our losses"[12]—and for that reason she feels compelled to write poems that have that potential.

In choreographer Anna Halprin's philosophy, "dance could once again become an integral part of people's lives. I am driven by a desire to see all the different ways dance can be meaningful to us."[13] To *us*—not just to her. She's known, in part, for her use of non-dancers in her pieces, sometimes without the presence of an audience, so that the dancers and the audience are actually the same thing. She's taken some criticism for this, but in one interview she responded, "Participatory dances that have no audience are based on art because an experience that enables people to find the full depth of their humanness *is* an art experience."[14]

Enabling people to find the full depth of their humanness sounds a lot like the *kohen*'s job, doesn't it? If we view being an artist this way, whether we do participatory work or not, we have an expectation that an artist will be—should be—helping an audience, helping people, move toward fulfillment.

Some people have made this point still more strongly, arguing not only that art *can* help others, but that it *must.* Artists have the unique opportunity to lead people, in the words of Depression-era painter Max Weber, "from malady to health, from psychiatry and obscurantism to clarity."[15] Painter Hugo Gellert said, "Artists may fulfill a very important role. We may paint the way to the future."[16] Because art can offer a clear vision of an artist's values and understanding of the universe, it can show people

11. Levin, *Becoming Judy*, 235.

12. Moyers, *Fooling with Words*, 188.

13. Morgenroth, *Speaking of Dance*, 39.

14. Ibid., 31.

15. Baigell, "Jewish American Artists," 185.

16. Ibid.

something more ideal than what surrounds them already. Because that opportunity exists, say these artists, we must seize it. "Art must become part of the process that shapes a better world," argued painter Lev Landau.[17] Writer Norman Mailer wrote, "I feel that the final purpose of art is to intensify—even, if necessary, to exacerbate—the moral consciousness of people."[18] Painter and printmaker Ruth Weisberg put it like this: "What I do feel very strongly is that my desire to make art, to create meaning, and to be generative is a conscious commitment I make to being affirmative in the face of the knowledge of great systematic cruelty and inhumanity. To remember and to affirm have for me a specifically Jewish sense of renewal. It is the part I can play in the repair of the world."[19]

The Hebrew term for this repair is *tikkun olam*, and indeed this is a deeply Jewish idea. When Chicago says "I am interested in shaping values, making the world a better place," she also notes that "that's the rabbinic tradition in my work."[20] This obligation to repair, in Jewish understanding, applies to all of us—artists included.

But hang on—the idea that an artist has responsibility to an audience is not an easy thing for some to swallow. What about those who see their work as something that primarily challenges or provokes people rather than nurturing them?

This is not, however, inherently a contradiction. Another midrash about the *kohanim* suggests that the ear, hand, and foot needed to be anointed because Aaron at one point listened to the people's cries for a golden calf—an idol to worship—and ran to make it. This is, of course, a misuse of those body parts—parts that are supposed to be in service of the people, not in any old way the people request, but only as helps to bring them closer to God. Similarly, bringing an audience toward fulfillment doesn't mean answering to their whims. Take composer Arnold Schoenberg, never known for a crowd-pleasing kind of music. Fellow Composer Allen Shawn, writing about Schoenberg's complex opera *Moses und Aron*, made an important comparison: "Moses reminds us of Schoenberg himself, an artist who hears a 'call' that others do not and has the obligation to heed this call—paradoxically, for the very sake of those who mock him. The Golden Calf is the equivalent of 'giving the people what they want' (a

17. Ibid.
18. Mailer, *Spooky Art*, 161.
19. Baigell, "Jewish American Artists," 186.
20. Levin, *Becoming Judy*, 364.

nice, hummable tune, say); Moses' task, like Schoenberg's, is not to give them what they want but to give them the deepest and truest thing he has to give."[21]

This is where it becomes something of a circle. If we do have some obligation to help other people reach fulfillment, it may be that we honor that obligation somewhat by going inward, by finding the "deepest and truest thing" we have to give, by working toward our own fulfillment.

In this same *parasha* we see that objects that touch the sacred altar become holy themselves. The lesson is that holiness is contagious between things; maybe it's also contagious between people. Giving our own truth to the world—as opposed to striking a fake artistic pose or just giving the people what they want—can help the world move toward truth in general. The fact is that our work does go out into the world, does reach people, does affect them. All the more reason to approach our work with the purity of a temple priest, our minds and bodies all yearning toward the truth that can fulfill us all.

---

### In Your Mouth and In Your Heart:

Envision yourself creating a piece of art meant to help others in some way. What does it look like? Is it something you'd want to work on?

---

21. Shawn, *Schoenberg's Journey*, 231.

# Sh'mini

## Silence

### Leviticus 9:1—11:47

*P*ARASHAT *SH'MINI* OFFERS US, among other things, some difficult wisdom about tragedy. In these chapters, two of Aaron's sons, Nadab and Abihu, offer an *alien fire* (Lev 10:1) to God—and God consumes them both with flames. It is a shocking moment, one whose exact meaning has been a point of debate over the many centuries, though Moses, in one of his least compassionate moments in all of the Torah, immediately tries to justify to Aaron why it had to happen. Aaron hears what his brother Moses has to say, and then the Torah says, *And Aaron was silent* (Lev 10:3).

Now, this is the Aaron who was Moses' spokesman—his *mouth*, the text literally says in Hebrew (Exod 4:16)—when they were dealing with Pharaoh. This is the Aaron who *speaks readily* (Exod 4:14), whose personality enables him to lead the religious life of the Israelites, to stand before them and speak the priestly blessing to them. Here, however, he is silent.

Even the most articulate and expressive among us can be rendered silent in the face of deep tragedy.

In other places in this book, I have argued that art needs to look squarely at the broken and dark places in our world, and to express something truthful about them to the world. But this *parasha* suggests that there might be a limit to that. There might be some moments, some kinds of pain and tragedy, where the only possible response is silence.

For the first four years of George W. Bush's presidency, I sent him a poem or short story each month. The idea was to respond creatively to current events and to his policy moves, to test the possible relationship between politics and art. As I got started, I found it incredibly stimulating trying to find ways to talk about big and pressing things like the environment, poverty, religion, diversity—even stem-cell research—in a way that was on-topic but still art.

Then, in September of 2001, people hijacked airplanes and flew them into the Twin Towers and the Pentagon.

At the end of that month I had another mailing due. After a great deal of rumination, I wrote this in my letter to the president:

> I didn't write a piece this month that was critical of your actions, nor one that sang the praises of America. I guess there was too much pain for any of that. I did write several scattered poems about the tragedy itself, and about my confusion, and even about the guilt I feel just for being alive, when so many good people are not. None of these pieces, however, seem to capture even a corner of this tragedy. Truly, I'm at sea right now, and find myself unable to do justice to these emotions with words. In this context, they are indeed just words. So this month I am not sending you a poem or short story to accompany this letter. I am sending you a blank sheet of paper. I am sending you a blank sheet of paper to illustrate the futility of trying to summarize these times and our feelings about them.

I was something like a grieving Aaron then: a person comfortable with ex-pressing himself—a person whose life was devoted, in fact, to finding the means for expression—struck silent in the face of tragedy.

This issue, this idea about the places where art fails, comes up when we face personal loss, pain and struggle, and also when tragedy strikes more broadly. The problem is especially vivid for many Jewish artists in thinking about the Holocaust. Aharon Appelfeld, a writer and a survivor of the con-centration camps, has said, "The Holocaust belongs to the type of enormous experience which reduces one to silence. Any utterance, any statement, any 'answer' is tiny, meaningless and occasionally ridiculous. Even the greatest of answers seem petty."[22]

Some have made the point more forcefully. "To write a poem after Auschwitz is barbaric," philosopher Theodor Adorno famously said af-ter returning to Germany in 1951.[23] Even if we *could* find something to

22. Cohen, *Voices of Israel*, 130.
23. Kligerman, "Message," 8.

express about this tragedy, some believe that we cross an ethical line by doing so. As writer and survivor Elie Wiesel noted, "The Holocaust is not a subject like all others. It imposes certain limits."[24] The filmmaker Claude Lanzmann argued that the Holocaust "builds around itself a circle of flame. The limit should not be transgressed because a certain absolute of horror is intransmissible. To pretend to be able to do so is to make oneself culpable of the most serious transgression."[25] Lanzmann's fervor about this ethical imperative is, in the eyes of art historian Margaret Olin, like an ancient zeal against idolatry. "Had he found documentary footage of the gas chambers in operation," she wrote, "he would have destroyed it. Indeed, he attacks [the films] *Holocaust* and *Schindler's List* with all the energy of a young Abraham smashing his father's idols."[26]

And so one possible response to horror is no response—silence. Say nothing, write no poems, paint no paintings, sing no songs. This is the model that Aaron offers us, and indeed I think that there are times when this is the only possible response—the only thing our hearts or our consciences will allow us to do.

Yet sometimes there are, in fact, ways to express ourselves even in the face of unspeakable tragedy. Appelfeld, although he's said that "even the greatest of answers [to the Holocaust] seem petty," has written a number of novels that deal with the pain in their own way.[27] Many of his characters are assimilated European Jews in the years leading up to the Holocaust, and while the reader isn't shown the camps or the genocide, we are made to anticipate them while his characters proceed obliviously in their direction. He talks about the horrors without talking about them.

Despite Lanzmann's strong condemnation of attempts to capture the Holocaust in art, his film *Shoah* documents the stories of many concentration camp survivors. Notably, though, he doesn't include any archival footage of the camps or of anything else from that time—just the people telling their stories. And so he doesn't attempt to convey the horrors directly, but he does attempt to preserve the stories of those who lived through them.

24. Levin, *Becoming Judy*, 380.
25. Olin, "Graven Images," 40.
26. Ibid.
27. Cohen, *Voices of Israel*, 130.

Then, too, Adorno softened his stance over the years, suggesting that poetry after Auschwitz isn't "barbaric" if, according to scholar Eric Kligerman, it allows "the cries of the tortured . . . to be heard."[28] Apparently the poetry of Paul Celan, a writer who had lived through the experience, had made Adorno see the possibility of speaking about—and to—tragedy.

Some even see this possibility as an imperative. Israeli cultural theorist Adi Ophir said this about representing the Holocaust in art: "Do everything that you can to concretize the horror. Honor its intricate details. Present as much as possible of its creeping before the explosion, its day-to-day occurrences, its uncountable human, all too human, faces."[29] Obviously, his view is not shared by everyone—but neither is he alone in it. "I tell my story so that we can build bridges of understanding and avoid its occurrence in any shape and form to any people," said painter Alice Lok Cahana.[30]

In my own life after September 11th, 2001, I found that over time I recovered my voice and was able to return to poetry and fiction—even writing pieces that in some small way explored or addressed the horror, the anger, the grief that had been my experience of that day.

But none of this should overshadow the wisdom given to us by Aaron. It is possible that those of us who experience terrible tragedy will eventually be able to express ourselves about it. It's also possible that that moment will never come. In the Torah, Aaron never does find words for his loss. He returns to his work, he returns to his people, he gives his attention to his other children, but he never finds a way to express his grief over Nadab and Abihu. And sometimes these limits are immovable, and there is nothing to say.

In fact there is considerable meaning in silence. It may not be articulate, but it is rich all the same. It can contain a range and depth of emotion—not just grief but overwhelming awe and joy, too—in a way that a storyline or a sculpture cannot. Composer Allen Shawn noticed that Shabbat itself is the creation of a silence for God to inhabit, and that even in the Hebrew language "silence itself—the absence of a Hebrew letter—has a specific meaning."[31] Considering Aaron's situation, the Etz Hayim Torah

---

28. Kligerman, "Message," 8.

29. Levin, *Becoming Judy*, 362.

30. Baskind, "Alice Lok Cahana," in *Encyclopedia of Jewish Artists*, 67.

31. Shawn, *Schoenberg's Journey*, 234.

notes that "there are more possibilities—and more power—in silence than in any words."[32]

Ironically, these possibilities, this power, all come to us in moments when we are in some ways overpowered. There we humbly find a new kind of truth. As Rabbi Rami M. Shapiro put it in a poem, "As a symphony needs rest to lift music out of noise,/ so we need Silence to lift Truth out of words."[33] We may never be able to articulate our feelings about certain things, and these things may not be able to show themselves in our art directly—but hopefully we can simply give ourselves to the experience without worrying about how to turn it into an expression. Hopefully we can sit in the silence and just listen—to ourselves, to the universe, and to the truth that moves quietly, and sometimes painfully, between the two.

---

*In Your Mouth and In Your Heart:*

Are there subjects or events from your own life, or from the world around you, that seem beyond the limits of what art can or should address?

---

32. Lieber, *Etz Hayim*, 634.
33. Teutsch, *Kol Haneshamah*, 185.

# Tazria-M'tzora

## Tumah

Leviticus 12:1—15:33

**P**AGE AFTER PAGE, COMMENTARY after commentary, this book has suggested that artists can find themselves and their experiences in the Torah, that the text celebrates and encourages creativity—and that's all true. That doesn't mean, however, that the Torah is always perfectly comfortable with the topic. In fact, in some ways we find a profound discomfort in these pages, one that ought to make us see our work in a new light.

The double *parasha* of *Tazria-M'tzora* focuses heavily on the concept of *tumah*, which most people translate as referring to a state of impurity or uncleanness. These chapters explore some of the many things that can lead a person to become *tamei* (the adjective form of the word, meaning "impure"), and some of them make an intuitive kind of sense right away—for example, contact with a dead body makes a person *tamei*. However, many readers are surprised by some of the other causes. A woman is in a state of *tumah* when she's menstruating, for one thing, as is a man after a seminal emission, and as is a couple following sex. Furthermore, a woman is considered impure for a length of time after having given birth. That's the one that really feels unexpected—the Torah puts such a positive light on childbirth, raises it up as such a central goal, so how can it lead to *tumah*?

Nonetheless it does. A post-partum woman is impure for one or two weeks (depending on the sex of the child), and can't enter the sanctuary for another thirty-three to sixty-six days after that. At the end of all this, the woman has to offer a sacrifice, a burnt offering and a purification offering. It is no small thing.

Here's what I mean about the Torah's discomfort around creativity, a force that, in its most basic and original form, is primarily concerned with life and death. Here we see that the things associated with death *and* life—dead flesh, blood, semen, the experience of birth—make a person impure. As much as we traditionally value creation, there's something about it that leaves this text uneasy.

Unease, however, doesn't mean disgust. As the Etz Hayim Torah points out, you can become *tamei* simply by touching the Torah scrolls[34]—surely not a case of becoming polluted by some noxious thing. Rather, as in the case of childbirth, there seems to be a concern about people who have had contact with very powerful forces—and a need to separate them from the rest of the community until they are purified.

There are many examples of this happening in our tradition. I'm thinking of the marriage ceremony, which leaves the couple briefly in seclusion after the rituals, alone together in the wake of something so intense. I'm thinking of the story of Moses coming down from Mount Sinai, glowing with the light of his closeness to God, so bright that his face had to be covered when he faced the people. Just as Moses had to distance himself from the people because of the intensity of his state, so people who are *tamei* often need to be kept separate from community, alone in the power of their own experiences, until they are ready to return to everyday life again.

I'm thinking, too, of the lives of artists. In the midst of work, we tend to hole ourselves up in our studios, and many of us talk about the isolation and solitude that can set in. More striking, though, is what can happen to us after the work, work which often leaves us feeling shaken—and in some ways naturally removed from those around us who haven't just had the same kind of experience. This can be terrifying, of course, and it helps explain why painter Amedeo Modigliani felt so depleted after a burst of painting,[35] and why sculptor Louise Nevelson would often follow a period of productivity with an extended drinking binge.[36] Of course, there are healthier ways to handle these feelings, but there's probably no escaping the fact that immersion in creativity can temporarily set you apart from others.

34. Lieber, *Etz Hayim*, 649.
35. Meyers, *Modigliani*, 154–55.
36. Lisle, *Louise Nevelson*, 140.

At one point in my life I sometimes devoted entire days to writing. I would wake up before everyone else—I was in graduate school and had housemates—and wander off to coffeeshops and libraries and even laundromats to write and write and write, and I'd stay out well past dark, past the time that all my housemates would be asleep. These were intense days. A few times I made the mistake of trying to have a conversation with someone in the evening, calling a friend or chatting with someone in a bookstore, and in all cases I found it almost impossible to communicate. I was so caught up in my experience that I couldn't understand where other people were coming from, and they seemed to have plenty of trouble following me, too. I was, in my focus on art, *tamei*, and separate from others.

Given the potency of this kind of experience, it also makes sense that *tamei* people would keep their distance from the sanctuary. Think of a woman after childbirth, or even a couple after sex, if they are sufficiently present to the moment—there's enough awe to be had in the immediate circumstances without having to go to sacred communal space. Perhaps this is why some artists, regardless of whether spirituality drives their work or not, keep themselves at a remove from organized religion. Some must feel that they don't need any more than the awe that comes naturally from the creative process. Israeli writer Aharon Appelfeld said, "I count myself as a religious person—even if I'm not attending synagogue."[37] He is so invested in his purpose that attending synagogue, for him, is superfluous.

The Torah, though, sees this separation as being only temporary. Discussions of *tumah* tend to end the same way each time: with instructions for how to return to community. Generally there's some waiting involved. (After my all-day writing marathons, I generally had to have a solid night's sleep before I was ready to face people.) Then, when the proper time has elapsed, the *tamei* person in some cases offers a sacrifice (or more than one sacrifice), and in others s/he bathes and washes all of his or her clothes. There is some marking of the return, and some cleansing which allows the person to leave the experience of *tumah* behind. And then there is return.

What the Torah suggests, then—and the commentary in the Etz Hayim translation makes this explicit—is that there's a time for finding awe in the powerful moments in one's life, and a time for finding it in community.[38] For artists, this attitude can be the corrective to the potentially debilitating isolation that can set in; it may be impossible to avoid separation when in the throes of the work or in its immediate wake, but there is a model here

37. Cohen, *Voices of Israel*, 140.
38. Lieber, *Etz Hayim*, 649.

for return, too. In our days it doesn't involve a burnt sacrifice, but any of us can find a way to let sufficient time go by, and then to close the studio door and take a shower—and then, with our experience still in our bones but no longer all-consuming, we can reach out to others again.

*In Your Mouth and In Your Heart:*

Do you feel separate from others while working on art, and after working? What do you do to honor and make space for your individual experience of creativity? What do you do to return to community afterward?

# Aharei Mot

## Keeping Apart

### Leviticus 16:1—18:30

JUDAISM IS OFTEN CREDITED with a number of innovations: the extensive written text that is the Hebrew Bible, for example, plus *Shabbat* (the Sabbath), and even monotheism itself. Of course, there were probably other religions that tested these possibilities out earlier in one way or another, but people tend to see Judaism as a major turning point—if not the moment when these ideas were formed, at least the moment when they really took hold.

Certainly the Torah itself sees the Israelites' new relationship with their God as a shift, and specifically a shift away from the religious practices and understandings of the time. In the beginning of this relationship, Abraham has to leave the land of his father and start fresh in order to know God—and as the Israelites move through the desert, in the time between revelation and the promised land, they are repeatedly warned not to follow the ways of the many peoples that surround them.

In *Parashat Aharei Mot*, God says, *"You shall not copy the practices of the land of Egypt where you dwelt, or the land of Canaan to which I am taking you; nor shall you follow their laws"* (Lev 18:3). In other words, they are not to follow any crowds at all—not the ones they knew before or the ones they have yet to meet. We hear this kind of thing a lot from God, and several times in this *parasha*. And why? The answer comes at the beginning of the next *parasha*, *K'doshim*: *"You shall be holy, for I, the Lord your God, am holy"* (Lev 19:2).

Now, to modern ears this sounds a little cult-like: an authority figure demands that followers cut themselves off from everyone else and do just what the authority figure says. But I want you to hear this the way the people in biblical times would have heard this: they would have found in these lines reminders that their new religious tradition offered people immensely powerful new ideas—ideas so spiritually and morally earthshaking that they required a sharp break from the past. *Don't do what others do*, they would hear God saying, *because what they do just doesn't allow them to have this powerful divine experience that you're slowly beginning to feel yourselves.* That's what the *"You shall be holy"* is about. Surely we can appreciate that, too. Sometimes a person needs to part ways with widely accepted traditions in order to pursue something of great and undeniable import.

This is one of the primary lessons of the artistic life, in fact. As we've seen, an artist tends to need to step outside society, to see it from the outside, in order to respond to it with art. But the pull to be an outsider doesn't usually stop there, at least for people who want to use their creativity to do something truly new; often it means separating oneself from even the *artistic* understandings and movements of one's own time. When art historian Jeffrey Meyers describes the first two stages of the art student's development as "study" and "revolt,"[39] he is arguing for a sharp break from the past, one that replaces old creative ideas with new ones. Clinging to existing trends and schools of thought can squelch the revolution before it has a chance to start.

This is why Judy Chicago, as a young visual artist, said, "I won't show in any group defined as women, Jewish or California. Someday when we all grow up there will be no labels. And we give the professional categorizers pads and pencils and binoculars and birds to divide into groups."[40] Resisting categorization allows you the freedom to go wherever the creative impulse takes you. For example, this attitude allowed Chicago to work with ceramics, weaving, and stitchwork and call it all art, when everyone else was thinking of these things as craft. John Zorn—often labeled a jazz composer by others—makes the point a bit more strongly:

> The term "jazz," per se, is meaningless to me in a certain way. Musicians don't think in terms of boxes. I know what jazz music is. I studied it. I love it. But when I sit down and make music, a lot of things come together. And sometimes it falls a little bit toward the

39. Meyers, *Modigliani*, 24.
40. Levin, *Becoming Judy*, 129.

classical side, sometimes it falls a little bit towards the jazz, sometimes it falls toward rock, sometimes it doesn't fall anywhere, it's
just floating in limbo. But no matter which way it falls, it's always a
little bit of a freak. It doesn't really belong anywhere. It's something
unique, it's something different, it's something out of my heart. It's
not connected with those traditions.[41]

The key there is that last line—he is asserting that his work isn't even "*connected* with those traditions" (italics mine). Like the Israelites in the desert,
he is making a break with the past, and with the ideas of the present.

One thing that seems apparent from the Torah is that a break like this
is difficult to pull off. God tells the Israelites again and again not to act like
the other peoples around them, and just the fact of all that repetition seems
to indicate that people were deeply tempted to go along with the various
crowds. The Torah, for obvious reasons, spends no time warning us against
doing things we'd never want to do in the first place—there is no commandment against hitting oneself in the head with a hammer, for example.
But conformity? That had to be a very enticing thing, to account for all the
many warnings against it.

We know this from our own experience; it's hard to go one's own way
in the world, even as artists. Partly this is because the trends and schools
of thought around us tend to dominate artistic conversations. Could you
really be in a community of painters in the early twentieth century without
talking about cubism, and your relationship to it? Could you be a writer in
that same time period without thinking about how you connected to mod-
ernism? As painter R. B. Kitaj once said, "By now twentieth-century art is
such a maze of depersonalized 'isms' that an artist has to insist on exactly
how he does or does not fit in."[42] You see in this quote both a sense of the
inescapability of movements and also a disdain for them; when they are
"depersonalized," they are inherently in conflict with the highly individual
and personalized phenomenon of creativity.

Of course, there are reasons to find movements and traditions at-
tractive and helpful. As painter Camille Pissarro put it: "We have today a
general concept inherited from our great modern painters, hence we have
a tradition of modern art, and I am for following this tradition. . . . Look at
Degas, Manet, Monet, who are close to us, and at our elders, David, Ingres,

41. Milkowski, "John Zorn."
42. Jackman, *Artist's Mentor*, 173.

Delacroix, Courbet, Corot, the great Corot, did they leave us nothing?"[43] In other words, we don't need to reinvent the wheel in every generation. In fact, neither did the religion of the Israelites start completely from scratch; many of its stories and commandments and conceptions of God can be connected to other religious traditions that came before, put in the service of this new vision.

Something can be creative even when steeped in tradition, as long as the past is put in service of the future. As it happens, I left something important out of Pissarro's quote, right there at the ellipses. While he recognized the importance of learning from tradition, he wasn't about reproducing the work of the past. What he said was, "I am for following this tradition while we inflect it in terms of our individual points of view."[44] Even when we follow, we must make it new.

With this in mind, there's also a lot to be gained by involving oneself in the movements of one's time; while a young Judy Chicago refused to be in a "women's" show, an older Chicago did it all the time, when she decided that her work was, in fact, part of a larger movement, one that had the potential to be more effective and powerful as a collective effort than as a scatter of individuals. This did not, of course, prevent her from innovating—she continued to make art in ways that others never had—because she was, like other artists around her, leading the way rather than following. In a sense, this made her like one of those Israelites, participating in the new with others. As art critic Harold Rosenberg noted (and this is an ironic place for male-centered language): "How much the work of an artist owes to an art movement to which he belongs can never be determined exactly, if only because the movement derives its character from the individual creations of its members."[45] The point is that the movement doesn't have to control an artist—it can also be seen as the unconstrained collective results of a group of artists with similar goals or values.

In the Torah, the Israelites encounter many other peoples and some other ideas, and undoubtedly they are affected by them in one way or another. Yet still they try to stay true to their vision—a vision of a new way of being in the universe, a new way of being in relationship to the divine. We artists, too, will have many encounters and learning experiences in our

43. Ibid., 33.
44. Ibid.
45. Ibid., 86.

Leviticus

lives, and yet will always have to stay true to the newness and individuality of our own visions. As we learn in the Torah, that's no simple thing.

---

*In Your Mouth and In Your Heart:*

Are there traditions in your field of art that seem worth inheriting? Are there artistic movements in your time that feel relevant and exciting to you? What can you learn from them? In what ways do you need to break from them in order to realize your own unique vision of the world?

---

# K'doshim

## The Work

### Leviticus 19:1—20:27

JUDAISM IS, FIRST AND foremost, a religion of doing. Although we have certainly contributed philosophers and theologians to the world's ongoing conversation about spiritual matters, above all Judaism focuses on action: ritual, religious behavior, good deeds, work that moves us toward social justice. As we see in *Parashat K'doshim*, that emphasis has been with us from the beginning.

At the beginning of the portion we read "*You shall be holy*" (Lev 19:2), and we can therefore take what follows as an illustration of what holiness looks like to the author(s) of the Torah. It's interesting to see, therefore, that what follows isn't philosophy, abstract reasoning, or discourses on what the word *holy* might mean, but instead concrete instructions on how to behave. We're told to avoid doing certain things—idolatrous acts, stealing, gashing one's flesh—and we're also told what we must be sure to do: leave gleanings from our harvest available for the poor, keep Shabbat, show reverence for elders, and many other things.

Nothing shows the primacy of action more clearly, though, than the *hukkim*. Hukkim are laws that the Torah tells us to follow even though they don't necessarily make sense to us. Many of the commandments, it should be said, do make good sense—helping the disadvantaged, giving fair judgments, giving wages when wages are due—but then there are those that we're just asked to do without a full understanding of why. In this *parasha* we're asked to avoid mating our cattle *with a different kind*, to use only one kind of seed in our fields, and not to mix two kinds of cloth in one garment (all Lev 19:19). Why? Well, it's hard to say. We could speculate about why all this mixing would be bad (we've certainly done so, over the millennia), but it's certainly not immediately obvious, and the Torah doesn't spell it out—it just tells us to act.

As in other places in the Torah, a rebellious person might want to refuse these commandments precisely because we aren't given a good reason to follow them. To that person, it might feel like slavish, mindless obedience to do something just because we're told to do it. That's reasonable enough, and we must tread carefully to protect our own integrity—but what I see in the Torah isn't a call to slavishness but a call instead to realize that sometimes we come to understand and to grow *through doing,* and that waiting for a rational understanding before acting can keep us from some of the most powerful experiences available.

Nobody illustrates this more clearly than artists. Early each semester when I go into a creative writing classroom, I am sure to tell my students that we are not going to be engaging in the art of literary theory; we are going to be engaging in literary *practice.* There is a place for theory, even in art—but theory doesn't produce art. Filmmaker Woody Allen said: "Art in general, and show-business, is full of people who talk, talk, talk, talk. And when you hear them talk, theoretically they're brilliant and they're right and this and that, but in the end it's just a question of 'Who can sit down and do it?' That's what counts. All the rest doesn't mean a thing."[46]

It can be so tempting to keep art theoretical! Writer Norman Mailer wrote, "Writing is wonderful when you talk about it. It's fun to contemplate. But writing as a daily physical activity is not agreeable. You put on weight, you strain your gut, you get gout and chilblains. You're alone and every day you have to face a blank piece of paper."[47] Yet only action produces art—and very frequently we need to act without knowing what we're doing or why, in a state of doubt and uncertainty. We need to work past the point where it makes immediate sense to do so, to just keep at it no matter what. Mailer talks about how the initial excitement of working on a novel changes as you get into the middle: "It's the long middle stretches that call on your character—all that in-between!—those months or years when you have to report to work almost every day. You don't write novels by putting in two brilliant hours a week."[48]

46. Allen and Bjorkman, *Woody Allen,* 195.
47. Mailer, *Spooky Art,* 102.
48. Ibid.

This can be a shock to many would-be artists who think of the calling as a carefree, romantic kind of thing, a whimsical life. In reality, most committed artists talk about what they do as hard work, and they tend to measure their success by how much honest labor they put in. This is the difference, some say, between those who dabble and those who are really taking it on. In the words of visual artist Judy Chicago, "Amateurs work only if they feel like it. When you're a professional, you work whether you feel like it or not."[49] Mailer said nearly the same thing: "Professionalism probably comes down to being able to work on a bad day."[50]

Again, what all of this leads to is art, instead of talk. Many artists would prefer to let their work do all the talking for them. Photographer Andre Kertesz: "We became less and less inclined to talk about the photographs as we became more and more convinced that the best photographs talk for themselves, speaking in a language of their own, and that the less there is left to say about a picture, by way of explanation, after looking at it, the better it is as a picture."[51]

Perhaps this is what happens with the *hukkim* as well. We don't know why we do them, but in doing them we find that the value of the action speaks for itself, that the meaning of our lives is somehow enhanced—eventually, that is. Like art, we may go a very long time before being at all sure why we're doing what we're doing. It may even come to pass that we never really know. Art and life are both ongoing acts of faith. And that's the ironic thing—we often develop faith as a *result* of action, not the other way around. As Allen reminds us, hard work is a very good thing: "Making a film is a big struggle. But the fact that there's struggle helps me. I'd rather struggle with films than struggle with other things."[52]

---

### *In Your Mouth and in Your Heart:*

Is there a project that you've been talking about or thinking about but haven't actually managed to start? Stop talking, stop talking, and start working.

---

49. Levin, *Becoming Judy*, 273.

50. Mailer, *Spooky Art*, 103.

51. Jackman, *Artist's Mentor*, 170–71.

52. Allen and Bjorkman, *Woody Allen*, 268.

# Emor

## Perfection

### Leviticus 21:1—24:23

IN BIBLICAL TIMES, THE role of *kohen*, temple priest, was an extraordi-narily demanding one, and not just in terms of the workload. There was also an expectation that priests would attempt to do better than a good job—to approach, in fact, perfection in a variety of ways—and that any-thing that compromised this perfection would render the priest unfit for sacred duty. We've seen this in other *parashiyot* where God makes precise and detailed rules for the way a priest should set the temple up and maintain it, how a priest should conduct the sacrifices, even how the priest should dress. Again and again there is the sense that doing things a little bit wrong makes everything turn out extremely wrong.

This theme continues in *Parashat Emor*, where we learn about a va-riety of things that would make a *kohen* unfit for service. Contact with the dead—aside from close kin—makes a *kohen* impure, as do particular ways of shaving one's hair, gashing one's skin, along with marriages to women *defiled by harlotry* (Lev 21:7) or who are divorced. More exacting, though, are the demands on the *kohen's* body. According to the Torah, a variety of disabilities—blindness, limbs *too short or too long* (Lev 21:18), dwarfism and broken bones, for example—disqualify a person permanently from service in the temple. We find this kind of discrimination on the basis of disability disturbing today. Yet the point is that, however dubiously the To-rah defines *defects* (Lev 21:21), it's deeply concerned with them here—and what I always find the most startling about this section is that a priest is fully expected to be flawless in every respect, even down to physical details that would be utterly out of his control.

Tough to be a *kohen*, for sure, and perhaps understandably—these men were involved in the most important work of the community, work crucial to the soul. What they did on a daily basis could either elevate us toward the divine or, if done poorly, could leave us cut off, bereft. What they did mattered.

And what about others of us who are likewise concerned with matters of the soul, such as artists? Do we have to be perfect people?

Of course you can argue that this is all irrelevant to the artist—we're not priests, after all—but the *parasha* goes on to imply that these expectations might even apply to the rest of us. We end with an episode where a certain person blasphemes, and the Torah goes out of its way to point out that the blasphemer is only half-Israelite—his father was Egyptian. The mention of this implies that, according to the Torah, the Egyptian side of him may be what causes him to blaspheme. Certainly the xenophobic implications of this are offensive—but remember that the Torah's understanding of Egypt was that it was an idolatrous place that enslaved the entire Israelite people. Again, the point is that a flawed person (given the Torah's questionable definition of flaws) is essentially unfit.

In Chaim Potok's novel *The Gift of Asher Lev* (the sequel to *My Name is Asher Lev*), the main character, an artist, is in conflict with his family and his Hasidic community over the work that he does. They see an inherent contradiction between what he paints and his claims to be a religious Jew, while for him the two are not inherently contradictory. Asher Lev, in an argument with his father, says, "Niceness and greatness are two very different qualities"—niceness referring to being a good person, a good Jew, and greatness referring to his aspirations as a painter—and his father responds, "Not in Yiddishkeit, Asher. Not among Hasidim. What a person does is what he is." The artist cannot accept this, and he says, "Not in art."[53]

In the commentary on *Parashat Va-yera* I talked about the fact that many creative people suffer from mental illness, relationship problems, and difficulties navigating life well—and still they do astounding work. But of course those "defects" are just the ones that make us feel sympathy for the people who have them. What about the reputations of choreographer Anna Sokolow and composer Allen Schoenberg as arrogant and difficult people? (Sokolow, for one, once offered this advice to beginning dancers: "Go ahead

53. Potok, *Gift of Asher Lev*, 40.

and be a bastard. Then you can be an artist."[54]) What about the refusal of painter Amedeo Modigliani and sculptor Louise Nevelson to parent their respective children? (And what about her line, "If I'm selfish, I regret that I'm not more selfish"?[55]) What about the personal controversies surrounding filmmaker Woody Allen? (He once noted, talking about a fellow comedian, "I guess you can't be a genius without having personal problems."[56]) What about architect Louis Kahn's polygamy, each family kept in the dark about the others?[57] "The evidence—if the biographies of artists and writers are at all reliable," said writer Norman Mailer, "does support the notion that it is best to revere painters, poets, and novelists for their talent rather than their character."[58] Above all, what about the various lousy things that *you* and *I* do on an all-too-regular basis?

And so: if the question is "Do artists have to be perfect people to produce great art?" the answer is, pretty clearly, no.

Yet this doesn't mean that the two goals of goodness and greatness are, by necessity, mutually exclusive. What if you could pursue both? Take, as an analogy, the issue of broken bones in a potential Temple priest. The Etz Hayim Torah suggests that the reason this leads to a permanent disqualification is because in biblical times, broken bones were unlikely to set and heal properly, thus creating a permanent disruption in the body.[59] And here's a place where the Torah and the potential priest would have the same goal—both of them would be perfectly happy if there was a way to heal that bone completely. The same goes, presumably, for scurvy or crushed testes, both of which are mentioned among the list of physical problems. Now, that's probably not true for all of the disqualifications listed—many in the deaf community, for example, are adamant that deafness should not be seen as a deficit—but the typical person would be happy to do without the random injuries, anyway.

So, too, with the artist; given the time and the energy and focus to develop both one's art and one's self, I think most people would be inclined to do both. After all, many of the "flawed" artists I named above suffered

54. Sokolow, "I Hate Academies," 38.

55. Lisle, *Louise Nevelson*, 279.

56. Allen and Bjorkman, *Woody Allen*, 30.

57. Kahn, *My Architect*.

58. Mailer, *Spooky Art*, 170.

59. Lieber, *Etz Hayim*, 720.

a great deal as a result of their personal imperfections. Some of them even died far too young, depriving the world of all that they might have created—a tragedy that shows how personal problems can, when taken to an extreme, be barriers to art in themselves. As long as it doesn't interfere with the art—and that condition is critically important—it would seem natural to be open to alleviating one's depression, hostility, relationship issues, and so on.

And—really—why should we fear that spiritual growth would interfere with artistic growth? Certainly this book suggests that, far from being necessarily contradictory, spiritual and artistic growth could in fact be seen as complementary.

Perhaps Potok's fictional character Asher Lev is a useful model for us. After all, despite the conflict he has with his religious community, he himself feels no real conflict between his painting and his religious life. Both are so deeply a part of him that they cannot be disentangled from his identity—nor, really, from one another.

This is not just a matter of fiction. Real-life Israeli visual artist Michal Na'aman finds herself in a similar situation, though in her there is still some conflict between art and Judaism. Art historian Haya Friedberg writes, "Her art emphasizes her refusal as an artist and as a woman to be restricted by Jewish law. At the same time, by turning this tradition into an integral part of her works, she demonstrates a close connection to it."[60] Thus, conflict or not, there is still the fact of Na'aman's engagement with both these parts of herself.

And so, I return to the core question—Do artists have to be perfect people to produce great art?—and offer a somewhat different answer than I did before. The short version is still *No*—plenty of artists produce incredible things despite being fairly miserable human beings—but one thing the Torah consistently asks us to do is to go further than the short answer. In this case, the long version probably goes something like this: while perfection isn't necessary for the creation of art, neither does art require a person to be riddled with personal issues. Asher Lev may be right that niceness and greatness are very different things—but I read his story as a journey toward developing both. It turns out that neither one precludes the other—and that, in the end, they can sit in some peace with one another in the undivided heart of a deeply productive artist.

60. Friedberg, "Secular Culture," 267.

*In Your Mouth and In Your Heart:*

Do your personal and artistic growth seem to be in conflict with one another or compatible with one another? Think of something personal that you'd like to work on that would help you to develop both as a human being and in your creative work. Get to work.

# B'har-B'hukkotai

## Rest

### Leviticus 25:1—27:34

ARTISTS HAVE A DIFFERENT relationship to their work than people in other vocations: they are more dependent on their work for understanding who they are. For example: imagine an accountant, nurse, bricklayer, or rabbi who's been on vacation for a month. If you were to ask this person at the end of the month, "Are you still an accountant (or nurse or bricklayer or rabbi)?" you'd probably get a surprised stare and the response of "Of course—I'm just taking a break right now." Yet I've known many artists who, having paused in their work for a short time, begin to wonder if they are still really artists. Ask them the same question, and you might hear (in a panicked voice), "I don't know if I am—I might never create again!" Many of us are consumed with concern about whether we've done anything *lately*.

I think this happens for a couple of reasons. First of all, the creative muse can be awfully elusive, and we've all certainly heard stories of people who found themselves unable to create after one life event or another. Thus it can seem like there's a real chance that one's most recent song, say, will turn out to be one's very last song ever. Then, too, being an artist is very different from being in a profession where one can become more or less permanently certified. A lawyer who has passed the bar exam and a rabbi who has been ordained are both considered members of their profession in an ongoing way, even if they take a year off to write that memoir or just watch TV. On the other hand, the artist *is* what the artist *does*, and right now—if anything.

Leviticus

That said, while this self-imposed pressure is understandable, it's not completely reasonable. We see why in the Torah's double portion *B'har-B'hukkotai.*

In this *parasha,* God tells Moses some things about how the Israelites should manage the (promised) land once they finally enter it. What you might expect is that God would say something like, *Listen—when you get in there you're going to have a lot of people to feed, so work that land as hard as you can to get those big crop yields coming. And don't let up!* Yet the instructions aren't like that at all. Instead, in these chapters we learn about sabbatical years—years when *the land shall have a sabbath of complete rest, a sabbath of the Lord: you shall not sow your field or prune your vineyard* (Lev 25:4). In the sabbatical year the Israelites will be permitted to eat whatever the land produces naturally, but will not be allowed to actually work it.

There are two reasons for these surprising instructions. The main one given is that the sabbatical year (along with the jubilee year, also explained here) is a reminder that the land does not belong to the people. Indeed, land *can't* in any deep way belong to human beings. It belongs, instead, to weather, climate shift, a host of forces beyond our control.

This is certainly true of the creative process. We can force ourselves to come to our desks and easels and studios, but we are not, ultimately, in control of creativity. This is probably why Israeli poet Yehuda Amichai said, "I have had discussions occasionally with some American poets who think you have to write a poem, whether good or bad, every day to stay in form, like jogging. I don't believe in that. One should write only when the poetry comes."[61] Discipline is a crucial part of many successful artistic lives, but it has its limits.

The second reason for the sabbatical year is that, quite frankly, it works. Millennia before the term "crop rotation" caught on, the writers of the Torah recognized that the land needs to rest in order to continue being productive. This insight is so important, and for some people so counter-intuitive, that it needs to be restated: in order to do productive work, there also has to be rest.

The second part of this double-*parasha* makes this lesson clear in terms of managing the land. Not listening to these instructions will lead to a situation, God promises, where the sky will become *like iron* and the *earth like copper, so that your strength will be spent to no purpose. Your land shall not yield its produce, nor shall the trees of the land yield their fruit* (Lev

61. Cohen, *Voices of Israel,* 34.

26:19–20). This hard sterility is what develops when something is worked at too much.

Consider the cases of sculptor Louise Nevelson and painter Amedeo Modigliani. We have already seen how these two liked to create in a frenzy of production—and we've also seen how those bursts depleted them, much like an overworked field. Nevelson, for one, seemed to have a "lifetime pattern" with "periods of elation, exuberance, and exertion preceding an exhibition, followed by days of depletion, despair, and, increasingly, drinking."[62] This is the artist's equivalent of tilling a field into (hopefully temporary) barrenness. Choreographer and composer Meredith Monk, though happily living a less extreme life, nonetheless notes that the time after finishing a piece is "a time of emptiness."[63]

And so we must rest in order to work.

Sometimes the first rest comes before we start work at all. In the words of poet Allen Afterman, "I can feel when something wants to come out. I wait for it. I let it sit."[64] Filmmaker Woody Allen occasionally has this experience when he's got something brewing, but not enough to sit down and work with it: "Every now and then there'll be an idea that will come along that I just can't get a handle on. And so after a period of time I put it away and maybe come back to it two years later or something. I do a different film."[65] Yet the need to rest can happen at any stage of the creative process—in the dazed wake of past creativity before the next idea or urge hits, in the thick of creation, in the final steps toward a completed project. I once had to set aside a book-length fiction project for weeks because I was incapable of being productive with it—and then, when I sat down to work again, it turned out I only had one more afternoon of writing to do in order to complete the rough draft. After those weeks, I was ready.

I have also, at some points in my life, had a policy of giving myself a break every week for *Shabbat*. I've done this not because I always happen to have writer's block as Friday evening approaches but because including regular times of rest in my life allows me to survive the otherwise relentless pressure to produce, and it also allows me to refuel, to hopefully keep from ever reaching the place of exhaustion and depletion that so many artists experience.

62. Lisle, *Louise Nevelson*, 136.

63. Morgenroth, *Speaking of Dance*, 96.

64. Afterman, *Kabbalah and Consciousness*, 211.

65. Allen and Bjorkman, *Woody Allen*, 264.

The lesson that (I hope) we learn from the double *parasha B'har-B'hukkotai* is that genuine replenishing rest is not a luxury, not laziness, not something to be dodged or cheated—rest is an essential part of a productive life. You *are* an artist, even if you're not working for a little while—and much better that than working until you have nothing left to give.

---

### *In Your Mouth and In Your Heart:*

Are you working hard to come up with your next creation, but coming up empty? Take a break. Go for a walk, see a movie, spend a week having good conversations with friends. Are you stuck in the middle of a piece, unable to go forward? Take a break. Have you been working just fine for a long time, keeping a solid grip on things? Even so—consider taking a break all the same.

---

# Numbers

# B'midbar

## Playing Your Role

### Numbers 1:1—4:20

THE BOOK OF NUMBERS begins in just the way you might expect from its English name: the Israelites are brought together to be counted. The size of this people is impressively massive, and that in itself may make the census worth doing, but its real purpose is something more important. God wants Moses to count up all the able-bodied men (in other words, those eligible for military service) in order to decide how to arrange them to best protect this new and vulnerable nation. Who should camp where? Who should be in charge of what task?

Yet the census is not done on the people as a whole—it's done tribe by tribe. The understanding is that the people within a tribe, bound together by family ties and perhaps other things as well, will work well together as a unit and should not be split up. Thus, when duties are assigned to the Israelites, they're not assigned randomly to arbitrary subsets of the people; they're assigned tribe by tribe. Judah's group, for example, will camp in front of the *mishkan*, along with Issachar and Zebulun. Other tribes are assigned the back, the right side, and the left side. Each group has its role—and, perhaps surprisingly given this young nation of back-talkers, none of them protests. They are each happy to take on their particular job.

The Levites, too—not called to military service—are given the role of taking care of the *mishkan*, the sanctuary, and the clans within the Levites are further divided up to be given particular tasks; the clan of Kohath, for example, will carry the most sacred items between camps, and the Merarites work with the planks and bars and so on. These folks don't protest their assignments either. Rather, they settle into them very naturally.

Numbers

The Torah, as we have seen elsewhere, is often keen on making distinctions. In *Parashat Va-y'hi*, for example, we saw that the various sons of Jacob were all described as having different strengths and weaknesses, and different fates as well. Here, too, we see this interest in distinctions, but now not between individuals but between groups, and not in terms of characteristics but in terms of roles. The Torah here is telling us that different groups of folks have different parts to play in the work of the world.

And don't we? Of course, we sometimes hear stories of "Renaissance people" who seem to contribute to the world in a variety of domains—science, art, politics, and so on—but, as we saw in *Parashat Va-y'hi*, most of us, with our individual arrays of talents, are called mainly to one domain and not others. Some, like sculptor Joseph Epstein, give this process a negative frame—"Sculpture is an exacting and difficult medium, and I have known of sculptors giving it up after time and taking to painting . . . certainly less hard work and less expensive"[1]—but another way to look at it is that many artists simply feel called to one (or a couple of) arts, and not to others. Partly this happens because of talent—a person might be wonderfully skilled at conveying emotion through music, for example, but less skilled at doing so with movements of the body—but partly it happens because the different arts themselves may have different roles to play in the search for and expression of truth, and people might be drawn to one role and not another.

After all, the arts do differ, don't they? First of all, they differ in how they impact our senses. Photography reaches us through our eyes, for example, and music through our ears. Film uses both. Writing, on the other hand, depends on our brain to turn language, written or oral, into a simulation of sensory experience when we, say, read about a juicy apple and somehow start to taste it, without ever literally tasting it.

Composer Allen Shawn makes the case that music's relationship to hearing gives it a unique hold over the audience, one not shared with other arts: "The impression of a painting can be instantly escaped; we possess the ability to close our eyes without even looking away. But to escape music one must leave the space in which it is being played, attempt to hold one's ears, or reject it outright."[2] If you doubt this, consider how many murals, say, you've walked by without really seeing them, and then consider how many street musicians have caught your attention whether you wanted them to or not. Music may inherently be more aggressive in its expressiveness than

1. Jackman, *Artist's Mentor*, 201.
2. Shawn, *Schoenberg's Journey*, 166.

other art forms, and this is part of the reason why, for Shawn, "music itself has a unique power to disturb."[3] He also cites "the evanescent character of its substance, the mystery of its internal laws to nonmusicians, the potentially disturbing metaphorical nature of sound production—which mimics speech, breathing, the beating of our hearts—and the incomprehensibility of the connection between the physical principles involved and the emotions aroused, all make for a situation in which the listener feels vulnerable."[4]

That "mystery," that "incomprehensibility," is at the heart of one of the big divides talked about by artists: the divide between narrative arts—arts that tell a story, like fiction, opera, and much ballet—and non-narrative arts, such as sculpture and instrumental jazz. Painter Marc Chagall was talking about this distinction when he exclaimed, "I am against any sort of literature in painting."[5] Fellow painter Amedeo Modigliani used his "refined minimalism" to the end of keeping literature from visual art when "he portrayed, with a frank, unselfconscious vision, the natural appearance of his subjects, and by eliminating characteristic gestures and narrative elements forced viewers to see people differently and work a bit harder to understand them."[6]

Composer Leonard Bernstein took up this issue with characteristic eloquence in comparing music to literature. He wrote: "Music, of all the arts, stands in a special region, unlit by any star but its own, and utterly without meaning. . . . Without any meaning, that is, except its own, a meaning in musical terms, not in terms of words, which inhabit an altogether different mental climate"[7] and: "Nothing can be more different from the representational literary mind, with its literal conceptuality, than the nonobjective musical mind, with its concentration on shapes, lines, and sonorous intensities"[8] with the result that music "doesn't have to pass through the censor of the brain before it can reach the heart; it goes directly to the heart. You don't have to screen it, as you do words in a play."[9]

Now, to a writer this might sound like a snobbish dumping on the literary arts, especially when Bernstein suggested that "Most novelists, and

3. Ibid., 165.
4. Ibid.
5. Jackman, *Artist's Mentor*, 176.
6. Meyers, *Modigliani*, 155.
7. Bernstein, *Joy of Music*, 33.
8. Ibid., 15.
9. Ibid., 277.

writers in general, tend to put their feet in their mouths whenever they part lips to speak of music"[10]—but at the heart of his words is just the argument that each art has a unique effect on those who encounter it, and its own particular contribution to make. After indicating that music "goes directly to the heart," he went on to say this: "Of course, in a play, where there are only words to listen to, there is more chance for subtlety, and maybe profundity of ideas. There is more time to bandy words about, more chance to examine and re-examine, rationalize and justify."[11] So it's not that music is the only worthwhile art—it's that, in some ways, music and writing do different things in the world. Provoking an inarticulate, powerful feeling is different with leaving a person with a clear, concrete image or a linear story.

This insight helps us to see why the Israelites didn't complain about their assignments. The clan of Merari *could* feel bad about being assigned to carry planks rather than the sacred utensils of the altar, but the fact is that you'd have nowhere to put those utensils if the Merarites didn't do their job. It's also true that, while the Kohathites are honored to carry the most holy items, they are also the most endangered, in that touching these items can cause death, according to the Torah. The two jobs, therefore, are inarguably different, but you'd be hard-pressed to make the case that one job was really *better* than the other. And sculpting, though different from painting, is no better, and symphonies and novels do different things without one being superior to the other.

All this to say that we would do well to follow the example of the Israelites—to hear very clearly what kinds of art are calling to us, and to set up our camp right in that spot. A camp isn't permanent, of course, but it does give us the chance to find the soil that's best for us right now, and drive our stakes deep enough to build a home for a time there.

### *In Your Mouth and in Your Heart:*

Is there an art form in which you feel the most comfortable? What can you do with this art form that couldn't be done in another one? Start musing about a piece that will allow you to play to that strength of the art form. If you're a novelist, for example, put together a great plot. If you're a musician, on the other hand, grab the listener by the heart without the listener being able to explain how it happened.

10. Ibid., 15.

11. Ibid., 277.

# Naso

## The Collective Offering

### Numbers 4:21—7:89

ONE OF THE FRUSTRATING things about trying to understand creativity is that we encounter so many seeming paradoxes. We create; in so doing, we destroy. The question of why we create matters; at the same time, it doesn't. We are strong; we are vulnerable. There are unbending rules; ultimately, there aren't. We must work; we must rest. Then, too, as we saw in the commentary to *Parashat Yitro*, revelation—inspiration—comes to us as individuals; it also comes to us as a community. This is akin to the apparent paradox we encounter when considering *Parashat Naso* in the context of the last one we discussed—*B'midbar*. As we've just seen, we artists each have our distinct roles to play in the sacred activity of creation. As we'll see here, we're all doing essentially the same thing.

In this *parasha*, the work on the Israelites' sacred portable sanctuary, the *mishkan*, is completed, and Moses consecrates it. The dwelling place of the Israelites' spiritual life is ready. Prompted by gratitude, chieftains from each of the tribes come forward with gifts for the *mishkan*. They come one by one, each tribe on its own day—this despite the fact that each gift is exactly the same, and I mean *exactly*.

On the first day Nachshon from the tribe of Judah makes his offering, and it goes like this: *His offering: one silver bowl weighing 130 shekels and one silver basin of 70 shekels by the sanctuary weight, both filled with choice flour with oil mixed in, for a grain offering; one gold ladle of 10 shekels, filled with incense; one bull of the herd, one ram, and one lamb in its first year, for a burnt offering; one goat for a purification offering; and for his sacrifice of well-being: two oxen, five rams, five he-goats, and five yearling lambs* (Num 7:13–17). The next day Nathaniel of Issachar comes, and then Eliab of Zebulun, and so on. In each case, the gift is identical, and the Torah doesn't just say something like *And this guy gave the same as the last guy*. In each case, we start over with *His offering: one silver bowl weighing 130 shekels and one silver basin of* . . . and then we hear the same list of gifts, with the exact same wording—twelve times in all, with one offering for each tribe. Have you ever been in a synagogue when someone is chanting this section of the Torah? It sounds like the record is skipping.

So why list each offering separately, and at length? Why not just describe one offering and say that everyone else gave the same, or why not say that all gave equally and give the totals? One reason is that the Torah clearly wants to honor each of these tribes and not just brush off their gifts as more of the same. We can take from this *parasha* the general idea that, even if what people give in life is the same, it's all valuable and worthy of our attention.

We can also glean the converse: what's needed from one of us may be pretty much the same thing as is needed from everyone else. This is where we find our apparent paradox. In the last *parasha*, we saw how each tribe had a unique part to play in the ongoing journey of the Israelites. In this one, we see that each one is called to do something identical to what the others do.

And so it goes with artists. Consider composer Arnold Schoenberg, best known for his radical innovations in classical music. He said, "one must listen to [my music] in the same manner as to every other kind of music, forget the theories, the twelve-tone method, the dissonances, etc., and, I would add, if possible the author."[12] As different as his work is from the work of others, he wants us to approach it in the same way, as just another entry in this larger form known as *music*.

The similarities, actually, go even further, so that an artist working in one medium is not all that different from one working in another. Take poet Robert Pinsky, who also plays the saxophone: "Poets remind me in some ways of jazz musicians—people do it because they love the art, they're just crazy about it. Like jazz, poetry feeds other arts—creates ideas that find their way into the mass arts."[13] To some extent, these arts are all the same. Songwriter Bob Dylan said, "A lot of people paint if they got something

---

12. Shawn, *Schoenberg's Journey*, vii.
13. Moyers, *Fooling with Words*, 202.

they want to say, other people write plays, write songs . . . same place."[14] Indeed, the months I've spent writing at various artist colonies alongside painters, sculptors, composers, and filmmakers showed me just how many natural connections there are between all our work.

Some suggest that there is something universal and timeless about the creative experience, so that even artists working in very disparate time periods have more in common than not. When sculptor Louise Nevelson first saw ancient African sculptures, she felt a kinship with the people who had created those structures. "They were feeding me energy," she said.[15] Visiting Mayan ruins in Mexico, she said, "This was a world of forces that at once I felt was mine."[16] Painters Adolph Gottlieb and Mark Rothko also declared in a letter to the *New York Times*, "we profess spiritual kinship with primitive and archaic art."[17] Time changes many things, but perhaps not the goals or the experience of the artist.

For one thing, we all approach the world with the same keen sensitivity. According to filmmaker Woody Allen, "Any artist, any film artist, is giving you back his perceptions"[18]—but he was right in his first utterance of "any artist"; of course it's not just limited to filmmakers. Composer Allen Shawn wrote, "Any art presupposes a dialogue between what we perceive with our organs and consciousness and what we sense of a work that we do not consciously grasp."[19] So he, too, emphasizes the role of the creative person in recording and sharing perceptions—but he also notes one more thing that makes art timeless: its engagement with mystery, that which "we do not consciously grasp."

Art, in this understanding, is not defined by what form your work takes so much as how you approach your work. Photographer Alfred Stieglitz said, "Photography is not an art. Neither is painting nor sculpture, literature nor music. They are only different media for the individual to express his aesthetic feelings; the tools he uses in his creative work. . . . You do not have to be a painter or a sculptor to be an artist. You may be a shoemaker. You may be creative as such. And if so you are a greater artist

14. Cott, *Bob Dylan*, 3.

15. Lisle, *Louise Nevelson*, 102.

16. Ibid., 170.

17. Gottlieb and Rothko, Letter.

18. Allen and Bjorkman, *Woody Allen*, 353.

19. Shawn, *Schoenberg's Journey*, 295.

than the majority of painters whose work is shown in the art galleries of today."[20] This common creative engagement is what binds all of us together.

And so the Torah shows us offering after offering, each one exactly the same and each one honored for its contribution. It does overstate the point in order to make it, though; generally what a person offers the world isn't *identical* to what others offer. Here's where we get back to the apparent paradox: we are the same, and we are different. As for artists, although we are all pursuing similar goals, and are all similarly trying to express our perceptions, what we express is unique because no one person is exactly like another. Think of the creative drive as an unending source of light and think of us as crystals, no two the same. The light doesn't change, but the way it refracts through us does change.

In an artist's life, the typical way through a paradox is to recognize that in one moment one thing seems to apply—and in another, the opposite seems to apply. That's how you might approach this. On one day you will be caught up in doing the thing that only you can do; on another you will be aware of standing shoulder-to-shoulder with many or all of your fellow creators.

On both occasions, what you're feeling is absolutely true.

---

### *In Your Mouth and In Your Heart:*

Take time out to experience creative work that seems in some way distant from you—ancient sculpture or poetry, say, or work from another culture, or another medium than the one in which you typically work. Spend time with it. Get to know it. Can you express what these creators are expressing, in your own way?

---

20. Jackman, *Artist's Mentor*, 205.

# B'haalot'kha

## Envy

### Numbers 8:1—12:16

To write this book, I have surrounded myself with brilliant artists. I've read many biographies, including those of painter Marc Chagall and sculptor Louise Nevelson; interviews with poet Marge Piercy, songwriters Bob Dylan and Paul Simon and filmmaker Woody Allen; treatises on the creative process by composer Leonard Bernstein, painter Mark Rothko and writer Norman Mailer; the published diary of poet and war hero Hannah Senesh; and more than one Nobel Prize speech. I am surrounded by their wisdom, their talent, and also by their great success. What a gift!

Sometimes it just eats away at me.

It doesn't really matter that these people absolutely deserve their dazzling success. I recognize that they do—but I want it, too. I want to create art that illuminates the way theirs does. I want, I'll admit, some of the attention they get. On a day when I get a couple of rejections from publishers, I am full of want. On days like that I turn a hard eye on these artistic giants that loom over me on all sides.

I am not, as it happens, the first person to have ever felt this way. In *Parashat B'haalot'kha*, we see the prophet Miriam complaining to God about all the focus on her brother Moses. High Priest Aaron, her other brother, joins in, too. "*Has the Lord spoken only through Moses?*" they cry out. "*Has He not spoken through us as well?*" (Num 12:2). They are well-respected leaders of the community, a huge part of the Israelites' story—their names are in the *Bible*, for crying out loud—and still they want a little more credit. That's how powerful envy can be. In the Song of Songs we read, *passion [is] as mighty as Sheol* (8:6)—Sheol being an early conceptualization of hell—and in some translations, *passion* is rendered as *envy* or *jealousy.*

I believe that most artists spend some time, at least occasionally, in that hell. Unless you're Picasso or Beethoven or Graham or Shakespeare—and maybe even if you *are* them—there's always someone out there who's done something or got something that you wish you had done or gotten. A writer as well-known as Norman Mailer, in talking about the writer's plunge into "the jungle of his subconscious" (Mailer tended to use "his" and "he" for everyone), said,

> Most of us voyage out a part of the way into our jungle and come back filled with pride at what we dared and shame at what we avoided, and because we are men of the middle and shame is an emotion no man of the middle can bear for too long, we act like novelists, which is to say that we are full of spleen, small gossip, hatred for the success of our enemies, envy at the fortunes of our friends . . . and so there is a tendency for us to approach the books of our contemporaries like a defense attorney walking up to a key witness for the prosecution.[21]

Anybody out there with a whole lot of acclaim can be a target of envy, especially if the acclaim comes when the person is young. Here's a snippet from an article about fiction writer Nell Freudenberger: "Freudenberger writes from an enviable—and famously envied—position in the center of the literary elite. Five years ago, the Harvard grad was a *New Yorker* editorial assistant, until former fiction editor Bill Buford ran her story 'Lucky Girls,' the 'one story that I thought was worth showing to anyone in my life,' in the Summer Fiction issue, alongside a glamour shot of Freudenberger lounging on red velvet. Beautiful, poised, and, sure, a good writer, too, she was ripe for the inevitable bidding war—and the inevitable backlash. They even coined a term for it: Schadenfreudenberger."[22] Incidentally, a web search for the word "Schadenfreudenberger" turns up hundreds of hits.

It gets uglier. In 2007, Gawker.com (a gossip website) printed a brief article about writers Jonathan Safran Foer and Nicole Krauss (who are married to one another), who had recently bought a house in Park Slope, Brooklyn, for nearly seven million dollars. The article responded to the news with, "Oh, those crazy Safran Foer Krausses! We had almost managed to convince ourselves that they didn't matter anymore—after all, they've

21. Mailer, *Spooky Art*, 123.
22. Kachka, "Lonely Planet."

been too busy pooping out little scribblers to crank out any irritatingly overhyped books lately. But last night we heard this tidbit, from a source close to the writers, that made us feel the inadequacy of our lives and real estate holdings."[23] Okay—I'll admit that seven million dollars is a lot of money, and I have more than once envied the success of these two (very talented, in my opinion) authors. But why the venom in this piece? Why are the people at Gawker.com so desperate to convince themselves that these authors don't matter? And let me tell you—if you think the article has some bile in it, you should read the comments posted by readers underneath the article. None of them admit to envy, but it's hard to otherwise explain just how rabidly resentful people are about two (again, talented) authors doing well in the world.

This kind of resentment is not a healthy thing to encourage in oneself. In the Torah portion, we see what happens to Miriam as a result of her jealousy: *As the cloud [of God] withdrew from the Tent, there was Miriam stricken with snow-white scales!* (Num 12:10). Note that it doesn't say that God did this to her—God just left her presence, and she naturally became stricken with what we assume is leprosy. According to one of the Proverbs (in the 1917 JPS translation), *A tranquil heart is the life of the flesh; but envy is the rottenness of the bones* (14:30). In the Book of Job we read (in the same translation), *For anger killeth the foolish man, and envy slayeth the silly one* (5:2). Envy is a destroyer.

Just hear the distress in these words of visual artist Judy Chicago as she expresses a need to eclipse everyone else: "I want the focus to be on me—all the time. It's really awful. I either like to be alone or the star of the show."[24] Even when she's not the one feeling competitive, when it's someone else near her, envy does its damage; she complained at one point about having trouble finding a romantic partner because too many men were, among other things, "threatened by my work."[25] Envy can do great harm to a person's well-being.

It can also hurt a person's creative process. Mailer warned against having too much contact with the work of others while doing one's own. He wrote: "It's disturbing to read a novelist with a good style when you're in the middle of putting your work together. It's much like taking your car apart and having all the pieces on the floor just as somebody rides by in a Ferrari.

23. Gawker.com, "Jonathan Safran Foer."

24. Levin, *Becoming Judy*, 201.

25. Ibid., 117.

Now, you may hear a note in the Ferrari that isn't good and say, 'His motor needs a little tuning.' But nonetheless the car and its roar are still there in your ear while your parts remain on the floor."[26]

We need an alternative. Luckily, the Torah offers us one side by side with Miriam and Aaron: Moses. *Now, Moses was a very humble man, more so than any other man on earth*, reads the text (Num 12:3)—and we see clear examples of that in this Torah portion. In the previous chapter, when elders Eldad and Medad were prophesying and an Israelite tattled to Moses about it, Moses said, *"Are you wrought up on my account? Would that all the Lord's people were prophets, that the Lord put His spirit upon them!"* (Num 11:29). In other words, just before Miriam accuses him of hogging all the glory, Moses was offering to share it with anyone who wants it. He also rushes to pray for Miriam's healing after she is stricken with leprosy.

Now, you might be saying that it's easy to be humble when you're the person talked about like this in one of the very last verses of the Torah: *never again did there arise in Israel a prophet like Moses* (Deut 34:10). But Moses has always been humble. He gave up his privileged position as Pharaoh's son out of moral principle and worked quietly as a sheepherder until God caught his attention with the burning bush. Then, when God picked him to free the Israelites from Egypt, Moses said he wasn't good enough: *"Please, O Lord, I have never been a man of words . . . I am slow of speech and slow of tongue* (Exod 4:10). We learn from the Torah that Moses's greatness was made possible by his humility.

This may be our best avenue, too. Poet Allen Ginsberg once said, "When I was young I thought I was pretty dumb, so I decided I'd better be smart and shut up and listen, and be sensitive and innocent and shy and goofy, but really pay attention to what other people said—so I listened very carefully, always worried and anxious that maybe I was getting it all wrong, or that I was too stupid to understand—and I found that, actually, the people that were smarter than me *were* smarter than me, and they had something to tell me, so I heard it."[27] Ginsberg became one of the most beloved poets in his time, but never lost his humility. I offer him as a model for us to approach.

Comparing ourselves to others is not always a bad idea—it's just a bad idea if we bring bile (or its mirror image, self-loathing) to the comparison. In fact, there's a lot to learn from those who have done well in our chosen

26. Mailer, *Spooky Art*, 100.

27. Ginsberg, *Life and Times*.

art form. Ginsberg certainly did. Similarly, Mailer wrote, "Good writers are as competitive as good athletes. When I come across an interesting novel, I don't go at it as other people do. I read critically, the way one athlete will watch another's performance. Not watch it with venom—quite the contrary. . . . The ideal is to give a good novel its credit and never overlook its power by deciding too quickly that the work is overrated, which is exactly the dreadful tendency underwritten by the envy chronic to the writer's occupation."[28] In this way you survive the difficulties of the artistic life, and in this way you learn and grow.

The bottom line, though, is this: at times you may feel yourself ready to cry out in envy like Miriam and Aaron, and at times you may need to cry out just to give vent to the feelings—but you must not let them take over. You must instead find a way to get back to your studio, your desk, your keyboard. The only sure-fire answer to envy is work.

Get to it.

---

### In Your Mouth and In Your Heart:

Are there artists that you envy—people close to you or people you only know of through their work or their fame? What can you do to transform that envy so that you no longer resent them, but instead *learn* from them?

---

28. Mailer, *Spooky Art*, 107.

# Sh'lah L'kha

## Unrealism

### Numbers 13:1—15:41

THE WORD TRUTH COMES up a great deal when you're talking about art; it's certainly shown up many times already in this book. One of my core assumptions about art—and I share this assumption with hordes of other creative people—is that an artistic life is, by definition, a life spent in pursuit of truth. Truth about life, about the universe, about meaning, about the divine—about anything and everything.

What I want to suggest here is that this search for truth may be completely unrealistic.

*Parashat Sh'lah L'kha* finds the Israelites on the outskirts of the promised land of Canaan, wondering what to do next. God tells Moses to send scouts into the land to assess the quality of the soil and the size and strength of the inhabiting populations. Interestingly, like an echo of *Parashat Lekh L'kha*, God's command of *send, sh'lah l'kha*, can be translated *send for yourself*, meaning that God doesn't need the scouting mission; the people need it, presumably in order to encourage themselves to go forward. So Moses sends a chieftain from each of the twelve tribes, and they explore Canaan for forty days.

When they get back, unfortunately, they have a frightening tale to tell. According to the scouts, the land is inhabited by a variety of peoples, many with a reputation for strength and ferocity—and some of them are giants! Even though two of the scouts—Caleb and Joshua—assure the people that they can conquer the land because God is with them, the people panic and refuse to advance. God, furious again, declares that these faithless Israelites will be forced to wander for forty years and that none of the adults alive at this time will make it to the land—only their children will get to settle there. For their part, the fearmongering scouts succumb to a plague. (Caleb and Joshua are exempt.)

The Israelites are well-known for complaining, and they do it constantly in the Book of Numbers—but this is clearly one of their lowest points. They have turned their backs on the land, the gift that God had, for generations, held up for them as their sacred inheritance. And all because of fear.

It starts with the scouts, who mess up first by terrifying the people with their story. Their account is, in fact, so daunting, that a Torah reader's first temptation might be to assume that they're exaggerating. After all, *giants?* Yet the text gives us little reason to believe that they, in the context of this story, are lying, or even stretching the facts. When Caleb and Joshua protest, when they try to rouse the people to go forward into the land, they declare that the Israelites can succeed in their mission, that God is with them—but they never suggest that the scouts' intimidating report is in any way inaccurate. They never argue against the claim of giants, or the presence of many fierce warrior peoples, or even that *the country . . . devours its settlers* (Num 13:32). They are simply saying that *despite* all those things, the people can still conquer the land.

But why should the people believe them? They've just heard a unanimous report that Canaan is perhaps the most dangerous place on earth—isn't it fairly realistic to assume that they'll be slaughtered if they try to enter the land?

Is it realistic? Yes. Is it true? No. Later on in the story, in the Book of Joshua, the Israelites do successfully and safely enter the land. The two braver scouts will turn out to be right.

These Israelites in Numbers are on the cusp of their climactic moment of glory, and they recoil. Why? Because of an unhealthy dose of realism.

According to religion and philosophy scholar Earle Coleman, painter Marc Chagall "called spiritual reality 'unreality.' "[29] The call to a spiritual view—exactly the call God was making to the Israelites—means taking on a truth that is beyond the mundane reality we see all around us. In the words of poet Allen Afterman, this view "means transcending the eyes. Beyond the

---

29. Coleman, *Creativity and Spirituality*, 143.

range of vision is the future, the hidden essence of the present."[30] If the Israelites had been able to hold on to that truth, the one Caleb and Joshua were talking about when they said, "*Have no fear. . . . the Lord is with us!*" (Num 14:9), they would have marched forward and claimed their glory instead of only leaving it to their (perhaps less realistic) children.

Here is another place where the spiritual journey and the artistic one are essentially the same. Painters Adolph Gottlieb and Mark Rothko once wrote that the world of art "can be explored only by those willing to take the risks. This world of the imagination is fancy-free and violently opposed to common sense."[31] "Common sense," of course, is another way of saying "realism."

Many artists agree with Rothko. Painter Amedeo Modigliani, for example, said, "A work of art exists in its own right and not in relation to reality."[32] And, because of this attitude, according to art historian Jeffrey Meyers, Modigliani "rejected the limitations of the 'retinal' tradition and felt free to use, distort or ignore visible reality."[33] This, I think, is what makes his portraits deeply true without being photographically accurate.

Laurie Lisle, another art historian, describes the experience of sculptor Louise Nevelson in a similar way: "This ability to dissociate herself from objective reality and enter completely into the emotional truth of an experience proved to be essential to her development as an artist."[34] Lisle later offers an example of this from Nevelson's life (the inner quote is from Nevelson herself): "As she worked by day on large plaster figures, in her dreams at night they moved and glowed as if electrified, suggesting to her that 'there was a subterranean world, even if it was a dream world, where these bodies had a life of their own.'"[35]

Chagall, in his appropriately surreal autobiography, offers us an example from his life. He wrote,

> I roamed about the streets, I searched and I prayed:
> "God, Thou who hidest in the clouds or behind the shoemaker's house, grant that my soul may be revealed, the sorrowful soul of a stammering boy. Show me my way. I do not want to be like all the others; I want to see a new world."

30. Afterman, *Kabbalah and Consciousness*, 21.

31. Gottlieb and Rothko. Letter.

32. Meyers, *Modigliani*, 58.

33. Ibid., 155.

34. Lisle, *Louise Nevelson*, 68.

35. Ibid., 113.

As if in reply, the town seems to snap apart, like the strings of a violin, and all the inhabitants, leaving their usual places, begin to walk above the earth. People I know well, settle down on roofs and rest there.

All the colors turn upside down, dissolve into wine and my canvases gush it forth."[36]

Many artists seem to have a kind of constitutional discomfort with reality. "The actual world is too much for me," said Nevelson.[37] Filmmaker Woody Allen, too, feels enough discomfort to make it a central topic in his work: "If I have any one big theme in my movies, it's got to do with the difference between reality and fantasy. It comes up very frequently in my films. I think what it boils down to, really, is that I hate reality."[38]

But there's more to it than just discomfort. In pursuing a dream world, the artist pursues a deeper truth than the one that's with us in our waking hours: s/he offers us an alternative to the reality we've got. "I wanted to build my own world, not *the* world, *my* world," Nevelson said.[39] Woody Allen, again, echoes her: "What the writer does—the film-maker or the writer—you create a world that you would like to live in."[40]

Art may be one of the only ways to open up these alternative worlds. Writer Saul Bellow said so in his 1976 Nobel Prize acceptance speech: "Only art penetrates what pride, passion, intelligence and habit erect on all sides—the seeming realities of this world. There is another reality, the genuine one, which we lose sight of. This other reality is always sending us hints, which, without art, we can't receive."[41] By creating art, we *can* receive those hints—hints, that is, of truth.

Doing so also allows us to share the truth with others. According to literary scholar Joseph Cohen, writing about Israeli poet Yehuda Amichai, a striking metaphor allows us to see a connection beyond our current understanding of the world and so "enlarges the world for the poet and, subsequently, when read, does the same for the reader."[42]

Painter Max Weber saw this possibility of sharing as a duty. He said, "We workers in the field of the fine arts owe to this and future generations

36. Chagall, *My Life*, 94.
37. Lisle, *Louise Nevelson*, 166.
38. Allen and Bjorkman, *Woody Allen*, 50.
39. Lisle, *Louise Nevelson*, 52.
40. Allen and Bjorkman, *Woody Allen*, 51.
41. Bellow, Nobel Lecture.
42. Cohen, *Voices of Israel*, 24.

a legacy of as perfectly balanced a vision as our talents will afford."[43] Artists, in other words, need to show people that there's another world beyond what seems to us to be reality—a better one, in fact.

Sometimes the goal is to use art to make things concretely better around us. As we saw earlier, painter Lev Landau believed that "art must become part of the process that shapes a better world."[44] Feminist visual artist Judy Chicago put it succinctly: "I want to change the world," she said.[45] These artists do this by creating art that points to the problems with existing reality, and also by showing people that things don't have to be the way they are. They, like Caleb and Joshua, want people to see things differently than they currently do. "I'm interested in images that change consciousness," Chicago said. "I believe in the artist as a visionary."[46]

Realism means seeing the world as we currently understand it, with the limits and challenges and impossibilities we've decided are an inevitable part of life. If these artists are right, however, none of it is actually inevitable. Being a visionary means perceiving things that are not there—yet. For an artist, it means dropping realism whenever you need to, painting the way you see things in your deepest understanding of the world, composing music that sounds the way you hear things, creating movement that moves the way the world truly moves, or could move. It means standing with Caleb and Joshua, with their small protest against the many pessimistic scouts and the overwhelming mass of terrified Israelites and saying, *Yes, all these frightening things you hear are real—but what we can envision is still, is always, more true.*

---

### In Your Mouth and In Your Heart:

Create a piece that defies reality. Maybe it's a portrait (visual, verbal, auditory, etc.) that distorts the way things look or sound or feel in order to more truthfully describe the inner essence of things. Maybe it's a piece that offers us a glimpse of the way the world ought to be, or could be, or secretly already is—if only we have the guts to see it. Be as unrealistic and as truthful as you can be.

---

43. Baigell, "Jewish American Artists," 185.

44. Ibid.

45. Levin, *Becoming Judy*, 193.

46. Ibid., 327.

# Korah

## Authority

### Numbers 16:1—18:32

ARTISTS, WE HAVE TO admit, occupy an unusual position in society. Because our work involves making observations about the world, including the social world, in some sense we have to sit outside of it. Because we then share our observations, essentially telling other people *Here's how you seem to me*, we can be seen as putting ourselves *above* society.

As *Parashat Korah* vividly illustrates, people don't tend to like that.

In this *parasha*, a group of Israelites led by Korah confront Moses and Aaron, saying: *You have gone too far! For all the community are holy, all of them, and the Lord is in their midst. Why then do you raise yourselves above the Lord's congregation?* (Num 16:3) All sorts of trouble and carnage ensue, and by the end, Moses and Aaron are still on top, but the Israelites are much reduced.

We can understand the people's frustration—and, as we've seen before, envy—can't we? Aren't they right that everyone is holy? And can't we sympathize with their resentment of Moses and Aaron?

This hits home for me because it's so relevant to how artists are positioned in the community—or is it how we position ourselves? Filmmaker Woody Allen blames it on us: "I do think that . . . the artist considers himself not like other people, and in a secret way he considers himself in a way superior to other people."[47] Actually, some, like painter Amedeo Modigliani, aren't so secretive about it. He wrote, "People like us . . . have different rights, different values than do normal, ordinary people because we

47. Allen and Bjorkman, *Woody Allen*, 242.

163

have different needs which put us—it has to be said and you must believe it—above their moral standards."[48]

Sometimes this comes with noble motives, as when visual artist Judy Chicago wrote, "Maybe artists have to be like congress people—representatives of the needs, feelings, & aspirations of a group of people. At least that's what I want to be—to speak of the longings & yearnings & aspirations of women."[49] Yet even this can reasonably provoke resentment, as we see in these words of journalist Judith Lewis: "If women in the art world have been harder on Chicago than they have been on, say, Christo—an artist with whom she's been compared—they claim it's because she has set herself up as their representative."[50]

And are we really so special as to act as representatives for the people? Certainly Woody Allen doesn't think so: "I don't agree that the artist is superior; I'm not a believer in the specialness of the artist. I don't think that to have a talent is an achievement."[51] Songwriter Bob Dylan put it a little more gently, but still clearly: "I'm one of these people that think everybody has certain gifts, you know, when they're born. . . . Like somebody can make a cake, or somebody else can saw a tree down, and other people write. Nobody's really got the right to say that any one of those gifts are any better than any other body's. That's just the way they're distributed out."[52]

So okay—let's try this argument on. Let's say we're all the same, no one of us better than any other. That means that we artists are not superior to others—but it also means that we're not *inferior*, either. By that reasoning, we're certainly no *less* suited to making observations about the world than anyone else is. An artist may be just an individual, just one particular point of view, but there's no reason to believe that disqualifies her or him from pursuing universal truths. Indeed, "as Jews we know that the universal can only be truly discovered in the particular," according to composer Bob Gluck.[53] Why shouldn't that particular view be the focused lens of an individual artist? Art historian Mira Goldfarb Berkowitz said of painter Morris Louis, "Ultimately in the *Charred Journal* series, and certainly in the body of work that followed, Louis did achieve a universal tone. And

48. Meyers, *Modigliani*, 30.

49. Levin, *Becoming Judy*, 235.

50. Ibid., 375.

51. Allen and Bjorkman, *Woody Allen*, 242.

52. Cott, *Bob Dylan*, 10.

53. Gluck, "Jewish Music," 35.

perhaps his ability to arrive at a true universalist conception and message was made possible through confrontation with, and understanding of, his own particularism."[54] Fellow art historian Gannit Ankori had a similar feeling about the visual art of Hannah Wilke: "Wilke also uses her Self (through the vehicle of the body) to express broader, *universal* truths about the human predicament."[55]

This only works when it works, of course. An artist might make a wildly inaccurate observation about people or the world, or an artist might make a dazzlingly perceptive one. What I'm suggesting is that there's no reason for artists to be shy about giving it a shot.

By the way, I'm not sure I agree that artists are disproportionately to blame for finding themselves in positions of authority; people do choose to turn to the arts for these truths. In his Nobel Prize acceptance speech, writer Isaac Bashevis Singer said, "In their despair a number of those who no longer have confidence in the leadership of our society look up to the writer, the master of words. They hope against hope that the man of talent and sensitivity can perhaps rescue civilization."[56]

Given that, though, we do have to recognize the power that comes with expressing a view powerfully to the world—and be responsible about how we use it. I find one episode in the *parasha* at hand very telling: after God has asserted in a couple of different miraculous ways—we'll come back to this—that Moses and Aaron are the proper leaders of the Israelites, God tells Aaron at length that Aaron will be to blame if anything goes wrong with the sanctuary or with priestly matters. Woody Allen echoes this sentiment in his appraisal of the art world: "I do think that if you're lucky to have a talent, that with that comes a certain responsibility. Just in the same sense as if you were born rich."[57]

So what does "being responsible" look like? *Parashat Korah* has something to say about that as well. When the people first rebel, Moses reacts with a test. He says that if Korah is in the wrong and if Moses and Aaron are the Israelites' true leaders, the ground will open up and swallow Korah and his people. The ground does exactly that. (As we've seen repeatedly, biblical stories work a little differently from our everyday lives.) Now, you'd

---

54. Berkowitz, "Sacred Signs," 203.
55. Ankori, "Jewish Venus," 252.
56. Allen, *Nobel Lectures*, 138.
57. Allen and Bjorkman, *Woody Allen*, 242.

think that that would put an end to things—God couldn't have been much clearer—but in fact the people threaten revolution again the next day.

At this point, God devises a better demonstration; God has Moses collect staves from each of the tribal leaders, including Aaron, and says that the staff that miraculously sprouts will indicate the appropriate spiritual leader for the community. Of course, Aaron's staff is the one—and it doesn't just throw out a few sprouts. It produces blossoms and almonds, too. And *this* is the miracle that ends the rebellion.

I think we see here what responsibility means. When Moses asserts his authority with an act of destruction, he gets rid of Korah but does nothing to quiet the community's concern about his leadership. When Aaron's authority is demonstrated through an awe-inspiring act of creation—of beauty, even—the people accept it.

If artists occupy an unusual position in society, we are also unusually capable of earning it. We are creators—people who with our observations make something new in the world. If we set out not to harm but instead to offer something, perhaps we will find the people ready to receive us—no better than anyone else, to be sure, but certainly in possession of something unique and meaningful to say.

---

### In Your Mouth and In Your Heart:

What do you have to say—verbally, visually, aurally—about the world? Keeping guard against arrogance, put your wisdom into your art and let the world come to its own conclusions about whether you're onto something or not.

---

# Hukkat

## Mystery

### Numbers 19:1—22:1

THE TORAH IS, WITHOUT a doubt, frequently mysterious. We've already heard God tell Abram *Lekh l'kha* when a simple *Lekh* would have been clearer; we've seen an angel unexpectedly pounce upon Jacob; we've faced the unknowability of the divine; we've looked at the *hukkim*, the laws given to us by God that we follow but don't quite understand. Yet *Parashat Hukkat* offers up one of the biggest mysteries to be found in the Torah—one that, like any good mystery story, has life-or-death stakes.

The short version is this: the people complain about the lack of water during their wanderings, and God tells Moses to order a rock to produce something to drink; Moses yells at the people, whacks the rock with a stick, and out pours the water. The people are happy enough, but God tells Moses and Aaron that *"Because you did not trust Me enough to affirm My sanctity in the sight of the Israelite people, therefore you shall not lead this congregation into the land that I have given them"* (Num 20:12). In other words, God will see to it that both of these men, these venerated leaders, die before they reach the promised land—Aaron in this *parasha* and Moses at the very end of the Torah.

As you can see, this mystery is not a whodunit so much as a *why*dunit. Commentators have speculated endlessly about why God is so furious with Moses and Aaron—was it that they hit the rock instead of speaking to it, or that they hit it not once but twice? Was it that they called the people *rebels* (Num 20:10)? Was it that they said *"shall we get water for you"* (Num 20:10) rather than *shall God get water for you*? The text, in fact, offers no clear answers—and this is one important way that this story differs from a good mystery novel. In this story, we never solve the mystery; it stays with us.

Many readers of the Torah wrestle and wrestle with this turn of events. We question its logic, its fairness. We wonder if there's something we're missing. We may feel some anger at God, some pity for Moses and Aaron, and maybe even some doubt in them as well. How different this is than it would be if these two leaders had done something clearly terrible and then been punished appropriately. We might find that tale satisfying and never think of it again. Instead we find it unsatisfying and keep thinking. One of the lessons of this story is that, even when we're dealing with matters of the sacred, even when we might be tempted to lay out an easy moral, clarity is often much less compelling than ambiguity.

This is a lesson most artists learn well at some point in their careers. According to novelist Norman Mailer, "The wisest rule of thumb for the would-be moralist is: There are no answers. There are only questions."[58] And even if you think you do have some answers, songwriter Bob Dylan has warned us that there's no point trying to use your art to spread them to others. "Anybody that's got a message," he said, "is going to learn from experience that they can't put it into a song. I mean it's just not going to come out the same message."[59] Photographer Diane Arbus said, "A photograph is a secret about a secret. The more it tells you the less you know."[60]

If your goal is to get a clear statement out to the world, there are much better ways than using art to do it. In the words of Israeli novelist Amos Oz, "Whenever I am in total agreement with myself over anything, I don't write a novel or a story. I write an angry article telling my government what to do, sometimes, telling it where to go altogether. It's normally when I'm in a slight disagreement with myself that I hear more than just one voice in me, that I sometimes sense the embryo of a story or a novel."[61] When people try to create art out of that "total agreement" with oneself, it has trouble succeeding as art. Mailer made the same point about filmmaking: "Film is best when ambiguous. A truly good film will affect two people profoundly, but often, they will argue for hours over the message. . . . Bad film is when everyone laughs on cue, for then they are being manipulated."[62] About

58. Mailer, *Spooky Art*, 161.

59. Cott, *Bob Dylan*, 100.

60. Baskind, "Diane Arbus," in *Encyclopedia of Jewish Artists*, 21.

61. Cohen, *Voices of Israel*, 190.

62. Mailer, *Spooky Art*, 199.

novels, he wrote that "if a book is good enough, you cannot predict how your readers are going to react. You shouldn't be able to. If it is that good, it is not manipulative, and everyone, therefore, can voyage off in a different direction."[63] Inner agreement leads to manipulation; inner disagreement, which plays itself out in the audience as well, leads to art.

Painter and sculptor Ida Applebroog works with that fact instead of trying to resist it: "My pieces are like projective tests. When you are looking at them, they deal with how the viewer interprets the meaning. With each person the meaning shifts, so that no matter what you think you see in that piece, the next person will see something entirely different. It doesn't matter if it is what I wanted to say, or what I thought I was saying, or what it is that was built into that piece."[64] In saying that it "doesn't matter," she's let go of the need to control the experience of her viewer. She's also opened herself up to powerful new possibilities. Literary scholar Joseph Cohen noted about Oz that "in rejecting an ulterior sociopolitical motive, Oz releases his imagination to soar as it will, and soar it does to impressive lyrical and hallucinatory heights."[65] For Oz himself, he writes the way he writes "not in order to promote a political cause or to make a political statement disguised as literature, but as a way of observing the deeper and more mysterious dimensions of human existence and human experience."[66] To abandon moralizing and message-giving and manipulation is to open oneself to the enduring power of mystery.

When Aaron dies in this *parasha* and when Moses dies at the end of Deuteronomy, we may feel the shock that Aaron seems to feel—he dies without a word—and the frustration of Moses, who complains bitterly to (and about) the people before climbing the mountain to his gravesite. We may fail to understand. This all seems right to me; we're talking about death. How easy should it be? How much sense does it usually make? The same holds for life itself. If we are to produce an art that will compel the world, we must remember that the richness of life can't be captured in a moral or a message. Life drinks deeply from mysterious waters, and so must our art.

---

63. Ibid., 162.

64. Baskind, "Ida Applebroog," in *Encyclopedia Jewish Artists*, 19.

65. Cohen, *Voices of Israel*, 142.

66. Ibid., 188.

*In Your Mouth and In Your Heart:*

Is there some area of life—relationships, politics, meaning—that you feel you don't much understand, or that you see in conflicting ways? Make a piece of art about it. Cultivate your uncertainty, and put it into the work.

# Balak

## Listening

## Numbers 22:2—25:9

CREATIVITY, AS I'VE SUGGESTED elsewhere, is in part a matter of deep attentiveness—noticing the good and the bad, noticing the sensual details, noticing one's own inner states. This is one thing that makes art different from artifice. After all, being people skilled at expressing themselves in one way or another, artists (as we just saw in the last commentary) have the opportunity to be powerful manipulators, and indeed there is some manipulation in great pieces—but the centrality of the need to be attentive means that we can't set out to control the people who witness our work, and can't even really set out to control the work. We need to be controlled a bit ourselves.

This lesson comes through clearly in *Parashat Balak*, the strange story of a non-Israelite magician who's called on to curse the Israelite people as they near the land of Moab. This man, Balaam, has some ability to speak to God, and does so when he's asked to deliver the curses. God, unsurprisingly, doesn't want the Israelites cursed, and tells Balaam not to do it. Then, when Balaam asks a second time for permission (this time he's been offered riches), God says, essentially, "Go if you want." Not a ringing endorsement, but Balaam gets his donkey and sets out in a hurry all the same. God is furious—can't Balaam read between the lines?—and sends an angel of death to block the magician's path.

This is where things get a little unusual, even by Torah standards. The donkey sees the angel and tries to avoid it, swerving this way and that, and Balaam—who can't see the angel—beats the donkey again and again, never considering that the donkey might have a reason for acting this way. Lots of people think of pack animals as their slaves, really, so maybe we can understand Balaam's bull-headedness—but anyone who's encountered a donkey knows that they have a will of their own and that working with them demands just as much responsiveness as working with a person or with God. Balaam, however, doesn't know that yet. Then God lets the donkey speak, and this trustworthy animal complains about the beatings, but even in the face of this miracle Balaam won't listen—at least not until God opens Balaam's eyes so that he can see the angel standing there. This is one of those character-transforming moments, and the magician says to the angel: *"I erred because I did not know that you were standing in my way. If you still disapprove, I will turn back." But the angel of the Lord said to Balaam, "Go with the men. But you must say nothing except what I tell you"* (Num 22:34–35).

What exactly has changed in Balaam? As I see it, he has gone from being a man with his own agenda—getting rich, maybe—to being a man who is open to the agenda of the world around him. At first, he couldn't hear that God didn't really want him to go on this mission, and he was too busy abusing his donkey to pause to take in *her* point of view. After his brush with death, though, his listening skills improve noticeably; when he stands over the Israelites, for example, he hears God and offers blessings instead of curses, even though this means giving up all those riches. He's now interacting with the universe, being responsive to it, rather than trying to force his way blindly toward his own goals.

This is the kind of responsiveness that makes art possible. As painter Richard Serra said, "The significance of the work is in its effort not in its intentions. And the effort is a state of mind, an activity, an interaction with the world."[67] Rather than Balaam's inflexible intentions, a good artist has a readiness for activity, for interaction.

In the first place, we need to be receptive to insights about what creative journeys we must take and what journeys we must not, at least for the moment. An example: a sculptor might feel she *ought* to start a line of sculptures honoring her grandmother, say—but perhaps if she listens closely to her deeper instincts and to her reaction to actually *doing* the work, she might realize it's much more urgent for her to do something more abstract just then. An attentive artist therefore has a creative life that is somewhat out of control. In the words of sculptor Ibram Lassaw, "The

67. Jackman, *Artist's Mentor*, 165.

work is a 'happening' something independent of my conscious will . . . The work uses the artist to get born."[68] We see the same idea in Israeli novelist Amos Oz's complaint: "I have never enjoyed the freedom to choose a subject. It never works like this, you know, that I wake up in the morning and scratch my head and ask myself what it is that I'm going to write about next. Normally, a story or a novel for me begins with voices, with characters, not with global or local settings. Characters eventually bring with them the location, the settings and the time. What they do to each other is the plot. So I don't really have a choice."[69] Oz describes one such instance, when his character Hannah

> nagged me for a long time. She did not give up. She said to me: "Look, I am here, I will not let you go. You will write what I am telling you [to write], or you will have no peace." And I argued back, I excused myself; I told her: "Look, I cannot [do it], go to somebody else. Go to some woman author; I am not a woman; I cannot write you in the first person; leave me alone." But no, she did not give up. And then, when I wrote, to get rid of her, and return somehow to my own life, she nevertheless continued to argue about every line, day and night. She wanted me to write in a certain way, and to expand the story.[70]

Oz, of course, gave in. What else could he do? To resist these demands is to give willpower priority over art.

We see in his experience that the need to listen, to be responsive, goes beyond the initial moments when we choose our particular project and moves into the details of the work as well. Choreographer Meredith Monk said, "Each of my pieces creates a kind of world and part of my job is to let that world come into being without my getting in the way. Another part of my job is to ask what the laws of this particular world are. And the piece answers it."[71] Her pieces are not just expressions of her will—they are also expressions of something larger, something that she can enable if she's sensitive enough. Architect Louis Kahn put it bluntly: "I asked the brick, 'What do you like brick?' And the brick said, 'I like an arch.' "[72] Kahn would build an arch not because he wanted one but because the situation and the materials seemed to demand it of him.

68. Baskind, "Ibram Lassaw," in *Encyclopedia Jewish Artists*, 169.
69. Cohen, *Voices of Israel*, 184.
70. Ibid., 143.
71. Morgenroth, *Speaking of Dance*, 92.
72. Jackman, *Artist's Mentor*, 189.

Of course, the artist is not entirely a servant, a person who just carries out orders. Balaam, in his story, ultimately learns to *interact* with God. The creative process, as Serra pointed out, is also interactive. Painter Ben Shahn described the process in this way:

> From the moment at which a painter begins to strike figures of color upon a surface he must become acutely sensitive to the feel, the textures, the light, the relationships which arise before him. At one point he will mold the material according to his intention. At another he may yield intention—perhaps the whole concept—to emerging forms, to new implications within the painted surface. Idea itself—ideas, many ideas move back and forth across his mind as a constant traffic, dominated perhaps by larger currents and directions, by what he wants to think. This idea rises to the surface, grows, changes as a painting grows and develops. So one must say that painting is both creative and responsive. It is an intimately communicative affair between the painter and his painting, a conversation back and forth, the painting telling the painter even as it receives shape and form.[73]

This is how you make something great. From Balaam's example we hopefully learn to see our work not as a slavish pack animal that moves where we want it to with a yank on the reins or a whack from a stick but as a partner on our journey, a partner that—if we want a good journey—will have some input into where we go and how we get there. It's in this way that we arrive where we're actually meant to be.

---

### In Your Mouth and In Your Heart:

Go back to a piece of yours that just refused to work out the way you wanted it to. Maybe you wanted a certain kind of color array, a certain shape, a certain kind of plot. Go back to this piece and, instead of trying to make it bend to your original design, look for any sign of something unexpected and interesting and counter to your original design—an interesting and counter-intuitive character detail, visual pattern, movement—and use that as a starting point for a new vision of the piece. Only don't decide in advance which way you'll go with it. Feel it out, one detail at a time. What does each exciting sign lead to next?

---

73. Jackman, *Artist's Mentor*, 190.

# Pinhas

## Passion

### Numbers 25:10—30:1

PHINEHAS IS A MEMORABLE character in the Torah. In the last *parasha*, *Balak*, he witnessed an Israelite man and a Midianite woman having sex out in the open, in the sight of the Tent of Meeting and the whole community (which is still reeling from a plague), a culminating act of sexual audacity after the Israelites have already *profaned themselves by whoring with the Midianite women, who invited the people to the sacrifices for their god* (Num 25:1–2). This defiant act, done in the distressed faces the people, spurred Phinehas to act—and so, without pausing to think, he speared the couple through their bellies, stopping the plague. That's where *Parashat Balak* ended.

It's sort of a cliff-hanger; in the week between *Balak* and this next *parasha*, *Pinhas*, a new reader might be wondering what will happen to Phinehas. On the one hand, he put an end to the Israelites' bad behavior, and to their punishment; on the other, his act of violence is plenty disturbing in its own right. How will he be viewed by the Torah?

We get our answer immediately in *Parashat Pinhas*. It begins, *The Lord spoke to Moses, saying, "Phinehas, son of Eleazar son of Aaron the priest, has turned back my wrath from the Israelites by displaying among them his passion for Me, so that I did not wipe out the Israelite people in My passion. Say, therefore, 'I grant him my pact of friendship. It shall be for him and his descendents after him a pact of priesthood for all time, because he took impassioned action for his God, thus making expiation for the Israelites'"* (Num 25:10–13). In other words, God is thrilled—thrilled specifically about Phinehas' *passion*—and so much so that God names Phinehas as Aaron's replacement in the priesthood. It's quite a decision, designating this hot-blooded guard of the sanctuary to replace the generally even-tempered Aaron.

The nineteenth-century Torah teacher known as the Sfat Emet pointed out that "the priesthood had to be *given* to [Phinehas], since one who has killed a person is [ordinarily] disqualified from priesthood."[74] But if his action would typically disqualify him, *why* give it to him? Some commentators argue that the priesthood is intended to help calm Phinehas down, balance out his passion with some sobriety and deliberation. For example, another nineteenth-century commentator known as the Netziv wrote, "In reward for turning away the wrath of the Holy One Blessed Be He, God blessed Pinhas with the attribute of Shalom [peace], that he should not be quick tempered or angry."[75]

But I think that's only part of the story. It's a pretty big deal, handing over the Israelites' most important religious roles to Phinehas' line, if the only point is to give them some much-needed anger management therapy. I think that the God of the Torah would only do this if the priesthood had something to gain from Phinehas as well.

So what's to gain? Let me be clear: Phinehas' action is gruesomely violent, impulsive and extreme, and I obviously don't see how an action like this could be justified in everyday life—but because I see this as a story rather than a strict report of events that actually took place, I think less about whether murder is justifiable and more about what the Torah is trying to say allegorically about impassioned action. In this case, it *does* stop a plague—two die instead of thousands more—and, more to the point, its emotional content could be seen as fitting. Rabbi Shimon Felix wrote, "It would seem that the Torah realizes that the crime committed by Zimri [the Israelite caught having sex publicly] is the ultimate crime of passion . . . the passion of Zimri and Kozby [the Midianite woman] can only be matched by the passion of Pinhas, the zealot. The response to the emotional crime committed here must itself be emotional."[76] This is presumably why God, in praising Phinehas, specifically praised his passion.

74. Alter, *Language of Truth*, 264.

75. Alpert, "Zeal and Peace."

76. Felix, "Passion."

For me, *Parashat Pinhas* suggests that humanity and the world are not entirely sober and logical, and that we therefore can't always approach it with the calm poise of Aaron. The world also needs some zeal.

Visual artist Judy Chicago once wrote about her drawings, "The only way they work is if they're infused with emotion."[77] In the words of songwriter Bob Dylan, "My feelings come from the gut, and I'm not too concerned with someone whose feelings come from his head."[78]

Other artists make the point in stronger terms, saying that this isn't a matter of personal preference so much as a key to the understanding of art. "Motion comes from emotion," said choreographer Anna Sokolow more than once,[79] and writer Gertrude Stein said, "There can be no truly great creation without passion."[80] To these creators, art just doesn't make sense without an understanding of that "gut" that Dylan depends on. To wit, poet Robert Pinsky said, "If you live too much in your head, without any bodily sense of poetry, I don't think you'll truly get poetry"[81]

Emotion is generally, in fact, the avenue through which art reaches its audience. In the words of painter Lucien Freud, "The painter makes real to others his innermost feelings about all that he cares for. A secret becomes known to everyone who views the picture through the intensity with which it is felt."[82] Music, too, has its impact through non-rational channels, according to composer George Rochberg: "The ear remains the best judge of music, however composed, but this intuitive perceiver of sound is not susceptible to outside numerical or verbal logic."[83] Even written art, which can seem the least visceral of all the arts, works this way. Poet Muriel Rukeyser said, "Poetry is, above all, an approach to the truth of feeling. . . . A fine poem will seize your imagination intellectually—that is, when you reach it, you will reach it intellectually too—but the way is through emotion, through what we call feeling."[84]

All of this might sound lovely, really—but this is *Parashat Pinhas*, and one of the things this *parasha* is saying is that these emotions we need are

77. Levin, *Becoming Judy*, 253.

78. Cott, *Bob Dylan*, 270.

79. Warren, *Anna Sokolow*, 135.

80. Preston, *Creative Process*, 164.

81. Moyers, *Fooling with Words*, 211.

82. Jackman, *Artist's Mentor*, 197–8.

83. Shawn, *Schoenberg's Journey*, 292.

84. McIver, "Poetry and Radio," 178.

not all sweet ones. Consider Amedeo Modigliani, a self-destructive person but a magnificent painter, who said, "I need a flame in order to paint, in order to be consumed by fire."[85] In some cases the harsh emotion may not be directed inward but outward. The point is that zeal is not about pausing to consider whether one's emotion is "nice" or not. As painter Mark Rothko said, "I exclude no emotion from being actual and therefore pertinent."[86] Neither must we.

Phinehas would without doubt have to be considered a vigilante murderer if he did his hot-headed killing in our world. Furthermore, I'm not advocating for art that destroys the artist or others. I'm not even saying that all passion is constructive—after all, according to the Torah, if God had given into *passion*, the Israelites would all have been destroyed (Num 25:11). What I'm saying is that the creative process is not a logical process, not a sober or nice process. It is fueled by our passions, and those passions will allow us to reach others. God granted Phinehas the priesthood, the Israelites' most holy office, for his zeal. Surely you can find something of the sacred in your own emotional life—and surely you can find a place for that in your art.

---

*In Your Mouth and In Your Heart:*

Think of something in your life and in your world that arouses in you extreme emotion. Turn your heart in that direction, let that emotion become aroused and start work on a creative piece. Pour your zeal into the piece.

---

85. Meyers, *Modigliani*, 31.

86. Jackman, *Artist's Mentor*, 204.

# *Mattot*

## Vanity

### Numbers 30:2—32:42

A FTER A FAIRLY BRIEF discussion of vows and oaths, *Parashat Mattot* launches us into a bloody war of revenge, one called for by God because the target of the attack, the Midianites, had previously led the Israelites into moral degradation and threatened the sanctity of the community as a whole. On the surface level of the text—the *p'shat*, as it's said in Hebrew—it seems that the writer of the Torah is satisfied that this war is just and that its results (which include the killing of every last Midianite male adult and child, plus every woman that's not a virgin, and the claiming of all the remaining spoils—jewelry, livestock, and virgin women) are appropriate. A modern reader, on the other hand, is likely to feel some revulsion as the carnage is detailed, and then some more as the booty is counted up and distributed. However, that reader would do well to keep reading, to see what the Torah really thinks.

Right after the war against the Midianites—and putting two stories next to one another is often taken to be a significant thing in the Torah—the tribes of Gad and Reuben approach Moses to ask if they can claim land on the near side of the Jordan rather than the lots they had previously been assigned in the promised land in Canaan itself. Ultimately, Moses agrees, so long as the tribes go ahead and participate in the upcoming war to conquer Canaan. Yet all is not really well.

When the Gadites and Reubenites make their initial request, they ask for this excellent land in order to *"build here sheepholds for our flocks and towns for our children"* (Num 32:16). Notice that they focus first and foremost on their flocks—their possessions. Moses subtly chastises them when he responds *"Build towns for your children and sheepfolds for your flocks"* (Num 32:24), reversing the order, and these Israelites seem to get the message when they go on to discuss *"our children, our wives, our flocks, and all our other livestock"* (Num 32:26).

Still, even though they finally get their priorities in order, the damage has already been done. They were ready to give up their lots in the promised land because they were so focused on their *stuff*—some of which was the result of the recent war and that seemed to be such a point of pride earlier. Here, though, we feel Moses' (and the Torah's) disapproval of this materialism—and, perhaps, the things that these tribes have done in this *parasha* to *get* wealth. This disapproval carries forward in our tradition; when the tribes of Gad and Reuben are the first to be exiled, some point to their materialism as the reason for their misfortune.[87] Their greed corrupts them, and it leads to their downfall.

Our tradition does have some persistent concerns about a singular drive for wealth. The Book of Ecclesiastes—attributed to our famously wise ancestor Solomon—goes on about this repeatedly, and sometimes at length: *He that loveth silver shall not be satisfied with silver; nor he that loveth abundance, with increase; this also is vanity. When goods increase, they are increased that eat them; and what advantage is there to the owner thereof, saving the beholding of them with his eyes? Sweet is the sleep of a labouring man, whether he eat little or much; but the satiety of the rich will not suffer him to sleep.* (Eccl 5:9–11).[88]

That word "vanity" shows up over and over again in Ecclesiastes as a source of suffering, and materialism is one of its guises. In the writer's opinion, in fact, there is one main viable alternative to all this vanity: joy. We are mortals, temporary entities, and wealth can't change that—but allowing oneself to fully enjoy one's labor can sweeten the days we have.

This is certainly the kind of message you hear from artists, people who generally do what they do out of love. As composer Leonard Bernstein wrote, "Economic considerations cannot enter into this area. One is an artist by necessity, and there are other ways of making money."[89] Indeed, one of the things poet Robert Pinsky loves about poetry "is that there's not a lot

87. Lieber, *Etz Hayim*, 951.
88. Jewish Publication Society, 1917 *Tanakh*.
89. Bernstein, *Joy of Music*, 43.

of money in it. That can be beautiful, too. . . . people do it because they love the art, they're just crazy about it."[90]

Now, of course there's a danger here of romanticizing poverty, and there's nothing romantic at all about poverty. It can, among other things, even get in the way of a creative life, as we see in the life of Judy Chicago, who before attaining renown late in life sometimes found herself unable to work "due mainly to financial problems."[91] Painter Amedeo Modigliani suffered in this way, too, according to poet Anna Akhmatova: "I knew him when he was poor, and I did not understand how he survived—he didn't possess even a shadow of recognition as an artist. . . . All that was divine in Modigliani only sparkled through a sort of gloom."[92]

So I'm not talking about embracing a vow of poverty; as songwriter Bob Dylan said, "You don't have to starve to be a good artist."[93] I'm talking about making sure you have enough material success to sustain yourself and leaving it at that. Choreographer Anna Sokolow said it well: "I don't eat much, I don't care for expensive clothes, and I don't pay a lot for rent. What do I need money for? I want to work, and I want work that is stimulating and keeps me growing."[94] This could be right out of Ecclesiastes, if only she'd said "Vanity!" in there somewhere. The point is that, for most artists, the work comes first.

Bob Dylan said it, too—"I don't think in terms of economics or status or what people think of me one way or the other."[95] Filmmaker Woody Allen, for one, is insistent that the most important thing about making films is the work itself, and perhaps what that work can do in the world: "I learned one thing at an early age. If you just keep your nose to the grindstone, if you just try to do good work and don't get distracted from this work by either pain or pleasure or reviews or temptations, everything takes care of itself. Because over the years you accumulate work, and if you have anything to say that is meaningful to people, it's there. And hopefully there are always some people that you are communicating with. And you can never think about money."[96]

90. Moyers, *Fooling with Words*, 202.
91. Levin, *Becoming Judy*, 115.
92. Meyers, *Modigliani*, 88.
93. Cott, *Bob Dylan*, 235.
94. Warren, *Anna Sokolow*, 112.
95. Cott, *Bob Dylan*, 212.
96. Allen and Bjorkman, *Woody Allen*, 330.

Note that Allen points to another kind of vanity in this comment (and we heard it in Dylan's comment as well): the need for good reviews, for acclaim and recognition. For artists, this is probably a much more seductive temptation than the one that pulls us toward wealth.

Judy Chicago seems to have struggled with this issue all her life: "Even when I was a child, I always had to struggle & in every situation I started out behind the eight-ball, with people not recognizing my worth. Agonizingly, I would struggle until I received my rewards & people would acknowledge my worth."[97] The issue here isn't *being* worthy, but being *seen* and *talked about* as worthy. This concern has had a special poignancy for Chicago as a woman, in that women have often failed to get the recognition they deserved. "Famous women painters have been completely swallowed up w/ no remains," she wrote.[98]

But what happens if you don't get that reward? As Chicago seemed to recognize in this quote, it can eventually hold you back from doing your work: "I know I have a lot to give, & if the world will let me give it & acknowledge my gift, I'll become more relaxed & probably even be able to contribute more."[99] Without that acknowledgement, we have to assume, Chicago could only contribute less. Ironically, she also understood that "the only time you really have a chance of strong recognition is when you risk disapproval"[100]—and Chicago has met with plenty of disapproval over her career, all the while striving to be well-known.

Because this goal can be so destructive, many artists have to shut out all thoughts of recognition in order to work. Michael Chabon did so when he was writing his novel *Wonder Boys*: "I didn't stop to think about what I was doing or what the critics would think of it. . . . I just wrote."[101] In the words of author Lev Raphael, "You have to write what appeals to you [as opposed to reviewers or readers] first."[102]

Some artists actively avoid finding out what others think. "You can't look at reviews," Dylan once said.[103] Woody Allen has long had the same policy:

97. Levin, *Becoming Judy*, 46.
98. Ibid., 192.
99. Ibid., 189.
100. Ibid., 163.
101. *Writer's Almanac*, May 2008.
102. Buccini, "Lev Raphael."
103. Cott, *Bob Dylan*, 283.

I never read anything that's being written about me. I found out many years ago—many, *many* years ago—that the best way to work is not to read about yourself or watch yourself on television. I lead a very ostrich-like existence all the time. I never read the reviews of my movies. I don't read the articles about me. . . . If all the people liked my work, it didn't mean that the work was good—and it certainly didn't mean that audiences came to see it. If nobody liked it, it didn't mean that the work was bad.[104]

Chicago has been unable to avoid her reviewers, unfortunately. "I've been pretty beaten up critically," she's said. "So a lot of my focus has been on how to keep going, how to keep working and keep growing in the face of this incredible critical assault."[105] Instead of focusing entirely on work, she has to waste a lot of her energy on finding a way to weather the negative reviews.

Some artists are in a position where they honestly have to worry about money, and others are not. Some artists are indifferent to reviews, others manage to avoid them altogether, and still others take a beating that leaves deep bruises. The successful artist, ultimately, though, is not the wealthy one nor the well-reviewed one, but the one that manages, no matter what, to work. Unlike the Gadites and the Reubenites with their mixed up priorities, the other tribes just kept marching, on into the promised land. They should be our model of success: just keep marching.

---

### *In Your Mouth and in Your Heart:*

What "vanities" plague you, get in the way of your work? How can you keep them from interfering?

---

104. Allen and Bjorkman, *Woody Allen*, 269–70.
105. Levin, *Becoming Judy*, 398.

# Mas'ei

## Looking Back

### Numbers 33:1—36:13

JUDAISM IS A RELIGION that is heavily engaged—some would say obsessed—with the past. On Passover we tell the story of a millennia-old exodus from Egypt; on Yom Kippur we lament the deaths of Jews that happened centuries ago; and our weekly Torah readings bring us back to the creation of the earth, to distant historical events, to our first ancestors, to temple rituals that haven't been in effect since year 70 of the Common Era (when the second temple was destroyed). The Torah sometimes even pauses to look back at what happened earlier in the Torah.

The last *parasha* of the Book of Numbers, *Mas'ei*, offers one such pause. This section takes place at a significant moment—right before we hear Moses's final speech (which is the Book of Deuteronomy), the last prelude to entering the promised land. We begin with *These were the marches of the Israelites* (Num 33:1), and then we run through every place the Israelites have encamped since coming out of Egypt. It's quite a list—forty-one camps in all.

But why bother? We're probably a little impatient to get moving forward, and there isn't much news in this list, aside from a few stops that hadn't been mentioned earlier. If we've been reading the Torah all along, we were essentially there as they made these camps in the first place. Why go over them again?

I think the take-home lesson of these verses is that the past matters. There is much to gain from the simple act of reflecting on where we've been.

Certainly many artists seem to think so. Reading stacks of biographies in order to write this book, I again and again encountered artists' wistful or searching or pointed thoughts on their beginnings: the childhood baseball memories of writer Philip Roth and painter R. B. Kitaj; visual artists Judy Chicago's and Louise Nevelson's formative relationships with their fathers; the movies that filmmaker Woody Allen loved as a kid; poet Stanley Kunitz's recollection of seeing Halley's comet in 1910.

Then, too, there's the tendency to think back on where you started as an artist. Often you see just how much you've changed. Chicago described her eighteen-year-old self this way: "I was a young, idealistic, old-fashioned girl. I believed in art and truth and beauty. I didn't know anything about 'making it.' I was such a protected girl."[106] Woody Allen was apparently similarly innocent when he directed his first film, but fairly sure of himself all the same. He said, "It never occurred to me for a second that I wouldn't know what to do. I was guided by the fact that I knew what I wanted to see. So it seemed to me elementary how to get to see it."[107]

For all his confidence back then, Allen admits he had a lot of growing to do: "The films I made before [cameraman] Gordon [Willis] were, I think, fun and exuberant and the best I could do. But I didn't really know what I was doing, I was just learning. . . . It was not until later, when I did *Annie Hall*, that I became more ambitious and started to use the cinema a little bit. Then I could refrain from too many jokes; I tried to make the film more dimensional and searched for other values. That's how I developed."[108] This greenness was there in every aspect of filming: "In the first films I did, I did do a lot of takes and I printed a lot. Because I was insecure. Now I don't do that. Now I do long, long takes, and I have much more confidence."[109]

And how do you get that confidence? Experience. Allen later said, "Confidence that comes with experience enables you to do many things that you wouldn't have done in early films. You do tend to become bolder, because as the years go by you feel more in control of what you're doing."[110]

Looking back is about more, however, than the pleasure of seeing how you've grown. It's also about seeing and understanding yourself in a way that can further help your work. As choreographer Meredith Monk said,

106. Levin, *Becoming Judy*, 54.

107. Allen and Bjorkman, *Woody Allen*, 19.

108. Ibid., 22.

109. Ibid., 25.

110. Ibid., 244.

"After a while you find that you have to contend with the backpack of your past on a lot of levels," if only because "how [else] do you find something new? How do you explore something you haven't done before? How do you keep it fresh? How do you challenge yourself? How do you risk? How do you do something that really has a lot of life energy in it? All that has a lot to do with trying to consider yourself as a human being first."[111]

And so we look back. We try to understand who we were. For many artists this is an obsession as intense as it is for the religion of Judaism—and it leads to creative work. Said writer Nicole Krauss, "I rely on the past heavily. I'm in constant conversation with it, often without being aware of so being. Sometimes it is a vague conversation, and sometimes it is very pointed."[112] Painter Kitaj, who was American-born but lived most of his adult life in Great Britain, found that the past came knocking at his door every once in a while with a particular request: "From time to time I have to make a baseball painting to express a deep national love. By national I mean where you come from, grow up, get formed, national pride, etc., etc."[113]

In fact, artists return to their roots not just for subject matter, but for creative wisdom. It's true that we learn a lot to help us as artists as we get older and gain experience, but we sometimes lose essential things as well—and looking back puts us in touch with that essential stuff. Very early in his career Bob Dylan was already aware of the value of the past. In 1964, with three albums under his belt and another one on the way, he said, "From now on, I want to write from inside me, and to do that I'm going to have to get back to writing like I used to when I was ten—having everything come out naturally." What he meant by that was that "the way I like to write is for it come out the way I walk or talk"—and he saw that the innocent ten-year-old Dylan knew how to do that better than the sophisticated twenty-three-year-old version did.[114]

This search to return to his original creative impulse was a recurring thing for Dylan. Fourteen years later he described an elusive sound that was the inspiration for all his early work:

> I have to get back to the sound, to the sound that will bring it all through me. . . . That ethereal twilight light, you know. It's the sound of the street with the sunrays, the sun shining down at a

111. Morgenroth, *Speaking of Dance*, 98.
112. *Small Spiral Notebook.*
113. Jackman, *Artist's Mentor*, 111.
114. Cott, *Bob Dylan*, 16.

particular time, on a particular type of building. A particular type of people walking on a particular type of street. It's an outdoor sound that drifts even into open windows that you can hear. The sound of bells and distant railroad trains and arguments in apartments and the clinking of silverware and knives and forks and beating with leather straps. It's all—it's all there.[115]

Again, this is the lesson of this Torah portion: the past matters—or, in Dylan's words, it's all there. It may surprise or shock us to see where we've come from, and we might find ourselves overwhelmed, just as a reader of *Parashat Mas'ei* might after the first thirty encampments or so—but, as we see in these pages, with the Israelites poised to enter the promised land, we wouldn't do well to move forward without first taking a good look back.

---

## In Your Mouth and In Your Heart:

How have you grown over time as an artist? What material for your art do you find in your past? And what creative wisdom did you have then that you need now?

---

115. Ibid., 208–9.

# Deuteronomy

# D'varim

## Your Permanent Record

### Deuteronomy 1:1—3:22

THE BOOK OF DEUTERONOMY is also known as the *Mishnei Torah*, or the "repetition of the Torah." It gets this name because these chapters, the transcript of Moses's final words before the Israelites enter the promised land, are full of reminiscing. In the first *parasha*, *D'varim*, for example, Moses recounts the story of the Israelites wandering through the desert. It's not the most flattering tale, actually; in it is the episode where the Israelites sent spies into the promised land and then chickened out and had to spend another forty years wandering before they would get to enter.

Taking this walk down memory lane, the Israelites probably would have preferred Moses to skip the embarrassing parts. They might have been even more horrified if they could have known that their mistakes were going to be recorded in the Torah, and that people all over the world read about them year after year. They might think, *Man, you mess up one time* (or, in the Israelites' case, lots and lots and lots of times) *and it hangs on you forever.*

Many artists feel the same way. Mistakes, of course, are a big part of the artist's life. It has to be that way—as we've seen elsewhere, doing creative work means journeying into the unknown, trying new things and asking questions that haven't been asked before, or asking them in a new way. Inevitably some artistic experiments are less than completely successful. Filmmaker Woody Allen said, "I'm never happy with my films when I finish them. Just about always. And in the case of *Manhattan* I was so disappointed that I didn't want to open it. I wanted to ask United Artists not to release it. I wanted to offer them to make one free movie, if they would just throw it away."[1] Never mind that *Manhattan* is now one of Allen's most beloved films—that doesn't mean he ever came around to liking it. And yet it's out there, in the world, being watched by people—this movie that so disappointed him is now part of his permanent record.

That permanent record starts the minute the artist begins making work public—staging it, hanging it, getting it published. It can feel great at the time—getting a little attention for your work is a thrill. The problem is that, as we saw in the last commentary, artists are always in the process of growing, developing, learning—and that means that one's oldest stuff might not be as good as one's most recent stuff. According to songwriter Bob Dylan, speaking in an interview sixteen years after releasing his first album, "It's taken me all this time, and the records I made along the way were like openers—trying to figure out whether it was this way or that way, just what *is* it, what's the simplest way I can tell the story and make this feeling real."[2]

It's common to feel a mix of nostalgia and embarrassment looking back at one's earliest work. We recently heard Allen talking about how his first films weren't as good as the ones he made later, and he can learn from that as an artist, but it's not just there for *him* to see; it's all part of his public record, and—especially in an era when it's so easy to preserve and disseminate many kinds of art—it's nearly impossible to expunge any of it. It's a sobering thing, knowing that your growth curve is exposed for all to see. How do you deal with that?

Well, you could bide your time, wait until you've finally perfected yourself before you share your work with the world—but when would that be? If you're always going to be better later on, now is *never* the right time to add something to your record—no matter how long you wait for the right "now." Like it or not, if we're ever going to bring our art into the public sphere, we inevitably have to do it before we're as good as we're going to be later.

One way to weather that process is to just keep your eyes pointed forward. Dylan said, "I never listen to my albums, once they are completed. I don't want to be reminded. To me, I've done them. I find it like looking into a lifeless mirror."[3] If you keep from looking back, you don't have to think about how much less skillful you used to be.

1. Allen and Bjorkman, *Woody Allen*, 116.
2. Cott, *Bob Dylan*, 260.
3. Ibid., 400.

But we just talked about how useful it can be to look back! There is, luckily, another way to handle this phenomenon of developing in public: the artist can recognize that this phenomenon is, in fact, a gift to the world.

Reading *Parashat D'varim* reminds me just how generous a document the Torah is. It doesn't just portray our ancestors in the best possible light, at only their proudest moments. We see those moments, sure, but the Torah also shows us the low points, the times when people did things absolutely wrong—Adam and Eve disobeying, Joseph's brothers selling him into slavery, the people yelling for the golden calf and Aaron delivering, jealousy and griping all the way through the desert. This is a document that allows us to see the full humanity of the people in it.

Why is this generous? It's generous because seeing people do things right *and* wrong is the best way to learn from people. If our ancestors were painted as paragons of virtue and good sense, we wouldn't be able to relate to them, and we wouldn't know how to respond to our own mistakes. The same is true in the art world. When I read my favorite authors, it's a relief to see that the quality of their work varies, to see their humanity; after all, I'm a human, and I'm trying to do what they do. Seeing their flaws helps me believe I have a right to be among them.

It's more than that, though—it's also about learning from them. Honestly, I think I learn just as much from my favorite authors' worst books as from their best. I see things that I would do differently—and things that I know that they do differently when they're writing well. I see problems, and I have the chance to think about how to fix them. If I were only to look at artistic successes, seamless and whole and mysterious, I might never know how they were made. When I see a piece that's a little imperfect, I have a sense how work is done. What a gift that is for us!

That, I suppose, is how we and the Israelites ought to think about things. We should not be ashamed of our earliest work, work that we did with integrity and our best courage and all the wisdom we had at the time. We should not be embarrassed by growing in public. Instead we should realize that we give the world a gift by leaving our humanity on record, a gift that will be opened, with gratitude, by every person hoping to follow in our footsteps.

*In Your Mouth and In Your Heart:*

Are you embarrassed by your early creative efforts? Are there ways that you still need to grow? Make sure your imperfections don't prevent you from sharing your work with the world.

# *Va-ethanan*

## Opening the Closed

### Deuteronomy 3:23—7:11

A S I MENTIONED IN the last commentary, Deuteronomy is also called the *Mishnei Torah* because of all of the repetition we find here. Stories are repeated, and so are laws. In fact, *Parashat Va-ethanan* even features a full repetition of the *Aseret ha-D'varim*, what we often translate as the Ten Commandments.

What jumps out at many readers is that the repetition we encounter in Deuteronomy is very frequently inexact; details, words, and emphases are often changed. Most of these changes consist of Moses altering what he said earlier, but some of the changes even seem to come from God. The Ten Commandments offer a good example. You would think these were inviolable, unchangeable—but in fact they are somewhat revised here. In the Fourth Commandment we are told to *observe* the Sabbath (Deut 5:12) rather than to *remember* it (Exod 20:8) and we are told (for the first time) that it even applies to slaves, and the commandment is no longer justified by a mention of God's creation of the world; it's now resting on God's rescue of the people from Egypt. The wording of the Ninth Commandment is also slightly different, and the order of things we shouldn't covet is changed in the Tenth Commandment, which somewhat changes its meaning.

Why do these things change? Weren't the *Aseret ha-D'varim* good enough the first time? They may have been, but maybe they were originally shaped in order to best address the audience of Israelites gathered at the foot of Mount Sinai, and maybe that original version wouldn't have been as effective with the Israelites gathered on the border of the promised land.

Or maybe—as most readers assume—we have both versions so that we can learn by comparing them. In other words, maybe this new version isn't an improvement on an imperfect original so much as an addition that was planned all along.

Still—I can't help it. I'm a writer. To me, this looks like revision.

Those of us who are not God know that our first drafts are anything but finished. Filmmaker Woody Allen said, "My first draft is exploratory."[4] Songwriter Leonard Cohen said, "I find that easy versions of the song arrive first. Although they might be able to stand as songs, they can't stand as songs that I can sing."[5] Sometimes those first versions are so far off that they're almost unrecognizable, as in this experience of novelist Norman Mailer: "I began to go over the page proofs [of *The Deer Park*], and the book read as if it had been written by someone else. I was changed from the writer who had labored on that novel, enough to be able to see it without anger or vanity or the itch to justify myself. Now, after three years of living with the book, I could at least admit the style was wrong, that it had been wrong from the time I started."[6] In talking about writing his novel *The Yiddish Policeman's Union*, Michael Chabon said,

> I had made bad choices from the start. A lot of times when something goes wrong it's because an initial set of bad choices is made. . . . The point of view was wrong, it was in first person and that just didn't work, it was in the past tense and that didn't work, and the plot itself was grossly convoluted and didn't add up and had these extra elements that didn't work. When I started writing the draft that became the novel, I said to my wife, this is not a second draft, this is a sequel. I had the same character and that's all, it was a totally different story. I probably kept about 30 pages of the 600.[7]

Of course, it's not usually about just two drafts or versions. Writer Bernard Malamud was famous for saying, "I . . . write a book, or a short story, at least three times—once to understand it, the second time to improve the prose, and a third to compel it to say what it still must say."[8] Choreographer Anna Halprin described her process this way: "We would make a score, then open it up to improvisation. Then we'd close it. It's an iterative process. I

---

4. Allen and Bjorkman, *Woody Allen*, 249.

5. Zollo, *Song-Writers*, 331.

6. Mailer, *Spooky Art*, 35.

7. Greenwood, Chabon Interview.

8. Malamud, *People*, xi.

like to reach a point of having a definitive score, but then open it up again."[9] Allen again: "I always feel that, with a film, you're writing it every moment. You write it in the script, you rewrite it and change it when you cast, you rewrite it and change it when you see locations, and so on."[10] As Halprin said, "I never seem to be finished with anything. Nothing ever seems to be perfect."[11]

If this sounds like hard work, that's because it is. Chabon had this to say about rewriting his book *Maps and Legends*: "I went through and asked each piece to stand up and justify its presence in the collection. And if it couldn't fully justify its presence, I would rewrite it so it could."[12] Cohen described a similarly onerous process: "To find a song that I can sing, to engage my interest, to penetrate my boredom with myself and my disinterest in my own opinions, to penetrate those barriers, the song has to speak to me with a certain urgency. To be able to find that song that I can be interested in takes many versions and it takes a lot of uncovering. . . . to find something that really touches and addresses my attention, I have to do a lot of hard, manual work."[13]

But what can you do? It may be hard work, but you have to do it—don't you?

Some artists, it's true, claim to create a masterpiece in a burst of excitement and never go back to improve it. Painter Amedeo Modigliani, for example, "painted with great speed and completed most portraits in a single sitting," according to art historian Jeffrey Meyers.[14] Songwriter Bob Dylan claimed, "I don't spend a lot of time going over songs. . . . I'll sometimes make changes, but the early songs, for instance, were mostly all first drafts."[15]

So is revision optional?

Well, first of all it's important to note that Modigliani's process, for one, stood "in contrast to a traditional artist, who would spend months on a single work."[16] It's not a common thing to be able to knock off a painting in

9. Morgenroth, *Speaking of Dance*, 32.

10. Allen and Bjorkman, *Woody Allen*, 161.

11. Morgenroth, *Speaking of Dance*, 32.

12. *Boldtype*, "Michael Chabon."

13. Zollo, *Song-Writers*, 331–32.

14. Meyers, *Modigliani*, 155.

15. Cott, *Bob Dylan*, 435.

16. Meyers, *Modigliani*, 154–55.

one shot. As for Bob Dylan, his claim to do little revision on paper doesn't mean he did little revision. If you look at some of the other things he's said, it sounds like he does a great deal of reworking—just mostly in his head, before he ever starts writing anything down: "Songs don't just come to me. They'll usually brew for a while, and you'll learn that it's important to keep the pieces until they are completely formed and glued together."[17] So even here it looks like revision is part of the deal.

Besides, even if your first draft is good, why stop there? Writer Susan Sontag: "But is what you've written straight off never all right? Sometimes even better than all right. And that only suggests, to this novelist at any rate, that with a closer look, or voicing aloud—that is, another reading—it might be better still. . . . You think, If I can get to this point the first go-around, without too much struggle, couldn't it be better still?"[18]

Luckily, it's possible to get a lot of pleasure out of this aspect of creation. Sontag again: "And though this, the rewriting—and the rereading—sound like effort, they are actually the most pleasurable parts of writing. Sometimes the only pleasurable parts. Setting out to write, if you have the idea of 'literature' in your head, is formidable, intimidating. A plunge in an icy lake. Then comes the warm part: when you already have something to work with, upgrade, edit."[19] And Allen: "When I actually make the cut, to me it's like removing a tumour. I mean, I find it a mercy-killing. It's just great, it's such a pleasure. In the long run, when I look back now and at this much distance, I might think it's a shame I couldn't get that particular piece in. But when you are actually face to face with the film, and you want to move along, you take it out and suddenly it's like taking a weight off your back. It's just amazing."[20]

Now, I started this whole thing off by suggesting that we're acting like God when we revisit and change our work. That may seem audacious—but the Torah told us early on that we were made b'tzelem Elohim: in the image of God. I've been saying all along that one way we resemble divinity is in our creativity—so why not in this aspect of revision as well? Nothing *is* ever perfect, whether in our own work or in the universe itself. It makes sense that creators would go back over things that seemed closed at first and open them up again. So when you sit there uncomfortably pondering

17. Cott, *Bob Dylan*, 435.

18. Sontag, "Directions," 223–24.

19. Ibid., 224.

20. Allen and Bjorkman, *Woody Allen*, 313.

whether you should revisit a piece, remember that the God we read about was humble enough to do it. Shouldn't you be, too?

---

*In Your Mouth and In Your Heart:*

Do you have a piece you created in a burst of excitement that you secretly suspect is not so perfect? Get back to it and rework it. It's part of your job.

---

# *Eikev*

## What Got You Here

WHERE DID YOU COME from? How did you get where you are today? In *Parashat Eikev*, Moses asks the Israelites these questions— and answers them as well. He notes just how far they've come—from slavery to freedom and abundance; from being few in number to being a multitude—and from homelessness to the cusp of taking possession of their own promised land. If everything goes well, and Moses assures them that it will—the Israelites will soon have a home in *a land with streams and springs and fountains issuing from plain and hill; a land of wheat and barley, of vines, figs and pomegranates, a land of olive trees and honey; a land where you may eat food without stint, where you will lack nothing* (Deut 8:7–9). But how indeed has this ragtag people made it to this place of vast possibility? Moses follows these lines with this one: *When you have eaten your fill, give thanks to the Lord your God for the good land which He has given you* (Deut 8:10).

In fact, Moses returns again and again to the theme that the people wouldn't have much of anything without the help of God; he's clearly worried that the people will forget. He's worried that the people will say, *"My own power and the might of my own hand have won this wealth for me"* (Deut 8:17). Why does Moses have to hammer on this so much? God has dazzled everyone with wonders throughout the Torah, and continues to make appearances as columns of fire or cloud—you would think that the Israelites would have no trouble remembering that their success is not entirely their own. But therein lies the lesson—if *these* people can't stay grateful for what has been given to them, how much harder for us? Above all, how much harder for artists, people whose emphasis on creativity and originality seems to suggest they've come out of nowhere, invented themselves completely, have nobody to thank for what they've accomplished?

Many of us have consciously tried to break from our past. We have gone a different way from other members of our families. We have created our own style, one not quite like the style of any other person on earth. We are new, wholly new. It's all too easy to forget that we are not the only ones who got us here.

Yet even when we do forget, there can sometimes be a reminder. "Once in a while," wrote novelist Norman Mailer, "your hand will write out a sentence that seems true and yet you do not know where it came from."[21] This is a wonderful feeling, the feeling that one has received a mysterious gift from the universe. It's also an opportunity for humility. In the words of songwriter Bob Dylan, describing where his songs come from, "No one in his right mind would think that it was coming from him, that he has invented it. It's just coming through him."[22]

This is indeed an opportunity—an opportunity to recognize that our work is the product not only of our own insight and skill but also of all the many things that have come together to help us produce it. Composer Arnold Schoenberg, one of music's greatest revolutionaries, once said, "The appearance of the new can . . . be compared with the flowering of a tree: it is the natural growth of the tree of life."[23] The flower wouldn't exist without the tree.

Sculptor Chaim Gross described his resistance to this idea: "I had a brother, a great Yiddish poet, Naftali Gross. He used to say, 'Chaim, your work is Yiddish. You can tell. The way you are doing your figures. They are Jewish girls.' You can't get away, because I am a Jew. And you cannot get away from it. You can't get away mentally or physically. And maybe, if you try to get away from it, there is always something Jewish in your art."[24] Like it or not, Gross' work was influenced by his background. And why not like it? Poet Yehuda Amichai said, "I was lucky enough to be reared in a very Jewish home. My father was devoutly orthodox, and his Judaism was a treasure he passed on to me. Though I am not religious,

21. Mailer, *Spooky Art*, 68.

22. Cott, *Bob Dylan*, 242.

23. Shawn, *Schoenberg's Journey*, 141.

24. Baskind, *Encyclopedia of Jewish Artists*, xvii.

it is a marvelous treasure, and I use it."[25] He used it in his work, to be specific, and he knew it.

One's family is, of course, a powerful influence on one's work. Gross said that his "love of wood reaches back to . . . childhood," where, because his father was a lumberer, he "endlessly watched the processes of lumbering." "How I enjoyed the delicious, pungent smell of newly cut wood," he said. "Every evening after the day's work our household was a busy one with the peasants carving religious ornaments, household objects and utensils."[26] Art historian Samantha Baskind describes a similar influence on Saul Baizerman, another sculptor: "The approach used to make the hammered bronzes of *The City and the People*, and even more the hammered copper sculptures, has its roots in Baizerman's Russian childhood; his father, a third-generation harness-maker, hammered leather into harnesses."[27]

Those who have artists as parents must feel the influence even more keenly. Poet Allen Ginsberg was the son of another poet—Louis Ginsberg—and he said, "I got a good sense of rhythm from him, as well as real familiarity with American poetry in the twentieth century, in the lyric style."[28] He even claims that some of the rhythms and imagery in his father's poem "At the Grave of My Father" specifically influenced his own poem "Old Auntie Death, Don't Hide Your Bones."

Certainly we must acknowledge our debt to the artists who have come before us. This is what Schoenberg meant, above all, in referring to the tree that bears flower in the "new." We are that which grows on that which has grown before. As we've seen, painter Camille Pissarro once said, "We have today a general concept inherited from our great modern painters, hence we have a tradition of modern art. . . . Look at Degas, Manet, Monet, who are close to us, and at our elders, David, Ingres, Delacroix, Courbet, Corot, the great Corot, did they leave us nothing?"[29] Of course, as Pissarro himself acknowledged, we are not just repeating the tradition, not just imitating—"we inflect it in terms of our individual points of view," he said[30]—but the influence is there. Mark Rothko: "After I had been at work [on my Seagram murals] for some time, I realized that I was much influenced subconsciously

25. Cohen, *Voices of Israel*, 35.

26. Baskind, "Chaim Gross" in *Encyclopedia of Jewish Artists*, 133.

27. Baskind, "Saul Baizerman" in *Encyclopedia of Jewish Artists*, 36.

28. Ginsberg, *Life and Times*.

29. Jackman, *Artist's Mentor*, 33.

30. Ibid.

by Michelangelo's walls in the staircase room of the Medicean Library in Florence. He achieved just the kind of feeling I'm after."[31]

Generally we are happy to embrace this influence. Writer Saul Bellow, in his Nobel Prize lecture—at the height, in other words, of being appreciated for his unique gifts—took the opportunity to say, "I never tire of reading the master novelists."[32] Those novelists, after all, made up part of the powerful force that had brought him to that podium.

Every time we enter our studios, sit down at our desks, stretch in dance clothes in front of our mirrors, we are on the threshold of possibly wondrous discovery. We have done a great deal, shown courage and perseverance and skill in getting to that threshold. Still—we have not done it alone.

---

### In Your Mouth and In Your Heart:

Who have been your major influences? Think about the artists and other people who have helped you and your creativity get to this place. Can you envision a piece of work that would directly honor one or more of these people?

---

31. Ibid., 34.
32. Bellow, Nobel Lecture.

# R'eih

## The Open Hand

### Deuteronomy 11:26—16:17

IN MY EXPERIENCE, BEING an artist can sometimes feel like being a person who walks up to a deep, deep well and drops a pebble in—but it turns out the well is so deep that, strain as you might, you never do hear the splash. Except the real thing can be more painful than the analogy suggests because in the case of the artist you've actually *made* the pebble, made it with painstaking effort, and have probably loaded it with a great many hopes and expectations, and perhaps above all you really wanted to hear an excellent, affirming splash. Nonetheless, tired from the work and depressed from the lack of noticeable impact, all you can do is turn around and head back to do more work.

We pour ourselves fully into our art. Many artists—sculptor Louise Nevelson and painter Amedeo Modigliani come to mind—describe their creative process as being such a frenzy that afterward they are exhausted. Consider sculptor Saul Baizerman: "How do I know when a piece is finished? When it has taken away from me everything I have to give. When it has become stronger than myself. I become the empty one and it becomes the full one. When I am weak and it is strong the work is finished."[33]

This does not sound like something you'd sign up to do unless you were going to get some huge reward for your efforts. And yet in many cases your efforts not only go unrewarded—they might even go completely unnoticed. According to art historian Laurie Lisle, one of Nevelson's biggest difficulties was "the necessity of repeatedly unearthing and exposing her

33. Baskind, "Saul Baizerman," in *Encyclopedia of Jewish Artists*, 37–38.

deepest perceptions in the face of probable neglect."[34] Modigliani was, in fact, completely unknown in his lifetime.

And yet we persist. Visual artist Judy Chicago said, "It's really hard to keep on struggling—to push oneself forward—farther & farther—& yet, there's no going back & no standing still."[35]

This might seem crazy. Why on earth would people give and give and give without getting anything back from the world? This question certainly comes up for people who are not artists, puzzling about those who are—but it also comes up for those of us engaged in creative work, from time to time, when another pebble drops splashless into the well. At times, we are tempted to say that it's just not worth it. The Torah, however, would argue strongly that it *is* worth it, that it is our obligation to give even when we might not get anything back—even when it's very unlikely indeed.

In *Parashat R'eih* there is a substantial discussion of a phenomenon called *sh'mittah*—the remission of debts. As the Torah explains, every seven years we are supposed to forgive all the financial debts owed to us; no matter how little our fellow has been able to repay us so far, we are to let him or her off the hook for the rest of it.

It seems clear that this is meant to help the poor. Well-off people make loans and poorer people strive to repay, but they are prevented from entering a downward spiral of indebtedness when all debts are canceled every seven years. It seems like a compassionate and sensible system—but of course there's a flaw. Let's say the seventh year is almost here and a needy person comes to you, asking for a loan. You hesitate; after all, you've worked hard for your money, and if you give it to this person, with *sh'mittah* close at hand, it's unlikely you'll see much of your money repaid—ever. You'll be giving with no reasonable expectation of getting anything back. How likely are you to give, under these circumstances? What do you do?

The Torah, of course, has already considered this problem: *Beware lest you harbor the base thought, "The seventh year, the year of remission, is approaching," so that you are mean to your needy kinsman and give him nothing. . . . Give to him readily* (Deut 15:9–10). You are in fact *commanded* to give even when it's unlikely you'll get anything back. The Etz Hayim commentary on the Torah suggests that, in this case, "This is not so much a loan as an investment in a decent, compassionate, stable society."[36]

34. Lisle, *Louise Nevelson*, 162.

35. Levin, *Becoming Judy*, 237.

36. Lieber, *Etz Hayim*, 1078.

Artists feel this instinctually. We give because we are believers in this kind of investment. Composer Leonard Bernstein said:

> This somehow is the key to the mystery of a great artist: that for reasons unknown to him or to anyone else, he will give away his energies and his life just to make sure that one note follows another inevitably. It seems rather an odd way to spend one's life; but it isn't so odd when we think that the composer, by doing this, leaves us at the finish with the feeling that something is right in the world, that something checks throughout, something that follows its own laws consistently, something we can trust, that will never let us down.[37]

Even when our work makes no immediate splash, we go forward with the expectation that we are doing something good. Perhaps the more apt analogy is planting a seed; we see no sudden sprouts just after we cover the seed with soil, but nonetheless we have started something worthwhile in motion.

Yet we can't really be certain that the seed will ever sprout for others. We can't be sure that our art will ever reach a grateful and moved audience. And so that composer who gives everything "just to make sure that one note follows another inevitably" can't be doing so under the assumption that those notes will one day change the world. They might, in fact, never be heard by anyone else. That artist has to be doing it for the sake of doing it. In the words of writer Elie Wiesel, "Authentic writers write even if there is little chance for them to be published; they write because they cannot do otherwise."[38]

I think again of Modigliani, who died basically unknown. It happened that he went on to become posthumously famous, but he didn't know that while he was working. On one level—his poverty, for starters—that was a big problem in his life; on another, it didn't matter. Art historian Jeffrey Meyers suggested that "his haste to finish a picture showed that he cared more about the act of painting than the finished work."[39] This is probably how he was able to produce so much great art despite the fact that he was getting virtually nothing back for it. Painter Marc Chagall said that all he wanted to do as a painter was "to offer love with my dreams and colors and shapes."[40] "Offer," he said—and not in exchange for something else.

---

37. Bernstein, *Joy of Music*, 93.

38. Wiesel, "Sacred Magic," 262.

39. Meyers, *Modigliani*, 225.

40. Coleman, *Creativity and Spirituality*, 97.

"Write good poems and let go of them," writer Natalie Goldberg has advised us.[41]

And so, you stand at the well with the pebble in your hand; you kneel over fertile soil holding a seed; you stand in front of a needy world asking for help as *sh'mittah* approaches.

What do you do? You give.

---

*In Your Mouth and In Your Heart:*

What's the work you would do even if you knew it was never going to be seen or heard or appreciated by anyone else? Do that work.

---

41. Goldberg, *Writing Down*, 33.

# Shof'tim

## Appointing Yourself Judge

### Deuteronomy 16:18—21:9

ONE SENSES THAT A lot is going to change for the Israelites when they enter the promised land. Among other things, with the loss of Moses, the greatest prophet and closest confidant to God that we have ever had in our midst, God will inevitably be a little more distant from the people. Without Moses to act as such a faithful intermediary, the people may have to live without regular statements, commands and advice from God.

Thus it's no accident that *Parashat Shof'tim* begins with the line *You shall appoint magistrates and officials for your tribes, in all the settlements that the Lord your God is giving you, and they shall govern the people with due justice* (Deut 16:18). The people—all grown up now and ready to take possession of their inheritance—will need to find wisdom among themselves.

The nineteenth-century Torah teacher Sfat Emet wrote that this line was, in part, "a promise to the Jew, saying: 'You will be able to make yourself into your own judge and officer.'"[42] In other words, as we make this seismic shift, we are not only finding people in our community to help guide us—we are being empowered to, in fact, guide ourselves.

Here we have crucial wisdom for the artist, and particularly the beginning artist. It's natural, as we start out, to be heavily or even totally dependent on the feedback of others in judging our work. After all, we probably lack confidence, experience, clear knowledge of our own strengths and weaknesses. Filmmaker Woody Allen said, "When I was first making films, I used to have many screenings. And I would sneak into the back of the cinema and listen to the reactions and make my changes and cuts according

42. Green, *Menahem Nahum*, 311.

to that." Yet these were just the early films. Allen naturally became "more self-reliant over the years," so that his process of reworking things changed:

> Then I had less screenings. I had like maybe two big screenings. Then I started to screen the films in my screening-room. And now that's pretty much all I do. When I've finished a film, I screen it five, six times in my screening-room. I invite my sister and some friends. And when it's over I say to them, "Is there anything you want to tell me about this? Anything you don't understand or anything I should know?" And they might say that they liked it or didn't like it, or that there might be some scenes which were unclear or misunderstood. And then I take that into consideration. But basically, when I show a film to them, it's 99 per cent finished.[43]

Over time, he has become confident enough to decide for himself when he's doing well and when he's not.

One way or another, most successful artists come to this place of self-reliance. Visual artist Judy Chicago once wrote, "I know that I'm really doing good work."[44] Songwriter Bob Dylan said, "I kind of know myself well enough to know that the line might be good." Allowing himself to trust his judgment on that line has led him in productive directions: "It is the first line that gives you inspiration and then it's just like riding a bull."[45] Appointing oneself a judge of one's material allows you to go further into the work—and to do it well. According to literary scholar Joseph Cohen, the fact that novelist Amos Oz is such "an excellent judge of his material" makes Oz especially "accomplished in determining which literary structure is best suited to its exploitation."[46]

For some artists this development doesn't take years. Sculptor Louise Nevelson was more interested in her own opinion than in others' opinions from a young age, even dating back to early art classes she took. According to art historian Laurie Lisle, Nevelson had a teacher who suggested she wasn't ready for art, but she ignored that advice. "At the end of six weeks she was the best in the class, she claimed, which reinforced her belief in the importance of persisting and ignoring others' initial judgments," said Lisle.[47] This belief characterized her entire career. As she once said, "I hate

43. Allen and Bjorkman, *Woody Allen*, 267.
44. Levin, *Becoming Judy*, 187.
45. Cott, *Bob Dylan*, 226.
46. Cohen, *Voices of Israel*, 141.
47. Lisle, *Louise Nevelson*, 65.

the word 'compromise.' . . . My inner feeling dictates, and I will not change. I am dedicated to what has an intensity for myself."[48]

Of course, this self-reliance doesn't have to be completely inflexible. After all, the Israelites aren't *just* going to rely on individual judgment— they're also going to appoint those officials that God is calling for. Allen, for one, has continued to take in advice from others: "On the set, when I am filming the movie, everybody tells me how to do it—the script girl, the assistant director, the focus-puller. Everyone contributes with their comments. 'That joke is not funny, you should do this joke instead.' Or, 'That doesn't look real!' I mean, everybody has opinions. And I listen to all of them, and sometimes they are right and sometimes not. But nobody ever comes around in a serious way with suggestions of changes in the script. People feel I've made enough movies to know what I am doing."[49] More importantly, *he* feels that way, too. Having a trusted *inner* voice means having a key ally in your work, an ally that will challenge you, push you, and tell you when you're on the right track. Painter Ben Shahn described this collaborative-feeling experience like this: "The inward critic is ever at hand, perpetually advising and casting doubt. Here the work is overstated; there it is thin; in another place, muddiness is threatened; somewhere else it has lost connection with the whole; here it looks like an exercise in paint alone; there, an area should be preserved; thus the critics, sometimes staying the hand of the painter, sometimes demanding a fresh approach, sometimes demanding that a whole work be abandoned—and sometimes not succeeding, for the will may be stubborn enough to override such advice."[50]

The unsettling thing about this passage for me is the idea that "the inward critic" and the "will" (also presumably inward)—two separate judges—are able to go at it inside the artist. How many of our own voices will we ultimately have to listen to? Songwriter Leonard Cohen said this, speaking of his inner guides: "I bring all the people in to the team, the work force, the legion. There's a lot of voices that these things run through. . . . It's mayhem. It's mayhem and people are walking over each other's hands. It's panic. It's fire in the theater. People are being trampled and they're bullies and cowards. All the versions of yourself that you can summon are there. And some you didn't even know were around."[51]

48. Ibid., 179.

49. Allen and Bjorkman, *Woody Allen*, 277.

50. Jackman, *Artist's Mentor*, 190–91.

51. Zollo, *Song-Writers*, 343.

Sounds scary, but Cohen has had an enormously productive career. It seems that "fire in the theater" is a lot better for the artist than an empty theater. Here, in fact, is another place where good inner judgment ought to come into play. Rabbi Shefa Gold has said, "There are so many voices within that vie for our attention, all of them claiming to be the TRUTH. . . . In the pursuit of Justice, our Judge-within takes into account all the pushes and pulls of these forces of bribery. In the pursuit of Justice, she balances the powers of Love, Generosity, and Expansiveness, with the powers of Rigor, Limits, and Boundaries, while keeping the eyes of the heart wide open."[52]

Even this, this idea that we can sort through all these voices and truly know the truth, can be frightening. God's call to the Israelites in the beginning of this *parasha* is really a daunting call for them to take responsibility for their own community. Imagine what that must have felt like for a people that had so recently been entirely dependent on God in getting out of Egypt. Well, those lines also call on us as individuals, call on each one of us to take responsibility for ourselves. As artists of course we turn to others for fresh perspectives. In the end, though, only one person can—and should—act as the final judge on the matter. Luckily for us, that person, given a little training, patience, and self-awareness, is eminently qualified for the job.

---

### In Your Mouth and In Your Heart:

Do you have a piece that's still in progress and that needs some serious feedback? Try to give it to yourself. Think about your strengths and weaknesses, about the things you usually do well and the things you usually need to fix. Be your own judge. You know what this piece needs. Allow yourself to admit it.

---

52. Gold, "Shoftim."

# Ki Tetzei

## Preoccupations

### Deuteronomy 21:10—25:19

THE TORAH IS A document with preoccupations. I mean, the famous line about the Torah—*everything is in it*—seems to be true (this book may be evidence enough of that), but some things do show up more than others. That's often most evident in the sections of rules that are meant to govern the Israelites' lives. First of all, we see that God is preoccupied with the idea that the Israelites have to act a certain way in order to be holy—but there's more to see than that. *Parashat Ki Tetzei*, which contains more laws than any other *parasha*, is a good place to make the point.

The laws cover some things especially heavily. For one thing, there's a recurrent interest in social justice, in protecting the well-being of the disempowered, as in *You shall not abuse a needy and destitute laborer. . . . You must pay him his wages on the same day* (Deut 24:14–15), and *you shall not take a widow's garment in pawn* (Deut 24:17), and there's even a commandment that, if you encounter a nest with both a mother and baby birds in it, *do not take the mother together with her young* (Deut 22:6).

There are also a number of laws about marriage, sex, and family (though not always in that order), things that matter to a lot of people. Perhaps more peculiar is the deep and intense preoccupation with categories, with separating one thing from another. Men and women are not to dress in one another's clothing (Deut 22:5); your field should only have one kind of seed in it, rather than two or more (Deut 22:9); you shouldn't have a plow run by both an ox and a donkey (Deut 22:10); you shouldn't wear garments that are made up of both wool and linen (Deut 22:11). Over and over we see the Torah saying *This is not that; this is this and that is that.* It's not just in this *parasha*, either—think of the dietary laws, the different types of sacrifices one might make, the firstborn versus the secondborn son. For one reason or another, God cares a lot about making distinctions.

To put it more broadly, for one reason or another, God cares a lot about some things, and less so about other things. So one thing this section of the Torah does is demonstrate, once more, that we are *b'tzelem Elohim*—in the image of the divine. I mean, all the preoccupation in this *parasha* is kind of familiar; God has fixations—and so, of course, do we.

Artists often see this in their own work. Judy Chicago, for example, has spent a career making visual art about the issues informing women's lives, and using images that in some sense call up the experiences and physical forms of women. In graduate school, she found that "male instructors felt uncomfortable with [her] 'female' images, and made [her] feel that there was something wrong with [her],"[53] and as a result set this preoccupation aside for a while—but not for very long. It was too much a part of who she was. Even after creating her masterpiece *The Dinner Table*, Chicago has continued work in these areas.

Similarly, it could be argued that most of the novels of Chaim Potok tell the same story over again: a young person (usually a child) struggles because his or her developing individual needs and talents are in tension with the requirements of the surrounding Orthodox Jewish community. Or we could look at Amedeo Modigliani, who painted portrait after portrait after portrait, all in a signature style. There are Mark Rothko's many, many multiform paintings of blocks of color. Louise Nevelson made countless sculptures out of little discarded items, an interest that's been traced back to her childhood—"Even as a child she gathered pebbles, sticks, marbles, and other trinkets to display in little boxes"[54]—and her connection to her junk-dealing father. Or take painter Chaim Soutine; according to art critic Donald Kuspit, "one sees, in a Soutine picture, the same intimate thing, over and over again"[55] Visual artist Michal Na'aman has been determined to "confront themes of identity again and again."[56]

---

53. Levin, *Becoming Judy*, 103.

54. Lisle, *Louise Nevelson*, 29.

55. Kuspit, "Jewish Naivete?," 87.

56. Friedberg, "Secular Culture," 279.

According to painter Philip Pearlstein, "an artist needs a problem he can't solve."[57] Many of us can relate to this kind of persistent focus. Whether we get wrapped up in a topic or approach for a month or for a lifetime, many of us do find ourselves, at least for a time, working and working on one kind of thing, unable to shake it.

So here we have God as a model for our own sometimes-obsessive lives. In fact, in this we can see a model for our very individuality as creative people. What about God's somewhat idiosyncratic interest in making distinctions? This is a concern that not everyone shares, that seems sometimes a little strange—we really can't mix wool and linen? seriously?—and so in this we are reminded that each of us has preoccupations that mark us as distinctive, as individuals. Not everyone is as fascinated with little pieces of wood as Nevelson was; not everyone is as endlessly interested in bars and blocks of color as Rothko.

Yet it's also true that, if we take God as a model, we see that our preoccupations might often be relevant, or even helpful, to others around us—that they might respond to the needs of people around us. After all, God's tendency to return and return to the subject of family relationships is good news, given the fact that we mortals are pretty interested in those relationships ourselves—and the recurrent emphasis on social justice is something that has benefits for us, too. In other words, one's obsessions might be personal, but they are not necessarily only good for oneself when they're played out in the world.

Witness how much it moved painter Anna Walinska just to see Nevelson interact with a piece of string that had captured her attention: "I have never seen anyone open a cord so perfectly. . . . Not to cut it, but gently taking the time to open the cord, to respect the wrapping with a degree of sensibility that was astonishing."[58] Or take Judy Chicago again—her work exploring the experience and contributions of women has both served her interests *and* helped the world. Her installation *The Dinner Party* anchors Brooklyn Museum's Center for Feminist Art, a place where feminism can—through art, mainly—influence what we know and how we feel about the role and position of women across human history. When we honor our own fixations, we do work that turns out to matter to other people, too.

All in all, I see *Parashat Ki Tetzei* as divine authorization—authorization to get worked up, and to stay worked up, about the things that catch

57. Jackman, *Artist's Mentor*, 188.

58. Lisle, *Louise Nevelson*, 197.

and hold our interest. It may turn out that our preoccupations are of great value to the world, actually—but that's just a bonus; the real news is that they are already filled with the sacred, with the example of the divine.

---

*In Your Mouth and In Your Heart:*

What are your preoccupations? How do they show up in your art?

---

# Ki Tavo

## First Fruits

### Deuteronomy 26:1—29:8

IN *PARASHAT KI TAVO* we see Moses preparing the Israelites for their long-delayed entry into the promised land. We are, of course, on the cusp of a tremendously significant moment for this people, and Moses makes sure the people know it. When they do enter the land, he tells them, they must give an offering to God for getting them there, and, specifically, they must offer up the *first fruits* of their harvests from the land (Deut 26:2). Because this is such an important moment, it won't do to offer other gleanings from the harvest—it has to be the first fruits.

Why?

As artists, we know that our first attempts are not necessarily our best. Given that we see so many rough, rough drafts and unsatisfying initial sketches, it might seem strange to privilege the first fruits of someone's labors. Why not give the Israelites a whole growing season, or maybe more, to get the hang of things, and let them select the very best part of the yield?

Well, even if our early attempts aren't as high quality as what we'll produce later, they're extremely important—more important, as we'll see, than what we make in the long run. This is probably why God implicitly privileges rough things when demanding, elsewhere in this *parasha*, that an important religious altar be built from *unhewn* stones (Deut 27:6)—stones that are imperfect, unrefined, uneven. This is a statement of God's values—God wants to be worshiped not from a place of perfection but from somewhere humbler.

But why value imperfection?

216

Without a first fruit, without some rough thing to get things started and to show us how to do better, there will be no last fruit. Trying to perfect one's work before beginning is a creative dead end, and usually just another form of procrastination. Sometimes you just have to get going. As songwriter Bob Dylan once said, "You see, I spend too much of my time working out the *sound* of my records these days. . . . I've got a lot of different records inside me, and it's time just to start getting them *out*."[59] In other words, better to create and keep creating than to waste your energy on perfectionism.

As a matter of fact, though, those firsts can sometimes be our best. Writer Natalie Goldberg says that "first thoughts" "have tremendous energy," because they come from "the place where energy is unobstructed by social politeness or the internal censor, to the place where you are writing what your mind actually sees and feels, not what it *thinks* it should see and feel."[60] Those first thoughts can be surprising, even alarming, but generally they are more fertile than the safer ideas that come once you've had time to think things through.

The initial impulse can, in some cases, be more alive and better than what we make once we've refined things. Perhaps for this reason sculptor Louise Nevelson actively sought the "place of t[he] beginning-ness. The place of pureness, t[he] first place, t[he] one-ness & there you are. It is t[he] place you [tap] life itself."[61] Filmmaker Woody Allen gives his first thoughts a place of privilege as well:

> As the process goes on with making a film, from casting to shooting to editing, it gets worse and worse for me, because I get further and further away from the idealized perfection of the first idea. When a film is finished, I look at it and I'm disappointed and I dislike it very much, and I think that one year ago, I was sitting in my bedroom and I had this idea for a film that was so beautiful and everything was just great. And then, little by little I wounded it, in writing, in casting, in shooting, in editing, in mixing it, I want to get rid of it. I don't want to see it again. The wonderful part is getting the idea.[62]

59. Cott, *Bob Dylan*, 334.
60. Goldberg, *Writing Down*, 8–9.
61. Lisle, *Louise Nevelson*, 182.
62. Allen and Bjorkman, *Woody Allen*, 267–68.

This is not to say that the first fruits are the only good ones, and not all artists end up as disappointed in their final versions as does Allen—but it is to say that this *parasha* reminds us of the unique importance of our earliest ideas. Rather than seeing them as garbage to get out of the way, it might be more appropriate to see them as holy offerings, the most sacred gift a person can give to a universe that rejoices at every new creation.

*In Your Mouth and In Your Heart:*

Do you have a very rough idea for a piece, one that's nowhere near a polished thing? Get started on it. Don't worry about the problems. Just start creating.

# Nitzavim

## In Your Mouth and In Your Heart

### Deuteronomy 29:9—30:20

THERE ARE MANY PLACES of illuminating wisdom in the Torah—places where something crucial becomes clear. For me, there is probably no brighter moment in this respect than the one we find in chapter 30, verses 11–14, of *Parashat Nitzavim*. The people are assembled before Moses, hearing his final words, thinking about this covenant they're entering with God and one another, listening to some pretty exciting promises of blessings (if the people live up to expectations) and some fairly daunting threats (if they don't), and then Moses says this:

> Surely, this Instruction which I enjoin upon you this day is not too baffling for you, nor is it beyond reach. It is not in the heavens, that you should say, "Who among us can go up to the heavens and get it for us and impart it to us, that we may observe it?" Neither is it beyond the sea, that you should say: "Who among us can cross to the other side of the sea and get it for us and impart it to us, that we may observe it?" No, the thing is very close to you, in your mouth and in your heart, to observe it.

This is, of course, a pep talk, a reassurance: you can do it! It's also, however, a statement about ownership. Are the ideas of Torah in heaven? You would think so, if heaven is where God dwells—but in fact the Torah is *not* in heaven but on earth, in the people themselves. This wisdom and these commandments are rooted in human beings—not imposed on them. These words are also a charge: this Torah is yours, and so all the more reason that you'd better take it on. The minute that charge gets daunting, though, you can return to the sense of reassurance offered by these verses.

You can do this. It's yours. You must, in fact, do it.

It may already be obvious why I picked words from these verses for the prompts that conclude each chapter: "In Your Mouth and In Your Heart." That tri-fold message of reassurance, ownership, and obligation is a good message for artists to hear. If the Torah is a map of engagement with creation, and artists turn to it to navigate their own creation, these verses—all aspects of them—become awfully relevant.

First of all, many potentially creative people struggle with the issue of entitlement. Am I worthy of the arts? Do I have a right to claim a place as an artist? At times we all feel unworthy, but successful artists—those who do the creative work—are those who have found a way past this struggle. The working artist claims a place for her- or himself.

Sometimes this takes the form of just doing the work without settling the entitlement question. "You do it because you do it," writer Natalie Goldberg has said.[63] Similarly, art historian Donald Kuspit referred to painter Chaim Soutine's "radical naiveté"[64] or even "defiant naiveté"[65]—the artist instinctually doing things his way without concern for what the "old masters" might say. In other cases, though, one makes a more explicit claim, as in the case of visual artist Judy Chicago: "What is art? . . . That is debated all the time. I have a right to be thrown into the debate."[66] According to psychologist Otto Rank (as summarized by art historian Laurie Lisle), "The first step in becoming an artist . . . is when one calls oneself an artist."[67] Either way, doing it consciously or not, a working artist is someone who has overcome the entitlement problem.

To make your claim, you have to make the art form your own, to find it in your mouth and in your heart. Composer and choreographer Meredith Monk described her relationship to dance in this way: "I had to find my own style, my own way of thinking about movement, my own way of structuring in space."[68] Many artists go through a process like this, figuring out how to take personal possession of a form that has been in the hands of so many before them. Yet one of the central messages of this book is that art *is* yours for the taking, *is* yours personally, is in fact already in you.

63. Goldberg, *Writing Down*, 116.

64. Kuspit, "Jewish Naivete?," 97.

65. Ibid., 88.

66. Levin, *Becoming Judy*, 313.

67. Lisle, *Louise Nevelson*, 52–53.

68. Morgenroth, *Speaking of Dance*, 88.

Perhaps more dauntingly, the other message is that you *must* claim your creative life. Successful artists feel this urgency intuitively. "I have to make Art," wrote Chicago.[69] Composer Allen Shawn describes fellow composer Arnold Schoenberg as "an artist who hears a 'call' that others do not and has the obligation to heed this call."[70] Now, some of you might be protesting, "Well, that's Arnold Schoenberg. What does that have to do with me?" To my mind, what made the difference between Schoenberg and other people was not that he was called while others weren't, but, like Shawn suggests, he, unlike others, *heard* the call. Presumably it's out there for the rest of us, and not in the heavens, but close by, waiting for us to hear it. In other words:

You can do this.

It's yours.

You must, in fact, do it.

---

### In Your Mouth and In Your Heart:

What creative ideas have you rejected because they seemed impossible for you to carry out? Claim your place by starting to work on them anyway.

---

69. Levin, *Becoming Judy*, 113.
70. Shawn, *Schoenberg's Journey*, 231.

# Va-yeilekh

## Teaching

Deuteronomy 31:1—31:30

$P$ARASHAT VA-YEILEKH IS OFTEN paired with *Parashat Nitzavim*, read together as a double portion, and it's easy enough to see why that might be. First of all, they're both very short portions, and second, the two do seem to go together thematically. For example, in the last *parasha* Moses had just told the people that the wisdom of the Torah is not remote, but instead that it is in the hearts and the mouths of the people. In *Va-yeilekh* this idea comes up again, though in a slightly different way. God asks Moses to write a poem about the Israelites' divine covenant, and then says, *teach it to the people of Israel; put it in their mouths* (Deut 31:19). God is building on what's come before: each of us contains Torah, sure—but it's never a bad idea for a teacher of great wisdom, like Moses, to help us find it.

If we bring this back to the world of art, where we've recently explored how creativity is there for each person to claim, this *parasha* suggests the power of teaching to help everyone along. It also suggests that those who have something to impart ought to do so, for the benefit of others.

For sure, many accomplished artists throughout the centuries have taught other artists, whether taking on apprentices here or there or running a classroom. These days, it's commonplace; teaching is one of the main ways that artists manage to make a living. If what we hear in *Va-yeilekh* is right, this is a good thing for the students, as wisdom from successful people helps to bring out the wisdom in others—but is it good for the person doing the teaching?

In 1970, visual artist Judy Chicago broke ground by creating a Feminist Art program—the first ever—at the University of California at Fresno. She helped dedicated women to develop as artists in a male-dominated art world, to find their own relationship to their work. She and this program were part of a movement that ultimately radically changed the art world and the academic world. Yet it isn't so clear that all this was just as helpful for her. While at Fresno she complained, "I keep feeling like I *should* be working."[71] Of course, teaching is work—but it's not *the* work that passionate artists are driven primarily to do. "I feel it necessary," Chicago wrote, "to keep that part of me alive that got on the old #53 Bus in Chicago every Saturday & went off to the Art Institute."[72] To do so was a struggle.

Here's how writer Allegra Goodman described the conflict she's experienced in occasionally trying to balance teaching and writing: "I've taught a bit, but not regularly, no. I enjoy doing it, but I probably wouldn't be able to write nearly as much as I do if I had to teach. It's hard work. But I always have a great time when I'm teaching a seminar or something. I'm sitting there for two hours holding forth, talking about stories, and I'm thinking, *This is great! This is great!* Then about five minutes after the class is over I want to lie down. I think teaching in small quantities is probably good for me."[73] How do you pour yourself into doing right by your students and still have something left for your own work? By the time I get home at the end of the day, it's pretty rare that I'm still bursting with energy to write.

On top of that, there's the temptation, at least in higher education, to get caught up in scholarly work. Poet Stanley Kunitz was turned away from teaching at Harvard because he was Jewish, and he said later, "That almost broke my heart. And I think in the end it probably did me a great favor because it prevented me from becoming a completely preoccupied scholar."[74]

Then, too, there are the difficulties that can come from being part of an institution. After her next teaching post, a difficult experience at CalArts, Chicago decided to have "nothing more to do with full-time institutional jobs—it's just not possible to do anything significant for women & stay involved with institutions which are at best chauvinistic & at worst fascist."[75] Even the ones that aren't as bad as all that can leave you feeling that your

71. Levin, *Becoming Judy*, 155–56.
72. Ibid., 160.
73. Welch, "Allegra Goodman."
74. *Writer's Almanac*, July 2008.
75. Levin, *Becoming Judy*, 185.

individuality has gotten lost in something larger and not necessarily compatible with your artistic goals.

So why on earth do it? Aside from the money, that is—why would a person teach, other than to pay the bills?

Well, first of all, it gets you out of the house. As composer John Zorn said of the creative life, "It's hard work, and you get isolated."[76] Sculptor Louise Nevelson said, "An artist by his very nature works alone. He spends most of this time by himself, and it is *essential* that he have a public to keep him from going mad."[77] She could have used the word "students" just as easily where she said "a public." Human contact can be a very good thing, in whatever form it's available.

People also teach because they have something to impart, as in the case of Chicago herself: "I realized that I could actually begin to put out all this information I had about my own struggle, my own perceptions"[78]— and in many cases that kind of realization comes with a sense of obligation to pass on what one knows.

Sometimes the essential thing to convey is simply your fervor for art. Author Lev Raphael said, "the greatest thing about teaching is transmitting your excitement."[79] Think of Moses again. When he finishes reciting his poem in the next *parasha*, he says, "*Take to your heart all the words with which I have warned you this day. . . . For this is not a trifling thing for you: it is your very life*" (Deut 32:46–47). He's not just trying to get them to memorize a few things; he's trying to instill *passion* for what lies before them.

To teach is to do the important work that Moses does in this *parasha*, to help others develop a sense of ownership of the very thing that has been so powerful and meaningful for you. It's an amazing thing to witness, and, if a teacher is sensitive to this process, s/he can be reminded on a daily basis just why s/he *is* an artist. It's there on the students' faces.

I will also say that teaching, perhaps ironically, becomes a way to learn. By becoming fluent in conveying your understanding of your art, that understanding deepens and broadens. By listening to your students, you encounter wisdom you couldn't have generated on your own. By putting yourself into a hungry artistic community, you connect to the ongoing conversation between artists that's been going on forever, and perhaps you

76. Goldberg, "John Zorn."

77. Lisle, *Louise Nevelson*, 225.

78. Levin, *Becoming Judy*, 160–61.

79. White, "A Conversation."

even remember the larger point of the creative endeavor, the point that's larger than any one of us.

*In Your Mouth and In Your Heart:*

Do you teach your art? If so, how do you balance it with your artistic work? If not, would you like to? Why or why not?

# Haazinu

## Success

### Deuteronomy 32:1—32:52

IN 2001 I WAS on a bit of a roll. I had been submitting my work to literary magazines for six years by then, and in all that time I had published just five short stories and no poems at all—but things changed in 2001. From December 2000 through September of 2001—only nine months—three stories and three poems were accepted for publication, and one story was selected to be read dramatically in a theatrical production. All of a sudden it felt like I had figured the game out, had conquered the publication world. I would meet someone at a party and, after introducing myself as a writer and getting the question that *always* comes in response to that—"Are you published?" (how unhelpful and off-the-point this question is!)—I would sigh a contented sigh and say something like, "Oh, sure. The big thing for me now is to get the book in print, now that I don't have any problem publishing individual stories and poems."

You can see where this story is going.

After that last acceptance in the early fall of 2001, I got nothing but rejection letters until June of 2003—twenty-one straight months of only hearing the answer *No*.

Over those dry months I became, as you can imagine, increasingly distraught. It wasn't as though rejection was a new idea for me—the typical writer who's trying to get published receives rejections on a daily basis— but my string of successes had convinced me that maybe those old rules wouldn't apply to me anymore. I began to think I'd risen above it all. In the twenty-one painful months that followed my burst of publications I realized that success had been far more dangerous to my well-being than rejection ever had been.

This seems so counter-intuitive—you would think that success (as measured in these terms) would make a person ever more grateful for those positive things, ever more aware of just how precious and rare these treasured moments can be. Instead, I seemed to immediately start to take it all for granted.

Unfortunately, I am not alone in having this problem. We'll hear shortly from other artists who struggled with this, too, and the fact is that this has been a troublesome part of human nature for a very long time. For evidence of that, we need look no further than the Torah.

In *Parashat Haazinu*, Moses offers up a poem containing his final thoughts. This is his last moment with the people before he climbs Mount Nebo to die, and it's therefore his last chance to leave the people with the most essential wisdom he can give. It's significant, then, to see what he decides to focus on. Much of the poem is a complaint against the Israelites' ingratitude toward God. Moses reminds everyone what God's done for them—*Like an eagle who rouses his nestlings,/ Gliding down to his young,/ So did He spread His wings and take [Israel],/ Bear him along on His pinions* (Deut 32:11)—and then notes that the people met those acts of loving with thanklessness, that we *grew fat and kicked—/ . . . grew fat and gross and coarse* (Deut 32:15). The poem goes on to describe the people seeking after other gods. In other words, the very fact of having been given these gifts made us ungrateful for them, and left us only wanting more.

This is what Moses warns us about in his final words. He has only one more chance to tell us what we need to know, and he focuses not on how hard it is to respond to challenges but on how hard it is to respond to success. That tells you how deep this problem runs in us.

It is, in fact, a constant struggle for many artists. As we explored in the commentary on *Parashat Mattot*, striving for material or social success can be destructive. Here we see that it can be destructive to *attain* it. Consider the example of visual artist Judy Chicago, who in that commentary we saw consumed at times with the desire to have her worth recognized. What I didn't say in that commentary is that she did ultimately get what she wanted—Chicago is now very well-known. Getting it, though, wasn't all it was cracked up to be. She later wrote, "I really don't like many of the things about being a public figure & if I don't pull back now, it is likely that I will be consumed."[80] She suddenly found her work suffering because of all the demands on her time, attention, and psyche.

Author Norman Mailer is another interesting study, though his story was quite different. Rather than laboring for many years to get recognition, he became famous with his very first novel—*The Naked and the Dead*. Mailer remained famous all his life, never really struggling seriously to get a book into print again (aside from some publisher squeamishness around the sexual content in his novel *The Deer Park*). Certainly many young writers would be happy to have such a big success so early on—yet they might want to consider the downside of Mailer's story.

First of all, at least until *The Executioner's Song*, a novel published thirty-two years after his first, nothing he wrote made quite the splash that *The Naked and the Dead* did. Some might argue that he never again wrote a book more successful than that first. What Mailer faced, then, was the problem of trying to *maintain* success, and trying to live up to his own hype—and dealing with the suffering that came when he couldn't do these things. He wrote:

> Some writers receive not enough attention for years, and so learn early to accommodate the habits of their work to little recognition. I think I could have done that when I was twenty-five. With *The Naked and the Dead* a new life had begun, however. I had gone through the psychic labor of changing a good many modest habits in order to let me live a little more happily as a man with a name which could arouse quick reactions in strangers. . . . I had learned to like success—in fact I had probably come to depend on it, or at least my new habits did.[81]

The problem is that the publishing world, the literary establishment, and the reading public are fickle and unpredictable, and one can't possibly hope to depend on ongoing adoration from any of them. Mailer had unwittingly set himself up for a fall: "I'd taken myself a little too seriously after *The Naked and the Dead*. Do that, and the book review world will lie in wait for you. There are a lot of petty killers in our business."[82]

Coming down to earth is awfully hard after your successes float you up way too high for safety. Mailer later wrote this about watching *The Deer Park* came out and seeing it do somewhat well in sales, but not incredibly

80. Levin, *Becoming Judy*, 204.
81. Mailer, *Spooky Art*, 40.
82. Ibid., 25–26.

well: "Like a starved revolutionary in a garret, I had compounded out of need and fever and vision and fear nothing less than a madman's confidence in the identity of my being and the wants of all others, and it was a new dull load to lift and to bear, this knowledge that I had no magic so great as to hasten the time of the apocalypse but that instead I would be open like all others to the attritions of half-success and small failure."[83] Mailer had to learn to deal with the fact that he was, after all, not much different from the rest of us, and that success (as defined by sales and reviews) was an absolutely undependable source of support.

Again: just as our striving for success can make us forget the point of our art, so can our *attainment* of success. As Ecclesiastes would say, this too is vanity. This, too, is a kind of idolatry that values the wrong thing and devalues the thing that is most crucial. If we are not careful, what we lose is the work itself.

Successful artists—truly successful ones, in the best sense of the word—are the ones who don't lose sight of the goal. When Chicago wrote, "I'm a painter, I teach at a good school for $14,000 a year (next yr's salary), I have a good marriage, some degree of fame—now I want to make simple, unadorned paintings,"[84] she was reminding herself that doing art is the goal, just as when she told her students, "The only thing that justifies your existence is work."[85] Not fame, not counting up gallery shows, but work. Similarly, as painful as it was for Mailer to see his later books received less enthusiastically than his first one, he wrote them anyway—forty books total over his lifetime. Ultimately he was able to develop some healthy perspective. He wrote: "Getting a bad review these days in the Sunday *Times* affects my wallet. My ego, however, remains relatively intact."[86]

As for me, I can't claim that I feel just as happy in times when it's hard to get things published as in times when it's easy—but I can claim that, either way, I get up in the morning and get back to the original task of writing. That's a measure of success I can believe in.

83. Ibid., 47.
84. Levin, *Becoming Judy*, 200.
85. Ibid., 204.
86. Mailer, *Spooky Art*, 53.

*In Your Mouth and in Your Heart:*

The next time you have a bit of external success with your work—a show, a publication, a staging, even a nice comment from someone else—find a way to celebrate a little. Go out to dinner, write about it in your journal, dance around the living room. Allow yourself to dwell on how nice it feels, maybe even overnight. The next morning, though, when you wake up, tell yourself, "That was nice—but where was I? What's really nice is the work. Let me go do some." And then do some.

# V'zot ha-B'rakhah

## Going Back, Going Forward

### Deuteronomy 33:1—34:12

$P$ARASHAT *V'zot ha-Brakhah* is the end of a long journey. We have now read all of the Five Books of Moses, dozens of *parashiyot*, encountering countless characters and stories, following the Israelites as they wander and wander toward the promised land—and now they're ready to enter at last.

Yet we also know that it's as much a beginning as an end. Each year at the holiday of *Simhat Torah* we read the end of this final *parasha*—and then we read the beginning of the very first *parasha* in Genesis. Before the Israelites even set foot into the land, before they complete their journey, we return to where we started, and we begin our journey all over again.

At first glance, this might seem like a bizarre anticlimax; we've come this far and we're just going to circle back to the beginning? On second thought, though, most readers start nodding their heads in recognition. This is, after all, pretty much how life works.

It's no wonder that choreographer Meredith Monk once said, "I don't think of my work as a line. I always think of spirals or cycles";[87] a line would take us into the Promised Land and bring us to a full stop there, but spirals and cycles bring us back to the work—and is the work ever truly done, truly complete?

We usually define being an artist not as *having created* but as being a person *who is in the habit of creating*. It is, by definition, ongoing. According to novelist Walter Mosley, "If you want to be a writer, you have to write

87. Morgenroth, *Speaking of Dance*, 92.

every day. . . . You don't go to a well once but daily. You don't skip a child's breakfast or forget to wake up in the morning. Sleep comes to you each day, and so does the muse."[88] Conceptual artist Eva Hesse was so committed to her work that she continued to create sculptures even from her deathbed. She had already achieved a great deal by then, but nonetheless, rather than resting on those accomplishments she always found herself starting at the beginning of a new piece.

This can be a scary thought, the thought that one is forever beginning again. Is there no change, no growth, no development?

Of course there is. When Monk talked about "spirals" she was talking about something that both circles *and* moves in a direction. Consider the experience of going through the Torah again every year. I can tell you that, in the experience of many, this text is new each time we encounter it. But how can that be? We've read these *parashiyot* before; we know these characters and stories. How can they possibly be new, when not a word has changed since the last time we read them?

What's changed, of course, is the reader. Consider the analogy of prayers which we repeat regularly in synagogue. According to Rabbi Reuven Hammer, "Of course, the main thing that is 'new' is oneself. Depending on my thoughts, my mood, my feelings, my existential situation of the moment, what I say, no matter how many times I have said it before, takes on new meaning."[89] Even when we engage with the same material again and again, we are not static, because we are changing and our understanding is growing. Painter Philip Pearlman said, "The lucky [artists] get into a problem that is unsolvable, so they keep going and there's a growth, evolution."[90]

There is a kind of accumulation that comes through Monk's spiraling. Visual artist Judy Chicago said, "The more I grow as a person, the larger my ideas become, & the larger the framework I have to build to accommodate those ideas."[91] In this way you move forward even as you go back—and of course you need to move forward. Choreographer Anna Halprin said, "For me to maintain creativity, I have to find new forms to reach out to people."[92] Writer Allegra Goodman has made the point that this need applies to all of us: "If you're going to be an artist, you have to do new things. I can't

88. Mosley, "For Authors," 161.
89. Coleman, *Creativity and Spirituality*, 158.
90. Jackman, *Artist's Mentor*, 188.
91. Levin, *Becoming Judy*, 239.
92. Morgenroth, *Speaking of Dance*, 27.

write The *Family Markowitz* every time. And I can't write *Kaaterskill Falls, Volume Two*—or, I could, but I'm not interested. You have to grow."[93]

What this *parasha* suggests is that you grow, in part, by returning. By returning, as Mosley would tell us, to our work, and by returning as well to our unsolvable problems and our main obsessions and issues. Songwriter Bob Dylan has over the years regularly talked about a need to get back to the way he used to see, used to write, used to think, in order to create the songs he wants to create—"I'm going to have to get back to writing like I used to when I was ten—having everything come out naturally" he said once.[94] By doing what he once did, he develops; as his nature grows, of course, what he produces "naturally" changes, too.

Monk, again: "After a while you find that you have to contend with the backpack of your past on a lot of levels. How do you find something new? How do you explore something you haven't done before? How do you keep it fresh? How do you challenge yourself? How do you risk? How do you do something that really has a lot of life energy in it? All that has a lot to do with trying to consider yourself as a human being first."[95]

We saw earlier in this book that growth often happens when we get close to—return to—who we are in our core selves. In these words of composer Arnold Schoenberg that we've seen before, "If we would live and grow, [we must] become ever more fully and nakedly what we essentially are."[96] We grow, and our growth causes us to return to the beginning, the essence; we return and that allows us to grow. The journey goes on.

Now, of course it's not quite accurate to say that the journey *never* ends. Ask Moses, who dies not only before the Israelites enter the land but also before the Torah ends, before we return to its first verses again. In his death we see that even truly great people pass away before their work is finished. At some point we get off this loop—done, without having completed what we meant to complete.

This is, for most people, terrifying. Filmmaker Woody Allen had this to say about the fear of death: "There is no other fear of significant consequence. All other fears, all other problems one can deal with. Loneliness, lack of love, lack of talent, lack of money, everything can be dealt with. In

---

93. Welch, "Allegra Goodman."
94. Cott, *Bob Dylan*, 16.
95. Morgenroth, *Speaking of Dance*, 98.
96. Shawn, *Schoenberg's Journey*, 83.

some way, there are ways to cope. You have friends that can help you, you have doctors that can help you. But perishing is what it's all about."[97] This fear may be more intense for some artists, whether obsessively engaged with an unsolvable problem or desperate to have a lasting impact or at least a real legacy. How do we face a possible end knowing that we just aren't done with our work?

The answer comes partly through a recognition that we are not alone in our work, and that there will be others to carry it on after we're gone. According to Dylan, "Usually the way things go is that someone else comes out, out of the crowd, of considerable ability who can cover what you're doing and take it another step."[98] In fact, usually they're waiting eagerly for the opportunity. Author Norman Mailer recognized that fact late in his career: "I think the younger writers are sick of Roth, Bellow, Updike and myself the way we were sick of Hemingway and Faulkner. When I was a young writer we never talked about anyone but them, and that feeling grew into resentment. Since they had no interest in us, we began to think, Yeah, they're great—now get off the stage! We want the lights on us!"[99]

And so, like a lot of other things, it's about acceptance—acceptance of the fact that we can't do it alone in a single lifetime, anyway, and that we are fortunate enough to have allies in our struggles. Eventually that acceptance can become generous indeed, as in the case of Dylan: "I don't know what's gonna happen when I'm not around to sing anymore. I hope somebody else comes along who could pick up on what I'm doing and learn exactly what it is . . . that makes it quite different. I keep looking for that somebody . . . not necessarily to cover me, but to take it a step further."[100]

In the meantime, though, there's work to do. That's part of what return is all about: it's fine to pause and reflect from time to time, as hopefully this book has allowed you to do, and of course it's natural to think about the future as well. But none of that is the point for the artist. Whether we've been on a long journey already or whether it's just beginning, whether we have a plan or whether we don't, whether we think we can get it all done or whether we have our doubts, wherever we are and whatever we've done, there is always the need to return to the beginning, to the task at hand. As

97. Allen and Bjorkman, *Woody Allen*, 106.
98. Cott, *Bob Dylan*, 239.
99. Mailer, *Spooky Art*, 294.
100. Cott, *Bob Dylan*, 324.

the *Mishneh* tells us, *It is not incumbent on you to complete the work, but neither are you free to abstain from it.*[101]

And tell the truth—would you really want the freedom to abstain?

---

*In Your Mouth and In Your Heart:*

Go back. Go back to the fundamentals of who you are, of your art, of your obsessions. What's still there for you to mine? Go back. Go back to work.

---

101. Shawn, *Schoenberg's Journey*, 301.

# Bibliography

Afterman, Allen. *Kabbalah and Consciousness and the Poetry of Allen Afterman*. Riverdale-on-Hudson, NY: Sheep Meadow, 2005.

Allen, Sture, ed. *Nobel Lectures, Literature 1968–1980*. Singapore: World Scientific Publishing, 1993.

Allen, Woody and Stig Bjorkman. *Woody Allen on Woody Allen*. New York, Grove: 1993.

Alpert, Rabbi Howard. "Zeal and Peace." No pages. Online: http://www.hillel.org/jewish/archives/bamidbar/pinchas/1997_pinchas.htm.

Alter, Judah Aryeh Leib. *The Language of Truth*. Translated and edited by Arthur Green. Philadelphia: Jewish Publication Society, 1998.

Ankori, Gannit. "The Jewish Venus." *Complex Identities: Jewish Consciousness and Modern Art*, edited by Matthew Baigell and Milly Heyd, 238–58. New Brunswick, NJ: Rutgers University Press, 2001.

Baigell, Matthew. "Jewish American Artists: Identity and Messianism." *Complex Identities: Jewish Consciousness and Modern Art*, edited by Matthew Baigell and Milly Heyd, 182–92. New Brunswick, NJ: Rutgers University Press, 2001.

Baskind, Samantha. *Encyclopedia of Jewish Artists: Artists of the American Mosaic*. Westport, CT: Greenwood, 2007.

Bellow, Saul. Nobel Prize Lecture 1976. No pages. Online: http://www.nobelprize.org/nobel_prizes/literature/laureates/1976/bellow-lecture.html?print=1.

Berio, Talia Pecker. "Mahler's Jewish Parable." *Mahler and His World*, edited by Karen Painter, 87–110. Princeton: Princeton University Press, 2002.

Berkowitz, Mira Goldfarb. "Sacred Signs and Symbols in Morris Louis: The Charred Journal Series, 1951." *Complex Identities: Jewish Consciousness and Modern Art*, edited by Matthew Baigell and Milly Heyd, 193–205. New Brunswick, NJ: Rutgers University Press, 2001.

Bernstein, Leonard. *The Joy of Music*. New York: Simon and Schuster, 1954.

*Boldtype*. "Michael Chabon." *Boldtype* (2008). No pages. Online: http://boldtype.com/160825.

Bolton, Elizabeth. "Toward a Jewish Theology of Creativity." *The Reconstructionist* 62:1 (1977): 16–22.

Buber, Martin. "I and Thou." *Contemporary Jewish Theology: A Reader*, edited by Elliot N. Dorff and Louis E. Newman, 60–64. New York: Oxford University Press, 1999.

Buccini, Max. "Lev Raphael on Being Gay and Jewish." *EDGE* (2007). No pages. Online: http://www.edgeboston.com/index.php?ch=entertainment&sc=books&sc2=features&id=4103.

# Bibliography

*Chabad.org.* "The Complete Jewish Bible With Rashi Commentary: Bereishit—Genesis— Chapter 3." No pages. Online: http://www.chabad.org/library/bible_cdo/aid/8167/ showrashi/true/jewish/Chapter-3.htm.

Chagall, Marc. *My Life*. Translated by Elisabeth Abbott. New York: Orion, 1960.

Cohen, Joseph, ed. *Voices of Israel: Essays on and Conversations with Yehuda Amichai, A.B. Yehoshua, T. Carmi, Aharon Appelfeld and Amos Oz*. Albany: State University of New York Press, 1990.

Coleman, Earle J. *Creativity and Spirituality*. Albany: State University of New York Press, 1998.

Cooper, David. *God Is a Verb*. New York: Riverhead, 1998.

Cott, Jonathan, ed. *Bob Dylan: The Essential Interviews*. New York: Wenner, 2006.

Falk, Marcia. "Response: The Poet as Liturgist: Marcia Falk's *The Book of Blessings*." *The Reconstructionist* 62:1 (1997) 73–84.

Felix, Rabbi Shimon. "Passion." No pages. Online: http://byfi.org/news/?q=comment/ reply/66.

Fogelman, Yaakov. "Toldos (Generations)." *The Jerusalem Jewish Voice*. 2008. Online: http://israelvisit.co.il/top/toldos.shtml.

Friedberg, Haya. "Secular Culture and Traditional Judaism in the Art of Michal Na'aman." *Complex Identities: Jewish Consciousness and Modern Art*. Edited by Matthew Baigell and Milly Heyd, 259–81. New Brunswick, NJ: Rutgers University Press, 2001.

Gawker.com. "Jonathan Safran Foer and Nicole Krauss Need Their Space." No pages. Online: http://gawker.com/244444/jonathan-safran-foer-and-nicole-krauss-need-their-space?tag=newsjonathansafranfoer.

Ginsberg, Allen. *The Life and Times of Allen Ginsberg*. DVD. Directed by Jerry Aronson. New York: New Yorker Video, 1994.

Gluck, Bob. "Jewish Music or Music of the Jewish People?" *The Reconstructionist* 62:1 (1997) 34–47.

Gold, Rabbi Shefa. "Shoftim." Rabbi Shefa Gold's Torah Journeys. No pages. Online: http://www.rabbishefagold.com/Shoftim.html.

Goldberg, Michael. "John Zorn." *Bomb Magazine* (2002). Online: http://bombsite.com/ issues/80/articles/2501.

Goldberg, Natalie. *Writing Down the Bones*. Boston: Shambhala, 1986.

Gottlieb, Adolph and Mark Rothko. Letter to the editor, *New York Times*. June 13, 1943.

Green, Arthur, ed. *Menahem Nahum of Chernobyl*. Mahwah, NJ: Paulist, 1982.

Greenwood, Helen. Michael Chabon Interview. *Sydney Morning Herald* (2007). No pages. Online: http://www.smh.com.au/news/books/michael-chabon-interview/2007/05/ 03/1177788267982.html?page=fullpage#contentSwap2.

Jackman, Ian. *The Artist's Mentor*. New York: Random House, 2004.

Jewish Publication Society, ed. *Tanakh: The Holy Scriptures*. Philadelphia: Jewish Publication Society, 1917. No pages. http://www.mechon-mamre.org/e/et/et0.htm.

Jewish Publication Society, ed. *Tanakh: The Holy Scriptures*. Philadelphia: Jewish Publication Society, 1985.

Kachka, Boris. "Lonely Planet." *New York Magazine* (2006). No pages. Online: http:// nymag.com/guides/fallpreview/2006/books/19723/.

Kahn, Louis. *My Architect*. DVD. Directed by Nathaniel Kahn. New York: New Yorker Studio, 2006.

Kaplan, Mordecai. "God as the Power that Makes for Salvation." *Contemporary Jewish Theology: A Reader*, edited by Elliot N. Dorff and Louis E. Newman, 72–80. New York: Oxford University Press, 1999.

Kligerman, Eric. "Message in a Bottle." *HaTanin* 19 (2008) 8–9, 15.

Kuspit, Donald. "Jewish Naivete? Soutine's Shudder." *Complex Identities: Jewish Consciousness and Modern Art*, edited by Matthew Baigell and Milly Heyd, 87–99. New Brunswick, NJ: Rutgers University Press, 2001.

Lerner, Michael. *Jewish Renewal: A Path to Healing and Transformation*. New York: Grosset/Putnam, 1994.

Levin, Gail. *Becoming Judy Chicago: A Biography of the Artist*. New York: Harmony, 2007.

Lieber, David L., ed. *Etz Hayim: Torah and Commentary*. New York: Jewish Publication Society, 2004.

Lisle, Laurie. *Louise Nevelson: A Passionate Life*. Lincoln, NE: Author's Guild, 2001.

Mailer, Norman. *The Spooky Art*. New York: Random House, 2003.

Malamud, Bernard. *People and Uncollected Stories*. New York: Chatto & Windus, 1990.

Matt, Daniel C. *The Essential Kabbalah: The Heart of Jewish Mysticism*. Edison, NJ: Castle, 1997.

Mayer, Egon. "Representing American-Jewish Acculturation: Reflections on the Photography of Frederic Brenner." *The Reconstructionist* 62:1 (1997) 85–88.

McIver, Don. "Poetry and Radio: Human Nerve Ending." *How to Make a Living as a Poet*, edited by Gary Mex Glazner, 177–80. Brooklyn, NY: Soft Skull, 2005.

Meyers, Jeffrey. *Modigliani: A Life*. Orlando, FL: Harcourt, 2006.

Milkowski, Bill. "John Zorn: One Future, Two Views." *Jazz Times* (2000). Online: http://jazztimes.com/articles/20521-john-zorn-one-future-two-views.

Morgenroth, Joyce, ed. *Speaking of Dance*. New York: Routledge, 2004.

Mosley, Walter. "For Authors, Fragile Ideas Need Loving Every Day." *Writers on Writing: Collected Essays from the New York Times*, edited by John Darnton, 161–64. New York: Henry Holt, 2001.

Moyers, Bill, ed. *Fooling with Words*. New York: Morrow, 1999.

National Endowment for the Arts. *Reading at Risk: A Survey of Literary Reading in America*. Washington, DC: National Endowment for the Arts, 2004.

Olin, Margaret. "Graven Images on Video? The Second Commandment and Jewish Identity." *Complex Identities: Jewish Consciousness and Modern Art*, edited by Matthew Baigell and Milly Heyd, 34–50. New Brunswick, NJ: Rutgers University Press, 2001.

Plaut, W. Gunther, ed. *The Torah: A Modern Commentary*. New York: Union of American Hebrew Congregations, 2005.

Poseq, Avigdor W. G. "Soutine's Jewish Bride Fantasy." In *Complex Identities: Jewish Consciousness and Modern Art*, edited by Matthew Baigell and Milly Heyd, 100–114. New Brunswick, NJ: Rutgers University Press, 2001.

Potok, Chaim. *My Name is Asher Lev*. New York: Fawcett Columbine, 1972.

———. *The Gift of Asher Lev*. New York: Fawcett Columbine, 1990.

Preston, John Hyde. "A Conversation with Gertrude Stein." *The Creative Process*, edited by Brewster Ghiselin, 159–68. Berkeley: University of California Press, 1952.

Ramban. *Commentary on the Torah*. Translated by Charles B. Chavel. New York: Shilo, 1971.

Revel-Neher, Elisheva. "With Wisdom and Knowledge of Workmanship: Jewish Art Without a Question Mark." *Complex Identities: Jewish Consciousness and Modern Art*, edited by Matthew Baigell and Milly Heyd, 12–33. New Brunswick, NJ: Rutgers University Press, 2001.

Roth, Philip. *The Facts: A Novelist's Autobiography*. New York: Penguin, 1988.

Rothko, Mark. *The Artist's Reality: Philosophies of Art*. New Haven, CT: Yale University Press, 2004.

Scherman, Rabbi Nosson, ed. *The Chumash: The Stone Edition*. Brooklyn: Mesorah Publications, 1994.

Senesh, Hannah. *Her Life and Diary*. Translated by Nigel Marsh. New York: Schocken, 1972.

Shawn, Allen. *Arnold Schoenberg's Journey*. New York: Farrar, Strauss and Giroux, 2002.

Singer, Isaac Bashevis. Nobel Prize Lecture 1978. No pages. Online: http://www.nobelprize .org/nobel_prizes/literature/laureates/1978/singer-lecture.html.

*Small Spiral Notebook*. Interview with Nicole Krauss (2011). No pages. Online: http://www.smallspiralnotebook.com/interviews/2007/11/small_spiral_notebook_intervie.shtml.

Sokolow, Anna. "I Hate Academies . . . Modern Dance is an Individual Quest." *Dance Magazine* (July 1965) 38–39.

Sontag, Susan. "Directions: Write, Read, Rewrite. Repeat Steps 2 and 3 as Needed." *Writers on Writing: Collected Essays from the* New York Times, edited by John Darnton, 223–29. New York: Henry Holt, 2001.

Spicehandler, Reena. "The Poetry of Liturgy; Liturgy as Poetry." *The Reconstructionist* 62:1 (2001) 65–71.

Sprecher, Rabbi Ephraim. "Mystical Message Of The Sacrifices (For the 21st Century)." *The Jewish Press* (2008). No pages. Online: http://www.jewishpressads.com/pageroute .do/30633/.

Taylor, Judith. *Selected Dreams from the Animal Kingdom*. Lincoln, NE: Zoo, 2003.

Telushkin, Rabbi Joseph. *Jewish Literacy*. New York: William Morrow, 2001.

Teutsch, David A., ed. *Kol Haneshamah*. Elkins Park, Pa: Reconstructionist, 2002, 185.

Warren, Larry. *Anna Sokolow: The Rebellious Spirit*. Princeton: Princeton Book Company, 1991.

Waskow, Arthur. *Godwrestling, Round 2: Ancient Wisdom, Future Paths*. Woodstock, VT: Jewish Lights, 1998.

Welch, Dave. "Goodman, Allegra." *Powells.com* (2001). No pages. Online: http://www .powells.com/blog/interviews/allegra-goodman-by-dave/.

White, Claire. "A Conversation With Lev Raphael." *Writers Write: The Internet Writing Journal* (1999). No pages. Online: http://www.writerswrite.com/journal/may99/raphael.htm.

Wiesel, Elie. "A Sacred Magic Can Elevate the Secular Storyteller." *Writers on Writing: Collected Essays from the* New York Times, edited by John Darnton, 258–62. New York: Henry Holt, 2001.

*Writer's Almanac* (May 24, 2008). No pages. Online: http://writersalmanac.publicradio.org/index.php?date=2008/05/24.

*Writer's Almanac* (July 29, 2008). No pages. Online: http://writersalmanac.publicradio.org/index.php?date=2008/07/29.

Zollo, Paul, ed. *Song-Writers on Song-Writing*. Cambridge, MA: Da Capo, 2003.

# Index

THE PRIMARY TOPICS OF this text's multiple, short chapters are not collected at "art" or "artists," but are indicated by boldface page numbers throughout the index.

# Index